ADOPTING
IN
AMERICA
How To Adopt Within One Year

5th Revised Edition

RANDALL B. HICKS
Attorney at Law

♦ ♦ ♦ ♦ ♦

WORDSLINGER PRESS
San Diego, California

[1]Book reviews on back cover are from prior editions. Cover review is from Hicks' *ADOPTION: The Essential Guide to Adopting Quickly and Safely* (Perigee Press). Cover-cited press/TV coverage includes author appearances and/or recommendations/references to Hicks' numerous adoption books.

Published by WordSlinger Press
9921 Carmel Mountain Road #335
San Diego, CA 92129

Distributed by SCB Distributors
15608 S. New Century Drive
Gardena, CA 90248
www.scbdistributors.com

Table of Contents

INTRODUCTION

I want to help you adopt.

I've been an adoption attorney for more than twenty-five years, and completed adoptions for more one thousand families. I believe that what I've done for them, I can do for you. More importantly, by the time you've finished reading this book, *you* will know that you can adopt as well.

I want to show you how to adopt quickly.

The key to success in any endeavor is *knowledge*. Adoption is no different. I will give you that knowledge in an easy-to-understand, step-by-step approach. In addition to the basic knowledge you'll need, I'll give you a strategy for success. And not just success, but *quick* success. I promise to give you more information than you thought was possible about how to succeed at adopting a child. This is true whether you wish to adopt a newborn child, an older child, a child with special-needs, or internationally. Some of these strategies you won't find anywhere else. But don't take it on faith. In less than one hour of reading from now you will know this to be true.

I want to show you how to adopt safely.

Every endeavor in life has risks, and adoption is no exception. I believe the biggest key in avoiding a failed adoption is to never start a risky one. Will there still be risks? Yes. Adoption is fraught with emotions, for both you and the birth family, so risks can't be eliminated entirely. However, I'll show you the red flags to watch out for to greatly minimize risk, and allow you to proceed into your adoption with confidence.

I want to show you how to adopt economically.

I don't practice law in Beverly Hills, or in Manhattan. The adoptive parents I work with are hard-working, middle-income people: teachers, fireman, electricians, accountants and the like. They can't risk spending their money unwisely, or where it will not produce results. Sadly, however, more and more adoptions in our country involve high costs. In this book I'll show you that it need not be that way. Beginning with key steps to finding the right attorney or agency, to the birth mother's pregnancy-related expenses, I'll show you how to reduce or even eliminate many typical adoption costs. Thanks to the 2012 tax year $12,650 federal adoption tax credit we will explore later, some people may even end up with a "free" adoption.

I want to show you how to adopt ethically.

Although this is a "how to" and "strategy" book, make no mistake that I believe the most important thing in every adoption is to not just do it legally, but with high morals as well. Shortcuts backfire. Illegality corrupts. Immorality taints. Run from people who tell you otherwise. Adoption is how you bring your child into your home. His or her unique adoption story will be a part of your family history, to be lovingly shared with your child as he or she grows. You want to look back on how each step was accomplished with pride. Your adoption can be, and should be, one of the most wonderful and rewarding journeys of your life.

Let's make this journey together.

CHAPTER 1

ARE YOU READY TO ADOPT?

Your readiness to adopt is the first critical step in your adoption. If you are not emotionally ready, all the knowledge in the world won't make adoption the right family-building option for you. Instead it will be the proverbial "house built on sand," destined to fail. You owe it to yourselves, and your future child, to be sure you are ready.

Readiness to Adopt

People often confuse being ready to *adopt* with being ready to *parent*. They are two vastly different things. Just because you are ready to parent does not mean you are automatically ready to adopt. Adoption means a full recognition that you are making someone else's biological child your own, as if born to you. This is an issue that can't be denied or ignored. Adoption can't be a healthy option if an adoptive parent views the lack of their own biological connection as a negative characteristic in their child. The biological diversity of an adopted child must not just be accepted, but embraced. As stated by two of the nation's leading authorities on the subject, Lois Ruskai Melina and Sharon Kaplan Roszia in *The Open Adoption Experience:*

> Children reflect both *nature* and *nurture*, though the exact interplay between those factors is still a mystery. Consequently, the child has a connection to both the birth parents and the adoptive parents, because each has made a significant contribution

3

to the child's development. This dual responsibility for who a child is and who he becomes also creates a connection between birth parents and adoptive parents. . . Through them, a human life is created and nurtured. . .

As an adoptive parent you must recognize that your child may look different from you (even if of the same ethnic group), or genetically be pre-disposed to different interests and skills. Of course, even biologically conceived children often have interests different from their parents or siblings, or don't look alike. Oddly, those differences are never questioned in biologically created families, just taken for granted as an extension of each person's individuality. In adoption, however, some people examine such differences with inappropriate scrutiny.

Another issue related to readiness to adopt, assuming you are adopting due to infertility, is that you have come to terms with infertility. For this reason, counseling is a normal and highly recommended part of the infertility process. For some, it is hard to give up the dream of a biologically conceived child, while others have little difficulty with the concept of adopting a person who is genetically from another family. For those who have difficulty with abandoning the dream of their own biologically conceived child, it is critical to come to terms with this issue before starting an adoption. To not do so would be like marrying someone while you are still in love with someone else. Everyone will suffer as a result, no matter how good your intentions.

Readiness to adopt means you have to look into more than your heart. You have to look into your mind. Are you adopting because you want be a parent? To have a family? If so, those are natural, healthy reasons to adopt. Some adoptive parents, however, are motivated by the desire to "save a child." Don't get me wrong; this is a good-hearted motivation by likely a wonderful person. It is the wrong reason to adopt, however.

Let me use marriage as an example again. If you were to marry someone to "save" them, perhaps from a life of loneliness and poverty, think how doomed that marriage would be. Either consciously or unconsciously, you would expect gratitude, and you would not get it. Instead, you would eventually get resentment. You'd feel they were ungrateful, and now we've got two people feeling resentment. Adoption is no different. The fact may be, particularly in older child and international adoption from some impoverished nations, that you are physically saving a child from a poor start in life and giving them a brighter future. Adoption, however, is about creating a *family* - a parent and child relationship - not living an act of charity. There are many honorable and much-needed ways to help children besides adoption, such as foster parenting, mentoring, volunteering time, and donating money. Let's leave adoption for true family creation, however, not human charity.

Talking to Your Child about Adoption

You might be asking a valid question right now. Why are we discussing talking with your child about adoption when you don't even have a child yet? Good point. There is a valid reason to bring it up now, however. A couple of reasons, actually. First, let's look at the practical side of it. If you are planning a newborn adoption, where the birth mother will likely be meeting with you prior to deciding if you are the right parents for her baby, a common question for a birth mother to ask you is, "How are you going to tell your child that he's adopted?"

If this is a question to which you've never given any thought, and you stumble out something simplistic and antiquated about the child "being special," you likely will not have impressed that birth mother. In fact, many birth mothers have already been given information, or met with a counselor, and learned about how and when adoption should be discussed with a child, meaning she already knows what the answer to this question should be. You want her to look at you as more than nice people who will be great parents, but who will be great *adoptive* parents. That means you took the time to be ready for these issues because you care about the subject, not left it to deal with at some uncertain point in the future. Failure to fully educate yourself in such vital issues means you might not be "birth mother ready" when you are selected by a birth mother, and she may come away unimpressed after meeting you. The result is she might select another adoptive family and you've lost what should have been your placement.

The second reason is that you owe it to your future child to do this kind of thinking in advance. It's just what adoptive parents *do*. It's part of the fantasy every future parent has, whether that family is created biologically or through adoption. As we look forward to parenthood, we all have fantasies about our child taking their first steps, playing catch on the lawn, opening presents at Christmas or Hanukkah, and sitting on grandpa's lap to hear the same stories we were told as children. The only thing different is that adoptive parents need to have a few additional fantasies, and talking to their child about how they entered the family is one of them.

Here is the introduction to a children's book, *Adoption Stories for Young Children,* which I wrote many years ago. Although it is a picture book for children, the first page is for parents regarding this very important topic.

Some adoptive parents feel very comfortable in discussing adoption with their child, while others have some anxiety. All adoptive parents, however, have one thing in common. They understand that not only does their child need and deserve knowledge of how their family was created through adoption, but also that his or her knowledge must be provided in a way which will give their child the pride and self-respect every person needs as a foundation in life.

What do you say and when do you say it? Every child - and family situation - is different, but there are many common themes which the adoption community has come to embrace. The practice followed by some parents many years ago of hiding any information about adoption until the child was "old enough" has been rejected. Although that policy may have been followed with good intentions, many problems resulted. Many children would accidentally learn from others they were adopted, instead of from their parents, creating confusion and parent-trust issues. Other children would wrongly assume their parents' silence was due to embarrassment about the adoption, creating shame in the child, unjustly believing something must be "wrong" with adoption.

Now, openness is embraced. Although your child grew in your heart and not physically in your body, you don't want to deny your young child the great joys every child receives when hearing about your anticipation of his or her arrival into the family, and how cherished and important a part of your family he or she has become. How your child views him or herself - and adoption itself - will depend almost exclusively upon you.

If you are adopting a newborn, talking about adoption starts at birth. True, the baby won't understand you, but that doesn't stop you saying "I love you," does it? You say "I love you" because you enjoy the giving and receiving of emotion the words bring. You don't wait until you are sure your child can understand the meaning of those words. Using the word "adoption" in a context such as, "The day we adopted you was the happiest day of our lives," makes the word a comfortable part of your family's vocabulary for when the time comes that the words are understood. And your child will know, even before the word "adoption" has any meaning, that is must be a "good" word, because mom and dad are always smiling when they say it.

Learning about adoption is a gradual process, like many things we need to teach our children about, such as "the birds and the bees" and "stranger danger." We don't sit down our babies or toddlers and give them a detailed lecture on those subjects. Neither do you do so when discussing adoption. Instead, you slowly lay the groundwork, and give information as your child is mature enough to understand it.

When you are adopting an older child, either in a domestic or international adoption, they will enter your home knowing they are adopted. In these cases, the focus is on why you have brought them into your home, and that you are going to be their parent forever. Many older children come from disrupted families, often filled with unreliable - sometimes even abusive - parents. Even if they were raised in foster care, they may have been moved often, unable to form normal attachments.

Regardless whether you are adopting a newborn or older child, it will be helpful to your child to know of other adoptive parents and their children to be aware there are millions of other people out there who entered their family in just the same way. Some of these people will be your friends and neighbors, or people in your community like your dentist or minister. It can also be some of the many public personalities, such as adoptive parents Steven Spielberg (director), Magic Johnson (basketball player), Walt Disney (entertainer) and Nicole Kidman (actress), who are very public about their adoptions. Famous adoptees (adopted persons) include Aristotle (philosopher),

Charles Dickens (writer), Edgar Allen Poe (writer), Faith Hill (country singer), Halle Berry (actress), George Washington Carver (inventor) and Mark Twain (writer). And why stop there? The Bible tells us Moses was adopted, not to mention Jesus (basically a step-parent adoption by Joseph as Jesus was not conceived with him, nor even by Mary I suppose, making it an unofficial full adoption - raising someone else's child as their own). The comics give us Superman, a superhero adopted by his earth family. Even two U.S. presidents were adopted via traditional or step-parent adoption (William Clinton and Gerald Ford). This knowledge creates the subtle message, allowing your child to think: "I'm not different. I'm like everyone else. I just entered my family differently than some, but exactly like many others." For an extensive list of famous adoptive parents, birth parents and adoptees, visit celebrities.adoption.com (the list includes step-parent adoptions).

This chapter is short, but don't think that is because these issues are not important. To the contrary, they are critical to your long-term success, and that of your family. One book can only do so much, however, and the goal of mine is to help you adopt. Issues related to emotional readiness to adopt and talking to your child about adoption are best covered by those who specialize in those fields. These subjects need, and deserve, entire books to adequately cover them. By touching upon these subjects, however, I hope I have demonstrated their importance, and that you will choose to explore them. I firmly believe that the small investment into an adoption library is the best money you will spend in your entire adoption. Visit adoption101.com for a list of recommended adoption books in all categories.

CHAPTER 2

THE FOURTEEN—YES,
FOURTEEN!—TYPES OF
ADOPTION

The normal approach in teaching you about adoption would be to start off by giving you a detailed outline of how each major type of adoption works: independent, agency and international. Sorry, I'm not going to do that. Instead, I'm going to approach this backwards. Why? Because you deserve it. I'm going to show you fourteen sub-types *first*. I want you to see right from the beginning that there are more types of adoption - meaning more options for you - than you ever imagined. It is in these sub-types, many of them greatly underused, where success lies for many adoptive parents. Many adoption professionals don't even know about them.

I'm also doing it this way to eliminate some preconceptions. I find many adoptive parents take their first steps into the adoption process armed with a basic understanding of adoption, and think they already know the best route to find, and adopt, their future child. You might be like that, firmly believing a traditional independent, agency or international adoption is the route you'll follow, and you just need help getting there. Don't be surprised, however, if by the time you peruse this overview of the fourteen different types of adoption that, you see there are types you didn't even know existed, and that one of them may be the best option for you. This is true whether you are seeking to adopt a newborn baby or an older child, or do an international adoption.

Want an analogy? Let's say a traditional adoption quest is like a cross-country road trip. So you get a Toyota Camry, a reliable car, and suitable for most situations. But maybe the path to your adoption actually requires a SUV to get up a sandy hillside for the adoption waiting on the other side. Without the SUV, that adoptive placement is lost to you, and went to another family who knew where to look, and was prepared how to get there. In fact, you drove right by, never knowing you came that close to the opportunity. Or, maybe you need a sub-compact to squeeze through a narrow roadway. The by-the-book Camry won't fit, so again you pass it by, unaware of the great adoption opportunity which was down that road. It's kind of like that classic old Cary Grant movie, waiting on the Eiffel Tower for his true love, but he passes her on the street, thinking he was stood up. Turns out she was right there; he was just looking the wrong direction.

To succeed in adoption, you need to be looking down every road, with the right equipment at your disposal. Wherever you live - a small town in Alaska with no adoptive placement options, an east coast state where independent adoption is not permitted, or a region with no qualified adoption attorneys or agencies - it makes no difference. You are not limited by your city, county, or even state. Your only limitation will be how open you are willing to be in exploring new options that may be different from your initial concept of how adoptive matches are made.

Of the fourteen sub-types of adoption, ten involve domestic (American born) children and four are international. The majority is centered on the adoption of newborns, while others deal with older children. Before we review them, however, it will be helpful to have a basic adoption vocabulary.

Domestic adoption: Adopting a child born in the United States.

International adoption: Adopting a child born overseas, born to a citizen of that country.

Birth mother: The biological mother of the child being placed for adoption.

Birth father: The biological father of the child being placed for adoption.

Birth family: A general term referring to all biological relatives of the child, such as the birth parents, siblings, grandparents etc.

Adoptive parents: The parents who will be adopting the child and becoming the child's legal and permanent parents.

Adoptee: The child being adopted.

Networking: The outreach effort to find women with unplanned pregnancies who might be considering adoption, and in turn have them consider you as adoptive parents. You can network on your own following my suggestions, or rely upon your adoption attorney or agency to do it based on their special relationships with health-care professionals leading to many referrals, and other strategies.

Independent adoption: An adoption typically initiated by an attorney, who helps "match" you with a birth mother and does the legal work required. Virtually all independent adoptions involve only newborns.

Private adoption agency: Private agencies can elect to serve the general public, or a selected group (usually based upon religious affiliation) as they elect. They can help "match" you with a birth mother and perform your home study, as well as other functions. Most of their placements are of newborns, but some may also work with older children.

Public adoption agency: Virtually every county in the nation has a governmentally operated adoption agency, usually a division of the state's department of social services. Although some county adoption agencies handle newborn adoptions, most have the duty of finding homes for older children, many of them dependents of the court due to their forced removal from their biological parents who were unable to care for them. Usually the agency's services to adoptive parents are free, or a minimal cost, to encourage the adoption of the waiting children presently under the county's supervision in foster care.

Okay, you've got the basic lingo. Let's take a quick look at the fourteen types of adoption. Thereafter, we have an entire book together to prepare you how to look at them in more detail, analyze the pros and cons, determine which ones are right for you, and map out a strategy for quick, safe, economical and ethical adoption.

Independent Adoption via an Attorney Located in Your Home State

This is the most popular option for those seeking to adopt a newborn baby born in the United States. You select an attorney located in your home state. He or she helps match you with a birth mother, or supervises your efforts to do so, then does the legal work thereafter all the way through finalization of the adoption in court. Your home study is done by an agency, social worker or state adoption office, depending upon the regulations of your state. (All states permit independent adoption except: Colorado, Connecticut, Delaware, Massachusetts and North Dakota.) In Chapter 3 we will be exploring this type of adoption in more detail. Chapter 15 provides a state-by-state review, detailing the exact laws and procedures governing independent adoption in your state.

This is a great method if:

- Your state has a large enough population base resulting in a sufficient number of birth mothers making adoptive placements.
- The qualities you possess as adoptive parents are those local birth mothers will find appropriate for their expected child. (For example, if you are Catholic and live in a state like Utah, with a predominately Mormon population, the birth mothers will most likely be Mormon, and less likely to pick you as non-Mormon.)
- Your region or state has attorneys who are well qualified and with reasonable fees.
- Your state's laws are fair to adoptive parents and not unduly restrictive.
- You are seeking to adopt a newborn.

Independent Adoption via an Attorney Located Outside Your Home State (An "Out-of-State" Adoption)

Instead of hiring an attorney who is located within your home state, you select one out-of-state. This could be in a neighboring state, or across the country. This attorney will usually be networking in his or her state for birth mothers, with the baby generally born in the attorney's state. Does this mean you have to stay six or eight months out of state with the baby until the adoption is completed? Not at all. When the child is born, after the necessary interstate approval, you return home with the baby, later finalizing the adoption in your home state's court. You would also be using a local in-state attorney for these proceedings, as normally many your home state's laws will apply. In addition to the more detailed information about out-of-state independent adoption in Chapter 3, the state-by-state review gives each state's unique laws and procedures, allowing you to learn about the laws and procedures in other states to determine the most advantageous ones in which to possibly start your adoption.

This is a great method if:

- There are not sufficient birth mothers in your state, perhaps due to a low population, or adoption is not a promoted or popular option.
- You live in a state that you feel is over-represented with waiting adoptive parents compared to the placements available.
- There are not enough well-qualified attorneys in your state.
- You belong to a particular ethnic or religious group and want to adopt a child matching your characteristics, but they are under-represented in your state, meaning few birth mothers to select you.
- Your state's adoption laws are unfair toward adoptive parents (such as giving the birth mother too long to change her mind and reclaim a child), some of which can be avoided by an out-of-state birth.
- Your state might be satisfactory, but you want to expand your options by including efforts in additional states.

- You don't mind traveling out of state, typically one or more times (certainly for the birth, but likely also for your initial meeting with the birth mother).
- You are seeking to adopt a newborn.

Independent "Non-Resident" Adoption

This is one of the most important types of adoption, and one of the least known. As with the above type of adoption, it involves hiring an attorney in a different state from your own. However, instead of finalizing the adoption under your own state laws and in your local court, you complete virtually the entire adoption in the attorney's state, where the child was born, under that state's laws.

As with *out-of-state* adoption, you can bring the child back to your home state after birth and reside there, having to return to the birth state later for a brief court appearance to finalize the adoption, just as you would need to do in your own city. The only service needed in your home state would usually be a local agency or social worker doing your home study, and reporting that you are caring for your child properly. More than half the states in the country permit non-residents to adopt in their state, only requiring that the baby be born there. These states are: Alabama, Alaska, Arkansas, California, Hawaii, Iowa, Indiana, Kansas, Louisiana, Maine, Maryland, Michigan, Missouri, New Hampshire, New Jersey, New Mexico, New York, North Dakota, Ohio, Oregon, Pennsylvania, South Carolina, Texas, Utah, Virginia and Washington. Chapter 3 provides more information about this critically important type of adoption, and the state-by-state review details the laws of the above twenty-six states which permit non-resident adoption.

This kind of adoption is ideal for adoptive parents for the same reasons as those listed above regarding "out-of-state adoptions," as well as the following:

- The laws of a particular state are attractive to you, as the birth state's laws will almost exclusively apply when you are also finalizing there.

- Adoption costs in your state are extremely high, and some of them can be reduced or avoided by completing the adoption in another state.
- You don't mind an additional trip out of state, as you will additionally normally be required to return about six months after birth for the final court appearance granting the adoption.

Private Adoption Agencies Located in the Adoptive Parent's Home State

This is the second most popular type of newborn adoption in the country. You select a private adoption agency located in your home state. The agency will help match you with a birth mother, or supervise your efforts to do so, do your home study and write a report for the court, then either has an in-house attorney do the legal work thereafter through finalization in court, or refer you to a local attorney to do so. This method is very similar to an independent adoption via an attorney in your home state, except you are selecting an agency, rather than an attorney, to be the primary entity. Chapter 5 explores the dynamics of an in-state agency adoption. Chapter 15 reviews the laws governing agency adoption in each state.

This is a great method if:

- Your state has agencies that are well-qualified, reasonably priced, and you meet their eligibility requirements.
- Your state has a large enough population base in your region resulting in sufficient birth mothers making adoptive placements.
- The characteristics you present as adoptive parents are those which local birth mothers will find appropriate for their expected child, such as religion and ethnicity.
- Your state's laws are fair to adoptive parents and not unduly restrictive.
- You are seeking to adopt a newborn (although some agencies do older child placements).

Private Adoption Agencies Located Outside the Adoptive Parent's Home State

Instead of hiring an agency located within your home state, you can select one out-of-state, either in a neighboring state, or a thousand or miles away. This is very similar to an independent out-of-state adoption, except you are retaining an agency rather than an attorney. The agency will usually be networking in its state for birth mothers, meaning the baby will likely be born in the agency's state. You can bring the child home shortly after birth, process the adoption primarily under your home state's laws, and finalize it in your local court. Your in-state agency will do your home study and prepare the report for the court. Chapter 5 gives more details about how out-of-state agency adoption works. Chapter 15 explains the laws within those states.

This is a great method if:

- There are not sufficient birth mothers in your state, perhaps due to a low population, or adoption is not a promoted or popular option.
- You live in a state that you feel is over-represented with waiting adoptive parents compared to the placements available.
- You are not pleased with the qualifications or fees of agencies in your state, or they have requirements making you ineligible.
- You belong to an ethnic or religious group and want to adopt a child matching your characteristics, but they are under-represented in your state, meaning few birth mothers to select you.
- Your state's adoption laws are unfair toward adoptive parents.
- Your state might be satisfactory, but you want to expand your options by including efforts in additional states.
- You are seeking to adopt a newborn (but toddlers and older children are available too).

Private Agency "Non-Resident" Adoption

Just as non-resident adoption can be done with attorneys, it can also be done via adoption agencies. You retain a private adoption agency located in another state, and finalize the adoption there, under that state's laws, where the child was born or the agency having custody of the child is located. It is not required that you stay in the child's birth state during the entire adoption. Instead, after interstate approval, you can return home with your child until it is time to finalize the adoption, when you normally return to the birth state. Usually the only services required within your state will be a home study by a local agency or social worker, who will write reports to the out-of-state agency confirming that you are caring for your child properly.

Thirty-one states and the District of Columbia permits non-residents to adopt in their state in an agency adoption. These states are: Alabama, Alaska, Arkansas, California, Colorado, Delaware, District of Columbia, Hawaii, Iowa, Illinois, Indiana, Kansas, Louisiana, Maine, Maryland, Massachusetts, Michigan, Missouri, New Hampshire, New Jersey, New Mexico, New York, North Dakota, Ohio, Oregon, Pennsylvania, South Carolina, Texas, Utah, Vermont, Virginia and Washington. You may have noticed that this list of states permitting non-residents to adopt is a bit larger than the list provided when *independent* non-resident adoption was discussed earlier in this chapter. The reason is that some of these states (Colorado, Delaware and North Dakota) are "agency only" states, and do not permit independent adoption, meaning non-residents can only adopt there if doing so via agency adoption. Also, some states do not allow non-residents to adopt simple due to the fact the child is born in the state, but do allow it if the agency having custody of the child is located there. Chapter 5 gives more information on this popular type of adoption and the state-by-state review provides the laws and procedures of each of the above twenty-two states.

This kind of adoption is ideal for adoptive parents for the same reasons as those listed above for out-of-state adoptions, as well as the following:

- The laws of a particular state are attractive to you, as the birth state's laws will almost exclusively apply when you are also finalizing there.
- Adoption costs in your state are extremely high, and you wish to reduce or avoid some of them by completing the adoption in another state.

Public/County Adoption Agencies

Almost every county in each state has a public adoption agency to serve both the children and adoptive parents in their region. This "public" or "county" agency is primarily supported by taxes, and their services to adoptive parents are either free, or greatly discounted. Although sometimes newborns are available via this method, in most cases the county adoption office has the imposing duty of finding homes for the older children in their care. Many of these children have been involuntarily freed through the courts due to inappropriate parenting, including neglect, abandonment and abuse. For more information about adopting through your local public agency please refer to Chapter 5.

This is a great type of adoption if:

- You like the people and procedures of your local county adoption agency, as normally it will be the sole "public" option in your county.
- You are looking for a free adoption, or one which has very minimal costs.
- You are seeking an older child, a sibling group, a child with special-needs and/or a child of an ethnic minority, as most, but not all, children will be in one of these groups.
- You want to share your love with a special-needs child but worry about the possible financial strain on your family. The existence of a possible monthly stipend even after the adoption is complete makes the adoption feasible for you.
- You want an adoption where everything is likely to be done in your home region.
- You possess the emotional qualities and training necessary to provide the extra nurturing a child from a disrupted family will require.
- You are open to a child who has been exposed to drugs during the pregnancy.
- Your income is limited and other adoption options are outside your needs. Public agency adoptions are often free, and even subsidies and special adoption tax credits exist if the child has special needs (discussed in those sections).

Adoption Exchanges

In addition to each county serving their own local children, there are state, regional and national adoption *exchanges*. They list waiting and special-needs children in an effort to find homes. In an effort to find the best homes for these waiting children, most exchanges welcome adoptive parents from any state, not just the state in which the child is located. For example, this would allow a Texas child with special needs, and no local adoptive parents available to meet those needs, to be matched with the perfect family who lives in New York. Although it is true that most of the children served by exchanges have been deemed to have special needs of some type, it may not always be a physical or mental challenge, as you may initially imagine when hearing the term "special needs." Some of the children have received that designation for no reason other than their age being past the toddler years, being part of a sibling group to be adopted together, or being of an ethnic group for which there are not enough adoptive parents. Please check out this virtually free option.

As discussed in more detail in Chapter 5, each state has its own adoption exchange. There are also regional exchanges and one national exchange. Generally, the exchanges charge no fees. Most exchanges have photo-listings so you can see the actual children available online right from your home. In fact, you could do it right now if you want. The state exchanges, and their phone numbers and websites, are listed in the state-by-state review. I'd suggest starting by checking your state registry, then the national exchange. The national and regional exchanges, and their phone numbers and websites, are listed in Appendix A.

This kind of adoption is ideal for the same reasons as those listed for public/county adoptions, as well as the following:

- You don't mind traveling several times to another region or state to meet, and slowly bond with, a possible child.

The Foster Parent Short-Cut

In the above two types of adoption (local county agencies and exchanges), the children are normally legally free for adoption when they are shown to you. This also means they are older and have waited longer to get to that point, perhaps having gone through one or more foster homes, and the potential trauma of multiple placements.

You can sometimes get to the "front of the adoptive parent line" by being a foster parent, caring for a child who may not yet legally be free for adoption. This often means the birth parents still have their parental rights yet have been denied custody, and it is believed the child is destined for adoptive placement. For example, the birth mother may have abandoned the baby in the hospital, or been under the influence of drugs at the time of birth, requiring the county agency to step in and take care of the child. In most situations the court will give the birth parents a limited time to prove they can be adequate parents and regain custody, but if they fail to do so, will terminate their parental rights. For this reason, the foster parent short-cut can be risky, as only some placements starting out as foster care turn into adoptions. Chapter 5 provides more information about fost-adopt placements.

This kind of adoption is ideal for the same reasons as those listed for public/county adoptions, as well as the following:

- You have the emotional constitution to be content with helping a child by giving him or her a loving home as a foster parent, knowing it may not turn into an adoptive placement as hoped.
- You feel you want to live with a child for an extended period and see if the family emotionally gels as you anticipate, prior to moving into adoption planning.
- You want to adopt but can't afford any legal or agency costs, and need the additional income provided as a foster parent prior to the adoption being finalized, to fully meet your child's needs.

Identified Adoptions

An "identified" adoption is a hybrid between an independent and a private agency adoption. Some people call them "designated" adoptions. These are adoptions where an adoptive parent likes some elements of an attorney-initiated independent adoption, but also likes the formality of an agency adoption, and combines the best elements of the two. In the most typical identified adoption, the adoptive parents retain an attorney to help find a birth mother and do the legal work, then when a birth mother is "identified," they use an agency to provide counseling to her, assist with her relinquishment of parental rights and conduct the adoptive parent home study.

This type of adoption can be combined with other sub-types of adoption. For example, you might select an out-of-state attorney to help find a birth mother and get the adoption going, but hire an agency in your home state to do the rest and complete the adoption in your home state. In so doing, you've now created a hybrid of sorts: an "identified out-of-state adoption." When you include the many hybrids possible, there are actually *more* than fourteen types of adoption available to you. Identified adoptions are discussed in Chapters 5.

This is a great option for you if:

- You want the flexibility of the characteristics of both independent and agency adoption.
- You want the option to do an in-state, out-of-state adoption or non-resident adoption, determined mainly by the laws of the state where you elect to hire your adoption agency and/or attorney.
- You seek to adopt a newborn.

Facilitators

A facilitator is not so much a *type* of adoption (so is not being counted as one of the fourteen types of adoption) as it is a *method* to start a newborn adoption. A facilitator is a person or business being paid a fee for adoption services, but which is not a licensed attorney or agency. They are the subject of a great deal of controversy. Some consider facilitators as "infantpreneurs," profiting from the placement of children, because unlike attorneys and agencies, they are not licensed to do legal work or conduct home studies. In fact, some states make it a crime to facilitate an adoption for a fee.

Most would agree a facilitator's primary function is to find birth mothers, usually via yellow page and internet ads. Those who support facilitators argue they are a viable, although often expensive, route to finding a birth mother. Also, remember that once you find a birth mother via a facilitator, you will still need to complete your adoption via either the independent or agency adoption method, and select an attorney or agency to assist you with those legalities, so you will have those costs as well. For more information about facilitators, and the potential risks in using them, please refer to Chapters 6 and 8.

This might be a option for you if:

- The state in which you are working permits facilitators.
- You are comfortable with the facilitator's methods of networking for birth mothers.
- You are content that the facilitator's fees might be more than that of an attorney or agency.
- You understand the risk of working with an entity not licensed as an agency or attorney.
- You understand that besides paying a facilitator, you will still normally need an attorney and/or agency to complete the adoption.

Private Adoption Agencies with InternationalAdoption Programs in the Adoptive Parent's Home State

Some of the private adoption agencies in your home state will offer international adoption programs rather than domestic placements. A few agencies do double duty, handling both domestic and international adoptions, although most international agencies focus only on that specialty. You will find that each agency normally has specific countries from which it makes adoptive placements. One agency might have a program only in Russia, while another might work in multiple countries, like China, Guatemala and the Philippines. Hiring an in-state international agency means that one entity can handle your domestic requirements such as your home study, as well as supervise the overseas portion of the adoption.

Because there are more than 1,000 agencies in the United States, and phone numbers, addresses and websites may change (perhaps making them invalid if listed within this book) it is recommended to obtain the listings online. This information is available on a state-by-state basis at both childwelfare.gov and adoption101.com.

This is a great method if:

- You want to adopt a non-newborn (usually from six months to 16 years, depending upon the country).
- You want one agency to do everything: your pre-birth home study as well as the international aspects of the adoption.
- Your state has qualified international agencies with programs in the countries of interest to you, and you meet the eligibility requirements of the agency.
- You are comfortable adopting a child where sometimes little medical history is available.
- You are willing to travel to the child's country and stay there for at least several weeks (although some countries use escorts to bring the child to you).
- You understand that your child, if of speaking age, will initially speak another language, and not know English.
- You are aware that at the time of the placement your child will usually be ten percent underweight, and about two months per each year of age regressed in physical and emotional development compared to other children due to lack of sufficient stimulation and nurturing in orphanages. (Most all of these children can and will quickly catch up to similarly aged children, however, if there are no other health factors causing the lack of development.)
- You understand a child raised in an orphanage or similar institutional setting may suffer from some degree of attachment disorder due to lack of prior nurturing, or bonding with a parenting figure.
- You want a "closed" adoption, as usually you will have no contact with the birth family.

Private Adoption Agencies with International Adoption Programs Outside the Adoptive Parent's Home State

As with domestic adoption, you might find that the agency with the best program, working in the country from which you want to adopt, is located in another state. No problem. In fact, this is very common. The out-of-state agency will handle the international aspects of your adoption (which is the critical part of an intercountry adoption), and will ask an agency in your local region to do the required home study. For more information on out-of-state agency international adoption, please refer to Chapter 7, and the state-by-state listing of all licensed adoption agencies at childwelfare.gov and adoption101.com.

The factors favoring this kind of adoption are the same as those listed above for private international agencies within your state, with these additional considerations:

- You feel there are no qualified international agencies in your state with programs in the countries of interest to you, or you don't meet their eligibility requirements.
- You don't mind working with two agencies: one to do your pre-placement home study, and one to handle the international aspects of the adoption.

Adoption Attorneys with International Adoption Programs in the Adoptive Parent's Home State

Most international adoption programs are operated via private adoption agencies. (It is the reverse of domestic adoption, where the majority is via attorneys.) Still, there are some attorneys who operate international programs. To some degree, every international adoption is an "agency adoption," as each one requires a pre-placement agency home study, and most all require a few post-placement visits as well. When we talk about international adoption programs, however, we are talking about much more: satisfying our federal laws governing international adoption, preparing a dossier to present overseas, having translators and drivers in the child's country to guide you during your visit, and much more. Attorneys can do this as well as agencies. Most foreign countries prefer to work with agencies, but in some attorney programs are common. For more information on international adoption please refer to Chapter 7, and the attorney biographies in the state-by-state review, which list which attorneys practice international adoption.

The factors favoring this kind of adoption are the same as those listed above for private agencies within your state, with the addition of the following:

- You will be working with two entities: a local agency to do your pre-placement home study, and the attorney for the international aspects of the adoption.
- Attorneys generally have less, or no, adoptive parent eligibility requirements regarding such factors as religion, as do some agencies.

Adoption Attorneys with International Adoption Programs Outside the Adoptive Parent's Home State

You might like the idea of working with an attorney outside your home state if he or she has an excellent international program in the country you prefer. This is usually no problem. You will need an agency in your local region to do the required home study, but the out-of-country work required in the international program can be done equally well whether you select someone in, or out of, your home state. After all, most of the work in the adoption will likely be occurring 10,000 miles away, in the child's country, so having an attorney in another state is usually not a big factor.

The factors favoring this kind of adoption are the same as those listed above for out-of-state international and in-state attorney international adoption

*   *   *   *   *

So, there you have it. Fourteen distinct types of adoption - more actually - when you count the many possible hybrids. And we've only touched the tip of the proverbial iceberg in learning about them. As you can see, there are many, many doors open to you. To find the right door, however, we need to explore each method in depth. We will be doing that by devoting individual chapters not only into independent, agency and international adoption, but additional chapters describing how to find the right attorney or agency. So much time is spent on this issue because success in adoption means not only having finding the right method to accomplish your personal goals in adoption, but also the right professional to help you make it happen.

CHAPTER 3

INDEPENDENT ADOPTION

The majority of newborn adoptions completed in the United States are done via *independent* adoption. You will often hear it referred to as *private, direct* or *open* adoption. Why independent adoption is so popular with both birth mothers and adoptive parents can be seen in its characteristics. In some ways it is very similar to private agency adoption, but in others it is distinctly different. The most popular elements of an independent adoption are:

- Almost all adoptions involve newborns.
- A pre-placement home study is not required in all states.
- There are usually no formal eligibility requirements.
- There is less bureaucracy.
- A match can often be made faster than via agencies.

In many states, the split between independent and agency adoption close regarding which is the most popular method is fairly close, while in others - like California - a whopping eighty-five percent are independent. To see the percentage in your home state, or states from which you are considering adopting, please refer to the state-by-state review in Chapter 15. Forty-five states permit independent adoption, while five require all adoptions to be done via only the agency method. Those states are: Colorado, Connecticut, Delaware, Massachusetts and North Dakota.

Here are the basic steps in an independent adoption:

1. Retain an adoption attorney (preferably one who has their own outreach program to find birth mothers to create adoptive matches and/or who has experience advising adoptive parents on the networking strategies they will be employing on their own).

2. Wait for the attorney to create an adoptive match for you (or find a match through your own networking efforts).

3. Have your attorney screen the birth mother to be sure it looks like a safe placement, and examine the case for potential legal problems.

4. Have a pre-placement home study done if one is required by your state. Your state law may provide that the home study be done by a social worker, adoption agency or state adoption office.

5. Get to know your birth mother personally so she has confidence in you, and you in her.

6. Help her with medical and other pregnancy-related expenses, assuming she has any, and if permitted by your state.

7. Be present at the hospital to share the birth experience.

8. Bring home the baby from the hospital.

9. The birth mother consents to the adoption (some states require this before the child is released to you from the hospital).

10. The birth father consents to the adoption, waives notice, or has his rights terminated because he can't be found or fails to object.

11. Do your post-placement home study (six months in most states).

12. Have your attorney complete all necessary documents and satisfy all legal obstacles to make sure the child is fully free for adoption.

13. Go to court to finalize your adoption.

14. Receive a new birth certificate naming you as the child's biological parents, as if you gave birth to him or her.

There are a lot of choices in how you do an independent adoption. That, in fact, is one reason for its popularity. The fact it is flexible, however, does not mean it is simple. To the contrary, there are many potential false steps in every adoption. Becoming aware of independent adoption's ins and outs and how to best use its flexibility to serve your goals are important steps to achieving success.

Eligibility Requirements

Asking what the requirements are for independent adoption is a bit of a misnomer. Why? Because there usually *are* no requirements. The restrictions commonly seen in many agency adoptions, such as your age, marital history, religion, financial status, number of children and proof of infertility, have little relevance in independent adoption. This is because there are usually no agency guidelines which must be satisfied. Instead, the birth mother personally selects the adoptive parents based upon factors *she* deems important. If she elects to choose a single woman as the adoptive parent, fine. If she wants to choose adoptive parents where both are fifty years of age, fine. If she chooses an adoptive family where the adopting father is Caucasian and Jewish with two children from a prior marriage, and the adoptive mother is African-American, Catholic and restricted to a wheelchair, fine. It's like choosing a spouse; everyone is attracted to different kind of people.

Does this mean anyone can adopt via independent adoption? No. You still have to be approved via a home study, but its requirements will almost always be very basic, generally establishing two things: 1) your present and past life indicates you can and will be good parents; and 2) you were honest in telling the birth mother about yourself, so she can make an informed consent about who is adopting her baby. We will discuss the home study in more detail shortly.

The Role of the Adoption Attorney

An attorney. Do you need one? And if you do, does it have to be an adoption specialist? That's up to you. Technically, you can do an independent adoption without an attorney. You could find your own birth mother, make sure there are no legal obstacles or risks (and solve them if there are), do all the routine legal work required, select a proper agency or social worker as required in your state to do your home study, prepare your final documents and finalize your adoption in court. Yes, it's possible, but do you want to try? The creation of your family is on the line.

Some adoptive parents think of adoption attorneys only as a route to be introduced to a birth mother to select them as adoptive parents. That is a valid reason for selecting one. Sometimes, however, finding a birth mother is the easiest part of your adoption. The real work is in screening potential adoptions, looking for legal risks (outlined in Chapter 12), noting red flags indicating risks beyond legal issues (Chapter 10) and doing the legal work needed in the adoption. By the time you've finished this book you will see how much analysis and work goes into each adoption, and why the chances of your adoption being successful increase dramatically with a qualified adoption attorney at the helm. To me, attempting an adoption without an attorney is like doing dental work on yourself. Rarely a good idea. As you learn more about independent adoption, you will see it is the adoption attorney who makes things happen in an adoption, and helps make them happen when and how they are supposed to. Because finding the right attorney is so important, Chapter 4 details forty-four individual steps and inquiries leading to finding the right attorney to best serve your unique needs.

The Home Study

The home study required in an independent adoption is usually considered less intrusive and time-consuming than in a typical agency adoption. In agency adoptions there are always two stages in a home study: pre-placement (before a child is placed with you), and post-placement (after a child is placed with you). In independent adoptions, however, approximately half the states do not require a pre-placement home study. The state-by-state review tells you which states waive this requirement. Surprisingly, a few states not only don't require a pre-placement home study, but the court can waive even a post-placement home study, meaning there is sometimes no home study at all. These states are Hawaii, Mississippi and Wyoming.

The fact that no home study is often required before a child is placed with you, and only occurs post-placement, might sound quite odd. The rationale behind it makes sense, however. In an agency adoption, as a legal matter the birth mother is technically placing the child with the agency, and the agency uses its judgment to place a child with selected adoptive parents. Whether or not the birth mother had a role in selecting the adoptive parents, it was the agency that officially made the placement, typically making it legally responsible. To protect itself from that liability, a home study is their safeguard. In independent adoptions, it is usually the birth mother who is personally making the placement, based upon her judgment of the adoptive parents, not those of an intermediary agency. Even if she met the adoptive parents through an attorney, as is typical in independent adoption, it is the birth mother who is the "placing person." Not an agency. Not the attorney.

As a practical matter, it is very, very rare for adoptive parents in an independent adoption to be denied due to their home study. Virtually all adoptive parents know from the beginning what their home study will entail for them, and don't attempt to start a process they know will not be approved. Plus it also helps that the standard is very basic, simply showing nothing indicates you will not be a secure and loving parent, and you were honest in describing your life situation to the birth mother, without the sometimes subjective approval of a private agency.

Each state has different regulations and procedures regarding who may perform an independent adoption home study. In some states a special state adoption office, usually a division of its social services office, has been staffed to perform all independent adoption home studies. Other states allow private agencies, social workers, or people approved by the court to perform it.

Home study fees vary. If a pre-placement home study is required, the cost may range from state to state between $500 and $2,500 and usually takes four to ten weeks to complete once started. The post-placement is more lengthy (usually six months) and frequently costs between $500 and $6,000. Most fall in the middle. If you live in a state where private agencies are the designated entity to do your independent adoption home study, the agency fee is usually significantly less than if the same agency were performing a full traditional agency adoption, where it would be performing more services for you and the birth mother.

A typical independent adoption home study will include the following:

- Your completion of forms describing your life history (health, employment, marital history, existence of other children, religion, age, religion, et cetera.). Unlike a private agency, however, which may exclude you based upon your answers, the independent adoption home study entity is simply collecting the information to provide to the court, and share with the birth mother when appropriate.
- You will be fingerprinted for a criminal and child abuse check.
- A basic physical, usually with your personal physician. (If you have a physical impairment, or one spouse has a reduced life expectancy, this will not necessarily disqualify you in an independent adoption, but is a fact which will need to be shared with the birth mother.)
- Several letters of reference from friends/neighbors, whom you select.
- Verification of marriage (if married).
- Verification of the existence of health insurance, or a plan to deal with medical costs if you don't have insurance.
- Verification of employment. (The issue is simply that you can meet your family's needs, not reach a designated high income level.)
- Proof that any prior marriages were terminated by a court of law (via a certified copy of the divorce decree).
- Reports from your child's pediatrician that you have been properly caring for the child.
- Verification of assets and any past bankruptcies. (The only concern here is if you show an inability to properly manage your resources, which could therefore put your family at financial risk. A prior bankruptcy, followed by financial stability, would rarely be seen to demonstrate financial instability.)
- Home visits by your social worker. Most states require between two and four, usually over a six month period. If a pre-placement home study is required, both adoptive parents must usually be present at home at the same time. In the post-placement home study, both adoptive parents and the child are usually expected to be present. In almost all cases these visits are by appointment, not "surprise" visits.
- Inspecting your home. Unlike becoming a foster parent, or even an adoptive parent in an agency adoption, an independent

adoption home study will usually not need to meet the same safety levels imposed upon foster or agency adoptive parents. The reason traces back to the rational that in those placements the agency is usually liable for any injuries to the child which might result from an accident. In independent adoptions, the birth mother is making the placement directly, usually without an intermediary taking over her role as the "placing person." For example, in a foster parent home study, the agency might require them to have latches on all toilets and cabinets, even if the child to be placed is, at present, a baby and unable to move from its crib. In an independent adoption, many states will only require that the adoptive parents make changes which are necessary for the child's safety at the present time, and simply recommend alterations to be considered when needed as the child grows. This is closer to the decision-making adoptive parents have the freedom to make when conceiving a child themselves.

The Children Available

Virtually all children available through independent adoption are newborns. They are of all ethnic groups, typically mirroring the ethnicity of the community in which they live. If you live in a region which is mainly Caucasian, most birth mothers will be Caucasian, meaning Caucasian placements. If your region is predominantly Hispanic, expect most of the placements to be Hispanic.

It is understandable why so many adoptive parents select independent adoption as their chosen method of adoption, but why do so many birth mothers do so? There are several reasons. Many birth mothers may feel a stigma about approaching an adoption agency and feel better about contacting a private attorney. (This stigma is unfair to most agencies, as the majority are staffed by non-judgmental, caring people, but the stigma still exists in the minds of many birth mothers.) Also, adoption attorneys are often more aggressive in their networking efforts to reach birth mothers, resulting in more referrals. Lastly, independent adoption has the reputation of being more open and direct, which is pleasing to most birth mothers.

Waiting for a Child

There is no absolute guarantee of adopting quickly, even in an independent adoption. The vast majority of adoptive parents, however, report they successfully adopt a baby within 1-18 months via this method. For many lucky couples the waiting time can be only a few weeks or months (and I will be talking in this book how you can be one of them). One reason for this is that there are usually no "waiting lists" employed in independent adoption, where the adoptive parents must wait to get to the top of a list to be considered for an adoptive placement. Instead, most independent adoption attorneys show all their waiting adoptive parent families and leave the decision of who is the best family completely up to the birth mother (assuming the adoptive parents want to be shown to that particular birth mother). Also reducing the time for a placement is that many states do not require a pre-placement home study, allowing you to start the process instantly, rather than wait several months or more to complete a home study.

Even if you live in a state which requires a pre-placement home study for independent adoption, you can still normally start networking for, and meeting, birth mothers immediately. You would just concurrently start the pre-placement home study, as typically it must only be completed before a baby is placed with you. Even if you met a birth mother almost immediately, she will likely not be due before you could complete the home study. (Compare this to most agency adoptions where you usually cannot start working toward a birth mother match until the pre-placement home study is complete.)

The Openness of the Adoption

Many people think of independent and "open" adoption as being synonymous. This is confusing as *open* adoption is a vague term and can mean many things. When used to describe independent adoption, it usually refers at minimum to the fact most all adoptive parents and birth mothers meet in person (or at least by phone if they live in different states), and share first, or more commonly both first and last, names. Each state has different requirements and traditions about openness. The state-by-state review tells you what to expect in your state.

For birth mothers, personally meeting and selecting you can be emotionally rewarding to her as she can develop complete confidence in you as adoptive parents, greatly enhancing her likelihood of placing the baby for adoption as planned. She can visualize you as the child's parents and the child being nurtured by you. She can also take pride in her active role in personally creating your family, rather than relinquishing that role to an agency.

You also benefit from becoming acquainted before the birth. You can learn more about your child's biological mother in person, rather than reading about her from an impersonal written analysis. You will be able to share important information with your child about how the adoption occurred and why their birth mother felt adoption was her most loving option for the child - issues of great importance to a child as he or she grows.

A small number of states allow for confidentiality in independent adoption, as is done in some agency placements. Usually this is done by the use of an intermediary, such as an attorney, who will provide information about the birth mother and adoptive parents to each other, allowing each individual to withhold their identities if they so desire. This practice is rare, however, and even when states permit it the birth mother and adoptive parents often voluntarily opt for sharing full identities.

This open relationship can continue post-birth. The overwhelming vast majority of post-birth arrangements call for the birth mother to receive pictures of the child and updating letters from you once or twice a year (often the child's birthday and Christmas) and a promise from you that you will be raising your child with the knowledge that he or she was placed with you out of love by their birth mother. It is not uncommon for her to give you a photo of herself, and perhaps a letter to the child describing why this was the best way for her to show her love.

Sometimes, even if you and your birth mother have become well acquainted before the birth, some birth mothers elect to have complete privacy after the birth and wish no further contact. Not all are comfortable with openness. Only about five percent feel this way, however. An equally small number wish to stay in contact with you, but expand that contact to what is usually called "cooperative adoption." A less technical term would simply be "a very open adoption." This would be where you and the birth mother agree that not only will you send pictures and letters, but maintain a face-to-face relationship, perhaps getting together from one to several times a year. Some adoptive parents embrace this openness, while others feel uncomfortable. Talking about the issue with an adoption counselor, as well as your attorney, and reading the many books on the subject (see recommended books at adoption101.com) will help you determine what is right for you and your child. Regardless of what you decide, the degree of openness your adoption will have should be discussed with your birth mother before the birth to be sure you all have matching expectations.

Fees and Costs

There are several areas of possible expenses in an independent adoption. The major ones are:

- Attorney fees
- Home study costs
- Possible medical and pregnancy-related expenses for the birth mother

An attorney is usually considered a necessity in an independent adoption as there is no adoption agency overseeing the entire process. Even if adoptive parents find their own birth mother, there are many legal issues to be addressed requiring an attorney's skill and knowledge. Although the attorney's degree of involvement will vary from case to case, thus affecting the cost of the adoption, most adoption specialists charge between $1,500 to $9,000 to handle all aspects of an uncontested, independent adoption, depending upon many factors. The three biggest factors are the extent of the services offered, their location and reputation. Attorneys in more populated cities and highly commercial states tend to have higher fees than small town counterparts. And, of course, attorneys with established reputations and a history of success, like in any profession, are going to charge more than those lacking those qualities. Also, some attorneys expend a great deal of time and money in networking and outreach efforts to locate birth mothers, who in turn select their waiting clients. This can greatly increase the attorney's overhead costs, so expect to pay a few thousand dollars more if your attorney is also performing that service.

For their fee attorneys typically do the following:

- Fully educates you on the laws and procedures in adoption, and advises you on how to plan a successful adoption.
- Uses an established outreach program to find birth mothers, or advises you how to effectively do it on your own.
- Screens birth mothers to eliminate inadvisable situations.
- Obtains necessary background and health information about the birth parents.
- Provides physician, counseling and hospital referrals to the birth mother.
- Examines the case for potential legal or practical difficulties.
- Attempts to contact the birth father and give any legal notices required.
- Handles any legal problems that may arise.
- Helps the assigned social worker process the home study by providing what is needed.
- Manage an attorney-client trust account to provide expenses to the birth mother or other parties (doctors, landlord, et cetera) on behalf of the adoptive parents.
- Prepares the necessary legal documents.
- Appears in court to finalize the adoption.

Expenses for the birth mother may exist. If she needs assistance with expenses related to the birth, such as her medical costs or her living expenses, you can usually assist her by paying some or all of those expenses. Such assistance allows a birth mother to stay in her own residence when she would otherwise be short on rent, rather than relocating to an agency-style maternity home which may not be comfortable for her. Or she may be without a place to stay and you can help get her into an apartment. Each state has different regulations regarding what assistance may be provided and for how long. A small number of states forbid adoptive parents to provide any expenses other than medical and legal costs, not permitting help with such expenses as food and rent. Generally, however, if the expenses are *pregnancy-related,* they are permitted. Financial assistance   can usually be provided not only during the pregnancy if she is unable to provide for herself, as well as after the birth for a month or two, while she recuperates.

Of course, in some cases, there may be no pregnancy-related expenses. For example, if a birth mother has health insurance (perhaps through her parents' policy or her own employment) or state-provided Medicaid, there may be no medical costs for the you. Similarly, although some birth mothers are impoverished and desperately need financial help to pay for basic food and rent during the latter stages of the pregnancy, there are many birth mothers who require absolutely nothing, as they have adequate employment or live with their parents or boyfriend with no rental expenses.

Other less substantial expenses may involve the purchase of some maternity clothes and arranging for adoption counseling to prepare for the birth and adoption experience. These expenses usually total several hundred dollars.

Many adoption professionals estimate the total cost of most attorney-assisted independent adoptions, including attorney fees, home study fees, medical and living expenses (if any), to range between $4,000 and $20,000. Usually costs only go significantly higher if there are medical complications not covered by insurance. Particular expenses, as well as suggestions to reduce or eliminate such critical expenses as medical fees, will be addressed in subsequent chapters.

Bringing the Baby Home

One of the nicest parts about independent adoption is that it normally allows you to bring the baby home directly from the hospital. There is virtually never an intermediate foster parent placement while you wait for the birth mother's consent to become irrevocable, or other procedural steps to be satisfied. (The popularity of immediate placements in independent adoption has caused many private agencies to duplicate the practice in their adoptions.) Most states allow the birth mother to release her child directly into your physical custody immediately upon the hospital's discharge of the baby, usually when the baby is two or three days old.

There is a great benefit to you in taking your baby home immediately. Every new parent, adoptive or otherwise, knows the early days of a child's life are precious and irreplaceable. Naturally, the child also benefits from being with you immediately as his or her future parents, rather than foster parents. But there is also a disadvantage. There is always a possibility you will bond to a child the birth mother has not yet permanently released for adoption and that she may seek to reclaim. This rarely occurs, but you have to be aware it is a risk.

Identified adoptions

An *identified* adoption (sometimes called a *designated* adoption) is a hybrid of an independent and an agency adoption. Sometimes adoptive parents like some aspects of an independent adoption and other aspects of an agency adoption. Combine them, and what you have is an identified adoption.

An identified adoption typically involves your selection of an adoption attorney to network for birth mothers, screen potential birth mothers, create your adoptive match, then refer the birth mother to an agency to provide counseling, do your home study, and perhaps witness her consent. Depending upon the laws and procedures of your state, the attorney and agency will divide their legal duties to you. Essentially, identified adoptions start as an independent adoption, but are finalized as an agency adoption.

What is the advantage of this type of hybrid adoption? Usually it is increased speed and/or safety. Let's say for example that you think an attorney will be more effective in quickly matching you with a birth mother, and spotting potential legal risks in the adoption. This makes independent adoption attractive. But maybe you live in a state which has different procedures in how a birth mother gives up her rights in each type of adoption, and agency relinquishments are faster. You want to reduce the at-risk time you face post-birth, so you want to complete the adoption as an agency adoption. Presto, a hybrid - identified adoption.

Working with an out-of-state attorney

The majority of adoptive parents will do every aspect of the adoption in the state in which they live. This is true whether they are doing an independent or agency adoption. They will hire an attorney there, the birth mother will live and give birth there, and the adoption will be finalized in their local court. If you live in a state with great attorneys from whom to choose, good adoption laws making you feel secure, and a sufficient number of birth mothers in your region or state, why leave your own state?

Many adoptive parents aren't so lucky. What if you don't like what the local attorneys have to offer? Perhaps there are few adoptive placements in your region or state. Maybe you are concerned that your state has laws which give a birth mother an excessively long period in which to change her mind. Or could it be that your state is fine, but you want to expand your options to increase the likelihood of being picked for an adoptive placement quickly. Clearly, there are many reasons to either do your adoption out of state, or work in both your home state and another state concurrently. Let's look at the two primary ways to do this.

Interstate adoption. Let's say you've found an exceptional attorney, but he or she is located in another state. Does that mean you can't work with that attorney because you are in a different state? No. In fact, it is getting more and more common to have an interstate aspect to adoptions. For example, you can hire the out-of-state attorney to help you find a birth mother and create your adoptive match, arrange for birth mother counseling, assist with her signing her consent to adoption, and have the child discharged directly to you from the hospital. Then, very shortly after birth, when the initial paperwork is done and you get interstate approval to bring the child across state lines (discussed in Chapter 12), you return home and raise the child there. Depending upon the laws of your home state, you would have an in-state attorney and/or agency. The agency would do your home study and write the final report to the court to complete the adoption, and the attorney would do any legal work needed in your home state. Doing an adoption involving two states sometimes creates a conflict between state laws, although rarely does this become a problem. This issue is discussed in Chapter 12.

A twist on the above is if the out-of-state attorney finds a birth mother for you and creates the planned placement, but perhaps the birth mother doesn't wish to stay in that state. Perhaps she has no place to live and has recently lost her job. To get to know you better and have you close for the moment the birth occurs, you can discuss having her relocate for the birth to your home state. After the birth she may return to her original state, relocate elsewhere, or decide she likes what your state has to offer and stay. In an adoption such as this, your local attorney and/or agency would be performing all the needed legal functions, other than the initial act of creating the adoptive match.

You might worry that using an attorney out-of-state, and another attorney or agency in your home state, would double the cost. That is not true, however. As discussed in more detail in Chapter 4 and Chapter 9, many attorneys and agencies only charge for the services they perform. Accordingly, if they are dividing their duties, their fees should be proportionally less. Not every adoption professional will work that way, but most will.

Non-resident adoption. Some adoptive parents want to do virtually the entire adoption outside their home state. You might choose to do this because your state allows a birth mother a long time to change her mind and the birth state's laws only permit a few days. Maybe you recognize birth mothers are more likely to start adoption planning if you are permitted to help them with their pregnancy-related costs, and your state does not permit them, but the laws of the birth state do. Or perhaps your adoption can be finalized in court much faster out-of-state. For these reasons, you might want to adopt from a state permitting independent non-resident adoption.

Many states permit independent non-resident adoption. They are: Alabama, Alaska, Arkansas, California, Hawaii, Iowa, Indiana, Kansas, Louisiana, Maine, Maryland, Michigan, Missouri, New Hampshire, New Jersey, New Mexico, New York, North Dakota, Ohio, Oregon, Pennsylvania, South Carolina, Texas, Utah, Virginia and Washington. You can learn more about each state's laws and the attorneys and agencies within that state in the state-by state review.

A non-resident adoption is basically just like the interstate adoption discussed above. You selected an out-of-state attorney to help match you with a birth mother. That attorney, however, continues to do virtually everything in the adoption, rather than transferring everything to your home state. After creating the adoptive match, he or she can make sure the child is placed with you directly from the hospital, arrange for the birth mother to sign her consent to adoption, do the legal work and finalize your adoption in court. An agency in your home state will only be needed to do any required home study work as determined by the laws of the state of where the child is born. Unlike interstate adoptions, where there a potential conflict of laws between the two states, in non-residency adoption generally only the laws of the birth state will apply as everything was done there. Non-resident adoptions can also be done working with an agency in both states, rather than an attorney, making the adoption an agency, rather than an independent, adoption.

When Independent Adoption is Not Permitted in Your State

Five states do not permit independent adoption, requiring that all adoptions be completed only by agencies. These states are Colorado, Connecticut, Delaware, Massachusetts and North Dakota. If you live in one of these states you either must do an agency adoption in-state, or work with another state. If you elect to do an out-of-state adoption, you may still be able to initiate the adoption with an attorney, as long as your home state completes it as a full agency adoption. Because each region within these states may differ on this policy, however, it is best to check with the agency which will be doing your home study and writing the final report to the court, to be sure they foresee no problems with your plan. Alternatively, you can do a non-resident adoption, which will virtually eliminate your state and its laws from the adoption. Even there, however, the out-of-state authorities will want to see a home study of you from an agency in your area, so check in advance to be sure they will cooperate in that plan. Usually, there are no problems.

CHAPTER 4

SELECTING THE RIGHT ATTORNEY

Here's what most people do to find their adoption attorney:

They open their local yellow pages, or they go online, and select a lawyer conveniently located.

And there you have the reason why most people fail at adoption, or take longer to succeed than they should have.

Think about it. If you're married, did you find your spouse in the town where you grew up? Did you buy your house down the street from your mom and dad's place? Did your find your career job around the corner from your high school? I'm betting the answer to several of these questions is "no." So why should you think the best attorney for you, and your unique needs, would just happen to be in your local phone book, just a short distance from your home?

That doesn't mean there isn't a well-qualified adoption attorney right in your region, and you might actually be hiring one of them. For most people, however, if that is the beginning and end of their search, the adoption is doomed from the start. Let's look at why that is, and what the right approach is to take.

Let me start with the basics of why you need an attorney. The attorney's role is to explain every aspect of the adoption process to you in advance so you fully understand what is ahead, then guide you through it. If you are planning a traditional *agency* adoption, you may not need an attorney at all, or for only minimal services, depending upon the state in which you complete your adoption. However, if you are like the majority of adoptive parents seeking to adopt a newborn through *independent* or *identified* adoption, the selection of your adoption attorney is critical.

In addition to their obvious legal function, many adoption attorneys also have a network of referrals leading to birth mothers being referred to their office, creating adoptive matches as well. Simply doing one of these two functions is of great importance. Doing both is monumental, making the selection of your attorney likely the most important decision in your adoption.

You might already have a general practice attorney in mind to assist you. This might be an attorney you previously used for a non-adoption purpose, such as drafting a will. Or perhaps a friend has recommended their family law attorney who does "some adoptions on the side." In most cases I think selecting such an attorney is a mistake. We live in an era of specialization. The world in general, and law in particular, is so complex it is almost impossible to be a "jack of all trades." Not a good one anyway. Would you consider consulting a dermatologist for a bad back? Or an orthopedic surgeon to examine your eyes? So why would you trust the formation of your family to someone who "dabbles" in adoption?

Finding the right attorney is not a difficult task if you know how to approach it. There are specific steps to follow to find not just a great attorney, but one who is right for your unique needs and desires. Let me list these steps, then we will look into each one individually:

1. Compile a list of possible attorneys.
2. Fine-tune your list.
3. Specific questions to ask the attorney.
4. Test the attorney's knowledge.
5. Determine if their personality and approach to adoption matches yours.

Compile a List of Possible Attorneys

There are tens of thousands of attorneys in the country, and several hundred who specialize in adoption. My advice is start with a wide net, and narrow it down to find an attorney not only well qualified, but with whom you feel personally comfortable. You may be looking only for an attorney in your home state, or in states other than your own. Regardless of the number of attorneys you will elect to hire to start your adoption quest, let's look at creating your list.

Only consider attorneys in your preferred geographical states. Your selected regions or states from which to adopt will be unique to you and different from other adoptive parents. You might live in a well-populated region in a state with advantageous adoption laws and a good percentage of birth mothers. If so, you will likely select an attorney in your home region and state. Another adoptive family may live in a state with very poor adoption options, so they've selected several states they feel are best for them, and will consider attorneys in those states.

To determine the right states for you, consider the many in-state and out-of-state options we discussed in Chapter 2, and the information provided in the state-by-state review in Chapter 15. Depending upon where you live, and the kind of adoption you want, different states will be best for each adoptive family. It is within only these states that you need focus your search for the best attorneys.

Consider members of the American Academy of Adoption Attorneys (AAAA). This membership organization has more than three hundred members nationwide and is limited to attorneys with demonstrated skill and expertise in adoption. The completion of fifty adoptions, twenty of them within the last two years, is a minimum requirement to become an AAAA member. Most have completed hundreds, however. Members are listed in the state-by-state review, including their biographies detailing important information about their background and experience, as well as contact information. Additionally, the AAAA website, adoptionattorneys.org. It lists all members by state, with full contact information.

Sometimes people fear a "specialist" will charge more. This can be true (although it is usually well worth it for the extra knowledge and experience), but the reverse is also true. Often hiring a specialist is actually less expensive. This is because a non-specializing attorney will not know the needed procedures and documents to prepare, and will charge you for that research time. The experienced adoption attorney typically already knows the needed information and has prepared the required documents hundreds of times, meaning less work hours are required, and less time for which you are billed.

Are there good adoption attorneys who are not in the AAAA? I'm sure there are, and we will get to how to find them in a moment, but the AAAA remains an excellent starting point. It is there you will find most of the nation's premier adoption attorneys. As the only national adoption attorney organization, why would an adoption attorney *not* be a member? The AAAA is more than a membership organization where attorneys pay a fee just to get a fancy plaque for their wall. There is a great deal of information-sharing between members, and attendance at periodic national educational conferences is required. Some attorneys apply for membership but are denied, or are removed from the organization due to their failure to meet or maintain the organization's high standards.

What if there isn't an AAAA member in your area, or you don't feel the closest member is right for you, but you want an AAAA attorney handling your adoption? Don't worry. First of all, as was discussed in Chapter 2, you don't necessarily need an attorney right in your home area, or even your own state. True, you will likely be finalizing your adoption in your local courthouse, unless you do a non-resident adoption, but that is the simplest part of the entire adoption. It's the equivalent of the "graduation ceremony" after years of college. The difficult work is in getting there. The smart thing to do is to find the best attorney for you, whether they are close or distant. Then if need be, that attorney can use another attorney right in your hometown to make the final court appearance, often at a token fee.

Check your local online and directory yellow pages under "adoption," or perhaps "attorneys – adoption/family law."

Although many of these attorneys may lack the qualifications you need and deserve, you might get lucky and find an excellent attorney who is not an AAAA member. This applies to your local yellow pages, as well as those in other counties or states you are considering. Out-of-region yellow pages can usually be found at your library. You can also access the same information anywhere in the nation via internet sites like Google by typing in something like "adoption, Los Angeles," or sites like yahoo.com's "yellow pages" feature, or yellowpages.com.

Join or visit local adoptive parent support groups. Many of the people attending these meetings have "been there, done that." They've completed the process you are just starting. They can tell you about their experiences with local attorneys, both good and bad, and perhaps some outside your region as well. To find out if there is an adoptive parent support group in your area, try calling local adoption agencies and attorneys who might know of some. Because these support groups are small, and sometimes just meet in members' homes, they are often not listed in the phone book.

Other resources listing adoptive parent support groups in each state are the *Adoptive Families* magazine's website, adoptivefamilies.com, and the Child Welfare Information Gateway (a federal government site, formerly known as the National Adoption Information Clearinghouse, childwelfare.gov (The sites are constantly redesigned, so giving you "first click here, then click here" directions would be futile. But if you explore the sites, you should find their listings of local adoptive parent support groups)

For more information about *Adoptive Families* magazine and the Child Welfare Information Gateway, please see Appendix B.

Join Resolve, or attend one of their meetings. Resolve is a very established and respected national infertility organization with regional chapters throughout the country. Part of their focus on infertility includes adoption. Many of their members are in the process of, or have completed, an adoption, and can talk about attorneys they used. To find a Resolve chapter near you, visit resolve.org.

For more information about Resolve, please see Appendix B.

Call your local bar association. Some bar associations have referral services based upon the attorney's specialty. Although this will possibly lead you to a good attorney, be aware that a local bar association "referral" is not as impressive as it may sound. Most local bar associations are merely voluntary associations which attorneys pay a fee to join (unlike the state bar, which is mandatory). Many of the attorneys being "referred" to you have done nothing more than fill out a form to be included in their list of recommendations. There is usually no requirement of demonstrating expertise or experience in adoptions. It is often the equivalent of a yellow page ad, but provided over the phone. Still, it is worth checking into when starting your list.

Call your local court. Each court has a different department which accepts Petitions for Adoptions (the document which starts the legal process in court) for filing. In some states this might be the probate court, or perhaps the family law court. Call the court's main number and ask to speak to one of the clerks who handle the filing of Petition for Adoptions. When you reach the correct person, explain you are planning to adopt and are compiling a list of possible attorneys. Ask which attorneys file a lot of Petitions within your county. Some clerks will be willing to share some names with you, and some won't. Remember, although the cases filed are confidential, you are only asking for the names of attorneys they see a lot in court on adoption-related matters. There is nothing confidential about that. The clerk's only remaining concern will be if he or she will be perceived as giving a recommendation by passing along some names (which they are barred from doing). Explain that you are not asking for a recommendation, simply the names of attorneys who are busy in their courthouse doing adoptions.

Talk to other adoptive parents. The more you start talking about adoption, the more you will find that people you already know have adopted. Often they have not previously volunteered the information, as there was no need to do so. But upon hearing you share that interest, they are happy to share their adoption experiences. There are millions of successful adoptive parents out there. You will find them everywhere: at work, in your neighborhood, at your place of worship. Ask who their attorney was, and other attorneys they've heard about from their friends who have adopted. Generally, adoptive parents tend to know a lot of other adoptive parents.

Talk to any attorneys you know. You may have used an attorney to draw up a will, handle a car accident, or whom you just know socially. Although they may know nothing about adoption law, they may know of other attorneys who specialize in adoption. Sometimes these referrals are more to "friends" than necessarily the best attorney. Still, sometimes these leads can be viable.

Visit the Adoption101.com and *Adoptive Families* websites. Adoption101.com is a leading information adoption website and

Adoptive Families is respected adoption magazine. Both their websites are quite helpful. Both have a state-by-state listing of adoption attorneys.

Talk to people you know in the health care industry. Adoption attorneys constantly work with doctors, counselors and hospitals regarding the care of the birth mothers they are working with. For this reason, some health-care professionals may be able to tell you about attorneys with whom they have had contact in prior adoption situations.

You will be surprised how quickly you can compile a list of possible adoption attorneys, and how large the list becomes. Don't worry if it seems unmanageably large. We will be paring it down fairly quickly.

Fine-Tune Your List

Okay, you've got the list. What now?

Depending upon the scope of your search, you might have only a dozen attorneys on your list, or more likely, many times that, and they will be located in one or several states. Now it's time to contact each one and get more information. Although nothing is wrong with calling and asking questions to each law office, I'd recommend you initially start by asking for their written materials. There are two reasons for this. One is that there is so much information for you to obtain about each attorney, it is almost impossible for any busy law office to verbally give all that information to every person calling. Remember, they have work to do and clients to serve. The other reason is that looking at the materials they send you is your first chance to see a sample of the attorney's work.

To fine-tune your list, and make it a manageable size, we now need to do some fact finding. Just because an attorney does some adoptions, perhaps even specializes in it, does not mean he or she is the right attorney for you. Different qualities are important to different people, and the best adoption attorney for one adoptive family may not be the best one for you. Here are some recommended steps to take, or questions to ask, to narrow down your list:

- Examine the written information provided to you by the attorney. Is it clear and concise? Does it give you bona fide information about the adoption process, the attorney's qualifications and the likely fees? Or is it a "puff piece" featuring a cute baby on the cover of a brochure, but little hard information? If the attorney can't provide you with professional, clear information to convince you to become a client, imagine how bad he or she will be once you've become a client and they've already got your money. Also, you are seeing your first sample of the attorney's work product. Is it well written, neat and professionally presented? If not, why would you expect their court documents prepared on your behalf, or correspondence to important people in your case, to be any better?

- When you ask for written materials, the attorney's staff may tell you the same information is available on their website. If so, by all means, check out the website. I still recommend, however, that you ask for their written materials. That is because the website is likely the work of a web professional. You want a chance to see the work of the attorney and/or his staff, and their written materials will give you that.

- In your initial phone call to the attorney's office, do you get a good feeling from the phone receptionist, secretary or answering machine message? Professional and friendly? Remember, this will be the same person or message a potential birth mother will likely get on the phone in her initial call. If the person or message is not warm and friendly, why would a birth mother be interested in staying on the line to speak to the attorney? That would mean fewer birth mothers to be considering you as adoptive parents through that office.

- Call the state bar association where the attorney practices, or visit their website. (Each state has a mandatory state bar association.) In most all states, records are available to the public regarding any discipline against the attorney for inappropriate conduct or malfeasance. Discipline by the state bar can result in disbarment, temporary suspension of the attorney's license or a public reprimand. Even the least severe discipline, a public reprimand, is seen as a quite serious among most attorneys. Be aware, however, that a "clean record" for an attorney is only confirmation he or she has not been disciplined for something. An attorney may still be a very poor practitioner, yet manage to have not committed any indiscretions requiring sanctions by the state bar.

Don't be surprised if you quickly eliminate half the attorneys you are considering just from the steps above. Does this surprise you? Sadly, the legal profession is no better than similar fields. Think of all the doctors you've met whom you didn't really care for and would not trust to treat you again. How about all the great, and bad, teachers you've had in your life? Attorneys are no better or worse. Just be glad you can so quickly eliminate some and not waste more of your time on the ones not right for you.

Specific Questions to Ask the Attorney

Now it's time to pare down your list to just a few attorneys, and lead to hiring the right one. Some of the following questions may be answered by the attorney's advance materials you have received, or provided by other materials, such as their biographies in the state-by-state review, or the attorney's website. Some questions, however, you will have to personally ask the attorney in a phone call or in a personal consultation. For adoptive parents seeking an attorney to provide legal services and help them be matched with a birth mother to start a newborn adoption, all the following questions will be relevant. If you already have your own birth mother, or don't feel you will need an attorney's guidance in being selected by one, some of these questions will not be necessary.

- *How many years have you been an attorney?* There is no perfect answer here. For example, an attorney with fifty years experience is impressive, but are they so advanced in years that a birth mother will not be able to relate to them? What about an attorney with only a few years experience? Likely they are younger and can work more effectively with seventeen-year-old birth moms, but do they possess enough experience? So what's the answer? It's a combination of things and requires answers to the next few questions, so keep reading.

- *Is your practice limited to, or does it primarily consist of, adoption?* The more specialized an attorney is, the more likely he or she is to be up to date in every aspect of adoption law, on both a state and federal level, as both can impact your adoption. If an attorney handles a few adoptions a year, as well as a few dozen bankruptcies, some divorce work, and the occasional drunk driving case, they show an admirable diversity, but will he or she have the same depth of knowledge as the attorney who focuses exclusively, or primarily, on adoption? (Let me revisit the comparison of doctors and attorneys. If you needed surgery on your spine, would you go to a general practitioner also who delivers babies, and helps the local teenagers with their acne? I'm guessing "no." You'd be seeking a specialist. In almost every case, the more specialized the professional is, the better trained they are within that narrow specialty. A general practice attorney who confidently tells you: "Adoptions are simple; there's no need to specialize in them," is only proving to you how little he or she knows about the field, and what can potentially go wrong. They just don't know enough to know it. In a few moments I'll even give you some "test questions" to ask the attorney, as a way to determine their knowledge.

- *How many adoptions have you done in your career?* The years of experience are important, as is their degree of specialization in adoption. More than anything, however, it comes down to numbers. Does this mean more is always better? Not necessarily, as long as the attorney has completed a significant number of adoptions to have sufficient experience. You will find some attorneys, particularly those in major metropolitan areas, who have completed hundreds and hundreds of adoptions, maybe even more than a thousand. That's impressive. However, that by itself does not make the attorney better than one who has completed only one hundred fifty. That is still an impressive number of adoptions, and enough to have seen most possible situations come up, and have experience handling them.

- *How many adoptions do you complete each year? How about last year?* This question is particularly important for you if you are hiring an attorney to not just do the legal work of the adoption, but to help match you with a birth mother. You will find that most adoption specialists complete from fifteen to seventy adoptions a year. Generally, the larger number is for attorneys in large cities. A high number of adoptions each year, particularly the most recent year, is impressive. As you will see in the next few questions, however, that information by itself can be misleading.

- *How many adoptive parents do you work with at one time waiting to be matched by a birth mother? Is there a maximum number you work with at one time? How many do you have at this moment?* These questions are all related, and critically important if you are looking to your attorney for his or her birth mother matching skills. Let's say attorney "Bob" completes sixty adoptions a year, and he works with one hundred adoptive parents at one time waiting to be matched with a birth mother. Attorney "Susan" only completes twenty, but she limits her number of clients waiting for a match to ten. Mathematically, Susan actually has a more successful ratio, as her clients on average are waiting six months for an adoptive match, while Bob's clients are averaging a wait of almost twice that long. Plus, assuming Susan isn't filling her time with other non-adoption cases, her smaller caseload may indicate she has more time to work on each case, and to get to know each client. (Sometimes bigger is better, and sometimes it isn't. There is no simple answer, which is why there are so many factors to consider.)

- *What is the average wait of your clients for an adoptive match? What is a soonest versus longest estimate of waiting time to be picked based upon prior clients?* On your own, you can "do the math" of a typical waiting time for an adoptive match based upon the attorney's estimates of the number of adoptions done annually divided into the waiting number of clients. Still, it is helpful to hear it from the attorney. For example, if the attorney does fifty adoptions a year and works with one hundred waiting clients (100 divided by 50 = 2), that tells you the average wait is about two years. If that same attorney tells you his clients' average wait is five months, something is wrong. Either the attorney is not being honest about some of those figures, or there is an explanation for the disparity. Ask the attorney to explain any confusion.

- *Are most of the adoptions you help arrange "open" or "closed?"* Sometimes the issue of an adoption being open or closed is due to state law on the subject. Other times, it is due to mindset of the attorney who consciously or subconsciously feels one type of adoption is best, and that feeling is picked up by birth mothers and adoptive parents working with him or her. (As a general rule, most newborn adoptions in the United States are to some degree, open. Usually this means meeting in person, and sharing identities. Slightly more open will include the adoptive parents sending the birth mother an annual picture and updating letter about the child until adulthood. Still more open might be where it is agreed the birth mother will have some continuing face-to-face contact with you and the child. Make sure that the attorney's philosophy, and his or her typical cases, matches your preferred degree of openness.)
- *Do some adoptive parents who hire you never get picked by a birth mother, or have to wait several years? Do you find these adoptive parents have any ethnic, religious or other qualities in common?* There are two reasons to ask this question. One is that if the attorney finds some families don't get picked by a birth mother, or have a much harder time being picked, you want to know if you fall into that category. For example, if you are a Hispanic couple seeking a Hispanic child, and you are hiring an attorney who is in a predominantly Caucasian region, there will be fewer birth mothers of your ethnicity to select you. It would likely make more sense for such couples to select an attorney in a border state, like California or Texas, with a higher percentage of Hispanics. This would make more sense than hiring an attorney in Idaho, for example. (The same issue can arise regarding religion. Parts of Utah would be an example of this, where the Mormon religion is quite prevalent. A non-Mormon family would likely find that attorneys practicing in Utah would be less effective for them. America is a very homogenous nation, however, and many adoptions cross cultural and ethnic lines. Still, the reality is that many birth mothers and adoptive parents' first choice is to stay within their ethnic group. If an attorney isn't suited for your particular individual characteristics, best to know it right away. The second reason to ask an attorney if some of their clients don't get picked is to judge their honesty.

The reality is that some adoptive parents desiring a newborn child won't get picked by a birth mother, just as some wonderful people out there will never find the love of their life and get married. Life is not always fair. To me, if an attorney tells you *every* client gets picked, this either means he or she has only handled a small number of adoptions over a short period of time, or the attorney is exaggerating his or her success. There is nothing wrong with an attorney telling you some adoptive parents fail. The key is how often does it happen and why. If only a small percentage of adoptive parents are not picked, such as less than five percent, the ninety-five percent success rate is actually incredibly successful. (Later we will discuss strategies to increase the chances you will not end up in the small percentage of adoptive parents who do not succeed.)

- *Does the state in which you practice allow you to find birth mothers for adoptive parents and create a "match??* Several states either bar attorneys from "finding" birth mothers to create an adoptive match, or may permit it but forbid the attorney to charge for it. These states include Connecticut, Georgia, Illinois, Maryland, Minnesota, New Jersey and New York. If you live in one of these states (and plan to finalize your adoption in your home state, as most do) it should not discourage you if your attorney can't introduce you to birth mothers. Although it is great when an attorney has the added benefit of finding a birth mother for you, let's not forget that an attorney's primary role – and a critical one – is to give you legal advice at all stages of your adoption. This is an especially important role in your home state. If you want an attorney to be networking for you, in addition to your own networking efforts (or in place of it), you can consider retaining an out-of-state attorney in addition to your home state attorney, as discussed elsewhere in this book.

- *What methods do you use to find birth mothers, or to help us do it, resulting in a birth mother selecting us.* There are many strategies you, as well as your attorney, can use to find women facing unplanned pregnancies and desiring to start an adoption. Later, I'll be sharing my most successful networking methods, including some unusual ones. Every attorney has their favorite methods, and you need to make sure you agree with the methods your potential attorney plans to use. (Some attorneys practice in states where it is not legal for them to attempt to find birth mothers (the state-by-state review tells you which these states are). Accordingly, in those states, the attorney will give you advice on what techniques he or she thinks is best. You will want to make sure that you see eye-to-eye on the methods to be used, as either you, or the attorney, may not feel comfortable with some types the other plans to use. Some networking strategies are very aggressive and public, which some adoptive parents might find uncomfortable. There are also many subtle and more private techniques. Regardless of the kind of networking campaign you plan to employ, you want to make sure the attorney shares your view.)

- *What percentage of the birth mothers you find are in-state, as compared to coming from another state?* If you don't care which state your birth mother resides in (affecting your travel costs, easy access to the birth mother pre-birth and at birth, and the state law which will apply) this may not be an important issue for you. However, if you are retaining an attorney in, let's say Washington, because you want a Washington birthmother, or you want to do a non-resident adoption there, why would you want to retain an attorney who finds all his or her birth mothers via a method leading to out-of-state birth mother contacts, such as out-of-state yellow page or internet advertisements.

- *When birth mothers contact you, how are we and other adoptive parents shown to her, giving us a chance to be selected?* Some attorneys show all their waiting adoptive parents, while some favor those who have waited the longest, showing those families at the exclusion of his or her newest clients. Others only show a few adoptive parents, selected to match characteristics of the birth mother. (I believe the best approach is to show every adoptive family to every birth mother, unless the birth mother has characteristics not desired by the adoptive parents (ethnicity, drug usage, projected expenses, open or closed adoption, et cetera.). The reason I favor that wide approach, rather than the subjective thinking of the attorney selecting the "right" families, is it assumes the attorney knows what the birth mother is truly looking for. The reality, however, is that often opposites attract. The "spark" of attraction is impossible to define. Furthermore, the more adoptive families the birth mother has to choose from, the more likely she can be truly happy with her decision. For example, is she more likely to find a family she truly likes, and therefore will follow through on her adoption plan, if she chooses from only two families. . . or from twenty? What would our chances to be a successful marriage if we had only two or three prospective spouses from which to choose? Adoption is no different.)

- *What percentage of your clients find a birth mother through your efforts, as compared to your clients finding a birth mother on their own?* If one of the key things you hope to accomplish in hiring an attorney is to have his or her help in finding a birth mother to in turn select you as adoptive parents, you will want to know how effective their efforts are. For example, an attorney may complete an impressive fifty adoptions a year, but if eighty percent of the adoptive parents found their own birth mother, it is not as impressive as an attorney completing twenty-five, all of which resulted from his or her own birth mother networking efforts.

- *Does your fee include your networking efforts to help us get picked by a birth mother, or is it a separate fee?* If the attorney is networking for birth mothers, leading them to contact his or her office to in turn select one of the waiting adoptive families, a lot of money is being expended by the attorney in that effort. This might take the form of mailings to health care professionals, yellow page advertising, internet promotion of their website geared to birth mothers, contributions of time and/or money to organizations which indirectly leads to referrals, et cetera. Just like with any attorney expenses, these costs are passed on to you as the client benefiting from those efforts. The question is if it is part of their standard fee, which includes their legal work, or a separate fee specifically designated for networking efforts. (It does not matter which of the two payment options the attorney uses. What does matter is that you know what you are paying for. For example, if one attorney's fee includes networking efforts, and he or she has demonstrated success with those efforts in the past leading you to believe an adoptive match is likely for you, it is understandable his or her fees will be higher than an attorney who does not offer those services. Sometimes this makes it hard to compare fees, as the services vary.

However, as you start contacting many attorneys and agencies, you will soon get a feel for what is a reasonable cost for birth mother networking efforts in a particular region. This might range from a few hundred, to several thousand dollars. The issue of networking, and its costs, is discussed in more detail in Chapter 8.)

- *Can we be listed with other attorneys and/or agencies while we are working with you, and proceed with whichever attorney or agency finds an adoptive placement first?* The goal of every adoption agency and attorney should be to help you adopt. To that end, if you wish to hire more than one attorney to obtain your goal as quickly as possible, you need attorneys who will work within that philosophy. Most all will be agreeable. Some attorneys, however, require you to only work with them. I believe this is wrong, as the attorney is making him or herself the central person in the adoption, not you.

- *Do we pay for your services as we work through the adoption, or do we pay it all in advance?* Some attorneys, especially in matters like criminal cases, charge their entire fee in advance, or require a retainer for their anticipated total fee, then bill against that and return any unused portion. Adoptions tend to be billed differently. For example, if you are waiting to be matched with a birth mother, it is not yet even known if you will *have* an adoption. For that reason, many adoption attorneys charge their fee in stages, so you are only paying for the services as they are provided. (Other attorneys may charge their entire fee in advance, but you should only accept such a fee arrangement if the unused portion is held in a trust account and any unused portion will be returned to you with a written accounting of all expenses. Be very cautious of attorneys who require a disproportionate payment, compared to other attorneys, in advance, particularly if it is non-refundable. While you might be led to think that paying more means you are getting more, this is often not the case. Often you will find the best, and most ethical, attorneys charge the most reasonable fees.)

- *What are typical birth mother expenses we will be expected to pay?* Almost all states allow adoptive parents to help with the adoption and birth expenses. Often this includes medical bills, and the birth mother's living costs while she is incapacitated due to the pregnancy. Some birth mothers have few, or no, expenses (they have insurance and are employed, or live at home), while others may have significant expenses. This question is important because some attorneys either practice in an area with a higher cost of living, or choose to operate their practice in a way which results in higher birth mother costs. As a general rule, expenses for a birth mother ranging from a few hundred to several thousand for total living costs during the pregnancy is not unusual. (When you get into significantly higher amounts, however, it is a sign for potential caution. For example, does the attorney "bribe" birth mothers to work with him or her by offering them an ocean view condo (at your expense) at quadruple the rent of a typical apartment? Does the attorney entice out-of-state birth mothers to travel to meet with you by providing them a first class plane ticket rather than coach? Needless to say, such behavior is not conducive to a successful adoption, or finding the right kind of birth mother.)

• *What is the fee for your initial consultation?* Some attorneys offer free consultations. You know this because you see them offered on TV, right? Other attorneys charge you for their time, and considering legal fees range from $150 to $300 hourly depending upon where in the nation you live, a two hour consultation with an adoption specialist will cost you approximately $300 to $600. A good consultation will completely educate you about the adoption process, not just the basic legal aspects. This would include: strategies to be used to find a birth mother, screening birth mothers, what happens when meeting a birth mother in person, the hospital experience, potential risks (the birth mother's time in which to change her mind and revoke her consent, et cetera.), birth father's rights, permitted expenses, interstate adoptions, the Indian Child Welfare Act, the home study, finalization in court and the federal adoption tax credit. The initial consultation will let you determine if you like the attorney. Does he or she explain things thoroughly? Can you imagine the attorney meeting with birth mothers and making them comfortable? (Let's get back to the enticement of free consultations. Sounds good, and in some cases, it may be. Generally speaking, however, while some attorneys, such as personal injury attorneys, are in the habit of offering free consultations, well-qualified adoption attorneys - or any specialist for that matter - are not. Usually free consultations are offered only when the attorney's practice is lacking in clients (not that they'd admit that's the reason). Think about it. Would a successful and established heart specialist, copyright attorney or dental surgeon sit down with you and spend two to three hours for no compensation? And then do it again for the next family after you? And the family after that? No. You generally get what you pay for. Well-qualified professionals get paid for their time, and to expect otherwise is not reasonable.)

- *Do you encourage counseling for birth mothers?* Placing a child for adoption will be one of the most emotional moments of a birth mother's life. The more prepared she is, the more likely it is she can make the placement as planned and handle the emotions of birth. Some state laws require counseling, and some do not. If an attorney feels counseling is not important, or in any way discourages birth mothers from receiving it, I believe it indicates a lack of not only empathy, but a basic understanding of the emotions at work, and the making of a successful adoption.

The answers to these questions should give you an excellent idea of the full scope of the attorney's services, fees, personality, and view of adoption. Do they match your vision of how an adoption should be handled? Do they make you feel comfortable and confident? Likely your list of possible attorneys is getting smaller and smaller, and those on it are getting better and better.

Test the Attorney's Knowledge

No, I'm not suggesting you hand your prospective attorney a #2 pencil and a written exam. Nor am I suggesting you be obvious, and perhaps offensive, that you are testing the attorney's knowledge. What I am recommending you do is ask about certain areas likely to arise in an adoption, which are normal questions to ask. The key here is that by the time you have finished this book, you will be savvy enough to know a good answer from a bad one.

Let's say you've narrowed down your list to just a few attorneys. It's now time to meet them in person, to see if you want to work with them. You might get some to speak to you on the phone if you explain you've read their materials and just have a question or two. For more than that, however, you will need to schedule a consultation.

Here are some recommended questions:

- *I've heard about something called the Indian Child Welfare Act. Can you explain what that is?* As we will discuss later in Chapter 12, this is a federal law, normally superseding state law. It provides that if a child is a member of an Indian tribe, or eligible for membership, the tribe must be given notice and certain procedures followed. If the attorney is unfamiliar with the Indian Child Welfare Act, or says it never applies in their state, beware. More and more adoptions are at least potentially touched by the Indian Child Welfare Act, such as where the birth mother is not actually a member, but has a small degree of tribal heritage which could make her a member. Noncompliance with the Indian Child Welfare Act can potentially invalidate an adoption, a high cost to pay for an attorney's ignorance. It is not necessary for the attorney know every aspect of the law off the top of his or her head, but should have some familiarity.

- *We may do an interstate adoption. Can you explain to me how the Interstate Compact works?* As we will discuss in Chapter 12, many adoptions are interstate, where you live in a different state than that of the child's birth/residency. The Interstate Compact for the Placement of Children provides that prior to a child being transported across state lines by adoptive parents, certain requirements exist, such as your preplacement home study, and approval from both states' Interstate Compact administrators. This is fundamental knowledge every attorney should have.

- *What are the birth mother and birth father's rights? Can they change their minds, and if so, for how long?* These issues are the most fundamental and important of all, so the attorney should know these issues frontwards and backwards regarding their own state. Do not, however, expect them to know this information for other states without some research, however, as each state has different laws.

- *Is there a federal tax credit for adoptive parents?* If the attorney does many adoptions, he or she should certainly know about the federal tax credit. The amount of the credit, and income eligibility changes each year. In basic terms, if the adoptive parents have a modified adjusted gross income of $189,710 or less for an adoption completed in 2012, they are eligible for a tax credit of $12,650 per child adopted. The income can actually go up to $229,710, but the credit is proportionally reduced when income exceeds $189,710. It is not reasonable to expect an adoption attorney to know the detailed tax repercussions of adoption. That is for a professional tax advisor. However, they should know the existence and basics of the tax credit.

The above questions are just a sampling of what an attorney needs to know, but they are diversified enough to give you an idea of an attorney's knowledge. Those particular questions may not even be applicable to your individual adoption, but it doesn't matter, as they are an excellent indicator of what your attorney knows, or doesn't know. If he or she is ignorant about these issues, the same is likely true regarding other important adoption issues. If you find you know more than the attorney, simply by reading this book, look for the door.

Determine if the Attorney's Personality and Approach to Adoption Matches Yours

Doing an adoption is a very emotional process, with many emotional highs, and potentially, some lows. Although high legal qualifications are mandatory in the attorney you choose, it is not enough. You want someone who views adoption the same way you do. Like a marriage, you need to be on the same page for things to go smoothly.

Remember, you've got an entire nation of attorneys out there. Tens of thousands of them in fact, with several hundred being adoption specialists, offering the exact service for which you are looking. And if you end up not being satisfied with the attorney options, there are more than a thousand licensed private adoption agencies to choose from, as discussed in Chapters 5 and 6. Your options are limited only by your own time and effort.

CHAPTER 5

AGENCY ADOPTION

There are two basic types of adoption agencies: *private* and *public*. Despite sharing the term "agency" adoptions, they are actually quite different. This is true in the services they offer, the fees they charge, and the children they place. In fact, most private agency adoptions are more like independent adoptions than they are like public agency adoptions.

In Chapter 2, we looked at fourteen different types of adoption in capsule form. Of those, nine types are fully, or partially, agency adoptions:

- Private adoption agencies performing services in your home state.
  - Private adoption agencies located outside your home state, but able to create matches for you, with the adoption to be finalized in the court of your home state.
  - Private adoption agencies located in states permitting non-residency adoption, allowing you to retain an out of state agency and finalize the adoption in the state where the child was born and finalized under that state's laws.
  - Identified adoptions, where an attorney and agency are working together, using elements of both an independent and agency adoption.
  - Public adoption agencies.

- The foster parent short-cut.
- Special-needs registries.
- International adoption by agencies located in your state.
- International adoption by out-of-state agencies.

Some of these methods can only be done via private agencies, while others fall into the domain of public agencies. To better understand these many options, we need to explore how agencies work, and how they can best be used to help you accomplish your adoption goals. It is interesting that only a few decades ago, almost all adoptions were done through agencies. Then as time went on, independent adoption became the most popular type (for newborn adoption). Agency adoption, however, remains a very viable adoption method, and in some states is still the most common way to complete an adoption.

Comparing Public and Private Agencies

Private agencies are privately-operated businesses. (Most are non-profit, yes, and we'l discuss this later, but the reality is their employees still need to be paid and there is overhead to cover, so the non-profit status is often more of a tax designation than anything else.) They are licensed by the state in which they operate to conduct adoptive parent home studies and/or place children for adoption. Some agencies only do one or the other, but most do both. Some additionally help match adoptive parents with birth mothers, creating adoptive matches, and may even actively network and advertise to make birth mothers aware of their existence. Most agencies only do domestic adoptions, but some do international adoptions. International adoption is separately discussed in Chapter 7. Adoption agencies are principally supported by the fees they receive from adoptive parents. A listing of every adoption agency in the nation can be found at childwelfare.gov and adoption101.com. (There are more than 1,000 licensed adoption agencies in the United States. Listing them within this book is not practical given the frequent changes of addresses, phone numbers and websites. All this information is provided on the websites referenced.)

Public adoption agencies are completely different than private. Public agencies are operated by the county or state in which they are located and are supported by tax dollars. The main function of public agencies is to find homes for children for whom the county or state has assumed responsibility. These agencies, usually referred to as *public adoption agencies,* are often a branch of your state social services department. You can find your local public adoption agency in several ways. The state-by-state review provides each state's central adoption office, which can direct you to the public adoption agency serving your area. You can also check your local phone book and look under government listings for your county under "adoption."

Although public adoption agencies are usually licensed to accept birth mothers' relinquishment of newborns, their most important function has evolved in recent years to finding homes for "waiting" children (in foster care and free for adoption) and children with special-needs or hard-to-place characteristics. For this reason, unlike private agencies, they rarely network or advertise their services in an effort to reach birth mothers.

Free seminars. A nice thing about adoption agencies, both public and private, is that they typically offer free seminars to learn about their services. Compare this to attorneys, who will almost always charge you for an initial consultation. The difference for the distinction, however, is that the typical agency free seminar is in a group setting scheduled at a time dictated by the agency, while attorney consultations are private and scheduled at a time you have agreed to. (Some agencies offer private consultations like attorneys.) When you attend agency seminars, I strongly encourage you to bring a question list so you leave fully informed. The seminar is your chance to learn exactly what their services are, and what they can, and can't, do for you, as well as at what cost.

The Agency's Licensing Status. Both public and private agencies are licensed by the state and a failure to perform their services properly can result in the revocation of their license. Agencies are also licensed to do different things. Virtually all are licensed to perform home studies. Some will be licensed to perform either domestic or international home studies, while a smaller number does both. Domestic agencies may also be licensed to place children for adoption, acting as a state-approved intermediary of sorts between the birth mother and adoptive parents. Agencies that do home studies *and* make adoptive placements are often called "full service" agencies. In some states all agencies are full-service, while other states issue separate licenses for each permitted service. For these reasons, you need to ask each agency:

1. Are they licensed by the state as an adoption agency?
2. Are they licensed to perform services in your county? (Many states require agencies to be approved on a county-by-county basis, with some being statewide and others approved in only one county.)
3. What services they are permitted to perform?

Clearly, there is no benefit to you in hiring an agency if they can't perform the duties you need done, so the above are threshold questions. The first inquiry about asking if they are "licensed as an agency" may sound unnecessary, but that is not the case. The reality is that you must verify the agency you are considering is licensed as an actual *licensed adoption agency* by the state in which it operates. Some individuals or organizations use names which sound like adoption agencies, when in fact they are not. Instead, they are generally what is referred to as *facilitators*. Facilitators are those who render the limited service of finding a baby for a fee. Chapter 8 addresses the risks of facilitators. To verify an agency's present valid licensing status, the state-by-state review provides contact information for the state office, usually called the State Department of Social Services or similar title, and located in the state capitol, and a department within that office will be responsible for overseeing adoption agencies and their licensing. Or even simpler is to ask the agency to see their license, as most states require that it be conspicuously posted.

Religious Affiliation. Private agencies can be divided into *denominational* and *nondenominational* categories. Denominational agencies are those affiliated with a particular religious faith. Generally, these agencies are easy to recognize based upon the agency's name (e.g. Catholic Family Services, Church of Jesus Christ Latter Day Saints Social Services, Jewish Family Services, et cetera.). However, the name can't solely be relied upon, as some agency names bear little relation to the religious entity to which they are affiliated.

The opposite is also true. A small number of private agencies employ religiously-oriented names with no official association with that faith, perhaps thinking it will boost business with birth mothers or adoptive parents by associating itself with that religion. For these reasons it is necessary to look beyond the name and question individual agencies to determine their status.

An important fact about denominational agencies not known by most people is that some denominational agencies do not require adoptive parents to be of the faith with which the agency is affiliated. This may be beneficial when you live in a region where there are few agencies from which to choose, or if you find the policies of one particular agency match you desires, even though the agency is affiliated with a different religion.

Public adoption agencies are different. They are forbidden to have any religious ties, or to use religion to determine the general eligibility of adoptive parents.

Eligibility Requirements of Adoptive Parents. Each agency, whether private or public, sets eligibility requirements for you as adoptive parents. These can vary from state to state, and even from agency to agency within a state. Speaking very generally, however, here are some typical guidelines followed by many agencies:

- Be no more than 40 years of age older than the child you will be adopting. If you plan to adopt a newborn, this means that you could not be older than 40. If you were seeking to adopt a child age 5, your maximum age would be 45. Be aware, however, that although there continues to be some age restrictions, more and more agencies are eliminating the age requirement, and taking more of a "whole person" view of the adoptive parents in finding the right parents for each child. The more "conservative" states, however, have held onto this requirement.
- Marital status. If you are married, you must be doing it in conjunction and with the agreement of your spouse. Almost all agencies will now permit singles to adopt.
- If married, be married a minimum number of years (usually two).

- Don't have what the agency may consider to be an excessive number of prior marriages. Some agencies will permit only one prior marriage per spouse while others will allow several.
- Live in a home suitable for a child. The days of requiring home ownership are largely gone. Usually renting either a house or apartment is acceptable, as long as the housing will be safe and appropriate for a child, and he or she will have his or her own bedroom. An agency social worker will visit your home to make sure it appears safe for a child. These visits are almost always by appointment, not the "surprise" visits which are part of agency adoption lore. The agency has the right to require certain safety precautions prior to a child being placed (safety gates, drawer latches, etc.).
- Be of reasonably good health with the expectation to live at least until the child becomes an adult, and not have any contagious diseases which could put a child at risk.
- Be medically unable to conceive a child, or show it is physically unsafe to give birth. The agency goal here is to be sure you are not adopting for an inappropriate reason, such as a goal to not gain weight during a pregnancy, or a "save a child" mentality which will result in the unreasonable expectation in a child to be grateful for being adopted.
- Have no more than one child already. (Many agencies are eliminating this requirement.)
- At least one spouse be securely employed with sufficient income to support a family. Being newly employed is usually fine if there is a history of employment.
- Some agencies require one spouse to be a full-time, stay-at-home parent, although most have eliminated this requirement and both parents can be employed. Almost all agencies, however, encourage one stay-at-home parent as one of many factors contributing to the best interests of a child, rather than be in the care of day care providers.
- No criminal record or child abuse history. This is a serious issue. In fact, most state's fingerprinting is in such depth that it will show even sealed and expunged adult criminal records. This does not mean that you can't adopt if you have made a mistake in your life. If a crime was of a non-violent nature (e.g. shoplifting or intoxication), and it was an isolated incident

where many years have gone by without a repeat of such behavior, it might be overlooked. If the arrest was for a violent crime, however, that single offense will almost always be deemed grounds to deny you.

- No history of serious financial mismanagement. The agency will want to be sure you manage your resources well, so your family will be financially secure. A history of financial problems, such as bankruptcies or repossessions, can lead to denial. Often a single bankruptcy, if followed by a significant period of financial stability to show it was an aberration, will not be deemed a reason to deny you.

Remember, these are *general* requirements. Your state, or certain agencies within your state, might be stricter or more lenient. Also, be aware that even within a single agency, their requirements might differ. Because they recognize the difficulty of finding homes for special-needs or hard-to-place children, many of the eligibility requirements (other than a criminal background) might be more flexible. For example, the agency will often allow adoptive parents to have more than a forty year of age differential. Single parents are also considered where they otherwise might not be. In fact, some states report one of every five agency adoptions is by a single parent. Couples who already have several children, or who are not infertile but wish to adopt, are often also not just considered, but welcomed. Those not interested in adopting a special-needs child can still apply to adopt through the public adoption agency, although often long waits are reported by those waiting for a newborn, with some never receiving a placement.

If you find the agency you hoped to work with, but it will not work with you because you do not meet their requirements, it's no cause for concern. You still have tons of options. You can work with more flexible agencies within your state. You can work with an out-of-state agency. Or, you can do an independent or international adoption.

Fees and Costs. Like other businesses, private adoption agencies offer services for a fee and must make a sufficient profit to remain in operation. Most agencies are *non-profit* agencies. Non-profit agencies may receive financial assistance from charitable entities. A small number of agencies are operated on a *for-profit* basis. As long as the agency is licensed by the state as an adoption agency, there is usually little difference between the services of a non-profit and for-profit agency, although some view non-profit agencies as more altruistic and reliable. Often, for-profit agencies charge higher fees, as they are solely supported by the fees earned from adoptive parents. Most states require all agencies to be non-profit.

The term "non profit" causes confusion for many. To most people it implies the people working there are doing so merely out of dedication for no pay, like a volunteer. To the contrary, however, virtually every key employee is earning a salary, just as they would at any job. The designation of a business as non-profit is principally a tax designation.

Fees can vary tremendously among private agencies. Depending upon the type of agency, the services being offered, and the state in which it is located, fees may range from approximately $500 to $25,000. The average fees fall between $4,000 and $15,000. Some agencies don't use flat fees and instead adjust their fee based upon your income and use a sliding scale. This sliding scale fee typically varies from 8% to 12% of your joint pre-tax annual income.

The fee usually covers the adoptive parent pre-placement home study, adoption education and counseling for you and birth parents, the post-placement home study and evaluation of the adopted child's progress in the adoptive home and the final court report showing your approval for the adoption to be granted. Not all agencies offer these complete services, however, so each agency you are considering must be questioned. Usually a portion of the agency fee is paid when the pre-placement home study is started, with the balance due when the child is placed in the adoptive home. Most all private agencies request additional funds from you if the birth mother needs assistance with her medical expenses or other birth-related costs, just as in independent adoption. Other agencies may include such costs in their agency fee and forbid any such expenditures directly by you. Usually these more restrictive agencies refuse to incur many pregnancy expenses, however, and offer little flexibility to a birth mother. For example, if she needs a place to live, they are more likely to insist she stay in their maternity home, rather than rent her own apartment. Many birth mothers don't like the rigidity and go to another agency or attorney.

The same fee flexibility can be seen in the agency's networking services, if it offers them. Some agencies will include birth mother outreach efforts in their flat fee. Others will make it a separate optional program. It doesn't matter which method is used, as long as you know what you are getting for your money.

Public agencies have a completely different fee structure than their private counterparts. Many offer their services for free, while some may charge a very minimal fee, often approximately $500. The expenses of public agencies are paid via taxes like other government services. The reason public agencies basically underwrite the adoptions they do is because:

1. Virtually all of the children are presently in foster homes, and would benefit from a permanent adoptive home.
2. Most of the children waiting for placement are in a hard-to-place category (physical or mental challenge, age, being part of a sibling group to be adopted together, being of an ethnic minority where there is a shortage of adoptive parents).
3. The continued placement of the children in foster homes, until age eighteen would cost the government even more money than underwriting the adoption.
4. The best interests of the children will be served by having the permanency of an adoptive home, benefiting not just the child, but society, in the long run.

Adoptive parents often wonder if they can use a "free" home study from a public agency, and use it toward an independent or private agency adoption, thereby saving themselves the cost of the pre-placement home study. The answer is almost always "no." Remember, the entire purpose of the public agency financially underwriting adoptions is to help encourage the adoption of the children in their care, desperately needing homes. To provide their manpower and services at no cost, only to have adoptive parents turn around and use those services for a private newborn or international adoption, would not serve the purpose for which the public agencies exist.

In addition to the lack of any significant fees, there are almost never any costs associated with a birth mother's medical or living expenses. This is due to the fact most children come into the county agency system after having been freed for adoption through the courts. Even the few voluntary newborn adoptions the public agencies might handle usually permit no payment by the adoptive parents for a birth mother's pregnancy expenses. This usually means the public agency will either pay those costs, make sure the birth mother is eligible for government aid to cover her costs (such as Medicaid and food stamps), or decline working with the birth mother, or refer her to a private agency or attorney where such expenses can be provided.

There are other limits in working with a public agency. The ability to "shop around" as with private agencies is usually not possible in the public sector. Virtually all public agencies will only accept applications from you if you reside within the county or territory they serve. Also, public agencies will normally refuse to offer their services to you if you have located your own birth mother and want the public agency to handle the adoption and take advantage of their low fee. This is because their function is to find homes for children for whom they are already responsible.

The Home Study. All agency adoptions, whether they are through a private or public agency, require a home study. Home studies are in two parts. Before the child enters your home, there is a pre-placement home study to confirm you will be appropriate parents for the type of child you hope to adopt. (The agency will consider the needs of a newborn versus an older child, and in excellent health versus a child with special needs.) The satisfactory completion of the pre-placement home study is a prerequisite to having a child placed in your home.

An agency social worker will be assigned to do the pre-placement home study and will want to have several meetings with you, some of which will be in your home. Home visits are required to see the potential environment for a child. These visits are almost always arranged by appointment, not "surprise" visits.

The vast majority of agency social workers are friendly professionals who are anxious to help you succeed at adoption, although a small number may be judgmental and take advantage of the power they have over whether a child will be placed with you. To avoid such an unpleasant experience, a list of suggested questions to ask potential agencies is provided in Chapter 6.

Because most agencies operate with almost unlimited discretion regarding with which of their waiting families they will place a child for adoption, it is important to show the agency you are the best waiting adoptive parents. Many adoptive parents waiting for a placement do not realize in many ways they are "in competition" with the agency's other waiting adoptive parents. To impress your agency, and make them be extra-motivated to specifically help you, consider doing these simple things:

- Return your required paperwork quickly, and complete it accurately and thoroughly. (You'd be surprised how many people take weeks or months to return their applications or subsequent paperwork.)
- When the agency seeks to make appointments with you for visits to your home or their office, don't ask the social worker to alter his or her busy schedule to fit yours. Show the meeting is important to you by agreeing to the soonest time they have available. Reschedule any conflicting and less important matters. They will think, "If you can't prioritize your life around a planned adoption now, how can you do it when a child's life will require it tenfold?"
- Attend all seminars offered by the agency to teach you about adoptive parenting and related issues. This includes non-mandatory seminars as well. They have valuable things to teach you about the uniqueness of parenting through adoption. Go because you want to, not because you have to.
- When asked by the agency why you wish to adopt, be honest regarding your motivation, instead of saying what you think they want to hear. For example, many social workers report that they question the motivations of adoptive parents who profess to be interested in adopting only out of humanitarian desires to make a home for a child. This motivation may be one of many appropriate factors when discussing adoption, particularly concerning children waiting for a home, such as special-needs children. Even in those cases, however, many social workers feel the primary motivation for adoptive parents should be the desire to share their love with a child and be a parent.
- Read recommended books regarding adoption and share what you learned with your assigned caseworker, and others on the agency's staff you deal with. It is tremendously impressive to the caseworker if you have read respected adoption books, especially if you have done so voluntarily before the agency

even begins your home study. Your advance reading shows you are strongly motivated and truly desire to learn all you can about the most important thing in your life - adoption. Adoption101 has a helpful list of recommended adoption books in all topics.

These basic suggestions toward establishing a beneficial relationship with your agency may seem absurdly simple. Surprisingly, however, many caseworkers complain that many of their agency's waiting families fail to show their sincerity and readiness to adopt by such simple acts. Remember, an agency's goal is to find the best homes for the children they place. The more educated and prepared you show yourselves to be can only serve to impress your agency (not to mention make you a better parent). With the few agencies where a waiting list is not used, the agency has sole discretion regarding with which waiting adoptive parents it will place a child. Make their discretion benefit, not hurt, your chances to adopt quickly.

Usually there is little difference between a private or public agency home study. The only exception is usually time. In most cases, private agencies can start and complete your home study faster than can public agencies. This is just the reality between the private and public sector. The people employed in your local public adoption agency may be the best and most dedicated social workers in the area. Still, as part of a governmental office, they will have a higher level of bureaucracy for you to work through. Another reason for this is that because they are offering their services for free, or close to it, they don't want to start home studies until they are sure you plan to stick to your decision to adopt through the public agency (and not stop the process after many hours have been spent on your behalf). This means they often "put you through the paces," to test your mettle. That, in turn, often means a longer wait to start a home study. Still, if they offer the services you want, it will be worth the wait.

So far, we've only discussed home studies as they relate to agency adoptions. Considering this is a chapter on agency adoptions, that makes sense. You should be aware, however, that in many states, private agencies can perform home studies for adoptions created via independent adoption. This can occur in an "identified" adoption (discussed in Chapters 2 and 3), where the placement begins via an attorney and is then converted to an agency adoption. Some states also give adoptive parents doing an independent adoption several choices where they get their home study done, perhaps getting to choose between a private agency or social worker, or a state adoption office specifically available to do independent adoption home studies. For this reason, many agencies have different fee structures, to distinguish such adoptions from ones where they helped create the match and spend additional time and effort in that part of the adoption. For this reason, you need to be very specific when you call agencies to inquire about home study services and fees.

The Children Available. The children available for adoption through private agencies handling domestic adoptions range in age from newborns to older children and are of all ethnic groups. Most of the adoptive parents retaining private agencies, however, will do so with the goal of adopting a newborn, often of their same ethnic group. Some private agencies additionally handle the adoption of waiting and special-needs children. The adoption of these latter two groups usually originates via county/public agencies, but sometimes is completed via the assistance of a private agency, as I'll describe momentarily.

Public agencies handle the vast majority of children in the *waiting* and *special-needs* categories. A "waiting" child refers to a child who has already been born and awaiting a home, likely living in foster care. Although all children in the foster care system are *waiting* children, not all waiting children are designated as special-needs. For example, a healthy young child would be termed waiting, but not special-needs. A "special-needs" child is usually a child the agency feels may require extraordinary parenting due to a physical, emotional or mental challenge. Special-needs children may also include children without disabilities, but who fall into a category the agency believes will make an adoptive placement difficult. Some prefer the term *hard-to-place* for children in this category. This could include a large sibling group to be adopted together, a child over a particular age and children of certain ethnic minorities where there is a shortage of adoptive parents.

Many of these children have been freed for adoption through the court system due to parental abandonment, abuse or severe neglect. These children are of all ethnic groups and of varying ages, although ethnic minorities are often over-represented. Some of these children will need extraordinary parenting due to the problems suffered by the child prior to the adoption, whether it is emotional, physical or intellectual difficulties.

There are approximately half a million children in America presently in foster care, and a large number of them either immediately available for adoption, or destined to eventually need an adoptive home due to their biological parents inability to care for them. Oddly, many Americans who consider international adoption (where many of the children are toddler or above) won't even consider adopting one of our own nation's waiting children. Sometimes this is because they want a child of a particular ethnic group and they feel that need can't be met in the foster care system. In some cases, that may be true and international adoption can best fit their needs. Sometimes, however, this preconception is incorrect.

Just who *are* these waiting children? The U.S. Department of Health has provided the following information about children in our country presently awaiting adoptive homes.

Age of waiting children:

Under age 1:	2%
Ages 1-5:	37%
Ages 6-10:	26%
Ages 11-15:	23%
Ages 16-18:	3%

Ethnicity of waiting children:

Caucasian:	32%
African-American:	51%
Hispanic:	11%
Native American:	1%
Asian:	1%
Unknown:	5%

As will be discussed later in this chapter, it is easy for you to see the children waiting in your home state, as well as other states. Thanks to adoption *exchanges*, you can visit your state's photo-listing website, and within a few clicks, see pictures and learn about thousands of waiting children.

<u>Waiting for a Child</u>. Historically, all agencies maintained waiting lists. Adoptive parents would simply wait their turn to reach the top of the list for their turn to adopt, and waiting several years was not uncommon if a newborn or very young child was desired.

Waiting lists have largely been discarded, however, and now most all agencies will now only consider which of their available adoptive parents could most effectively meet the needs of the child to be adopted. This evaluation may include judging the emotional readiness of the adoptive parents and matching the ethnicity, religion, and physical characteristics of the child and the adoptive parents. If all things are equal between waiting adoptive parents, often only then will the longer-waiting family get the nod. If the child is a newborn, and the birth mother has relinquished the selection of the adoptive parents to the agency, the agency will additionally honor any specific requests from the birth mother regarding the kind of adoptive parents she would like the child to have.

Because of these variable factors, and the ratio of placements that individual agencies may have at a given time compared to the number of their waiting adoptive parents, the wait for a child might be only months or it could be years. Remember, adding to this time is how long it will take to complete your pre-placement home study, as most agencies will not show you to birth mothers to be considered as adoptive parents until you are fully approved (unlike independent adoption where you can normally start being shown right away). For this reason, it is important to ask any agency not only how long it takes to *complete* a home study with them, but also how long must you wait to *start* the home study. If the home study will only take two months, but they can't start it for six months due to a backlog, factor in those eight months of forced inactivity into your timetable. Of course, not all agencies are backed up to this degree and many can start immediately.

In the past, if you were working with an agency, the birth mother matches could only come via the agency, not due to your own networking or other outside efforts. This was partially due to the agency tradition of not sharing identities between birth mothers and adoptive parents, which could not exist if you found the birth mother on your own. With a greater sense of openness, however, and agencies welcoming that new tradition, it has opened up the options you have.

This means most all private agencies will allow adoptive parents to speed up the process of being matched up with a birth mother by using their own contacts and initiative. This might include you hiring an attorney who is active in networking, or you might be planning your own networking campaign (discussed in Chapter 8). In these cases the adoption would then be completed as an agency adoption, even though they met outside the agency, making it an "identified" adoption.

Identified adoptions are becoming a very common type of agency adoption. These terms are derived from the fact you have brought your own "identified" birth mother to the agency, rather than the agency finding her for you. If your adoption agency is willing, they may also be willing to let you start your campaign to locate a birth mother before your pre-placement home study is completed, as they know your efforts may take several months to be successful, as long as any actual placement of a child will not occur until the pre-placement home study is completed.

Public agencies usually offer a shorter, or longer, waiting time for a placement than private agencies, depending upon the type of child you hope to adopt. If you are interested in adopting a special-needs child, often there is a substantially shorter waiting period for the placement, as many such children are already awaiting an adoptive home and few adoptive parents are available. Many public agencies are also willing to waive some of their normal restrictions regarding adoptive parents, creating a double benefit for you. With newborn placements, however, normally there is a much longer waiting time than with private agencies or independent adoption. This is because few birth mothers elect to place with their local public agency (they often view it as a "county facility" like a welfare or public health office), and prefer the private sector. Also, in many regions, a large percentage of the few newborn placements that do end up being handled by public agencies are those involving substantial drug abuse during the pregnancy. In fact, this is often why the public agency is involved, because Children's Protective Services was contacted by the hospital at birth due to the positive drug test and the child is not permitted to leave with the birth mother. Prenatal drug usage can occur in any type of adoption, but is more commonly found in the placements finding their way to public agencies.

Unlike private agencies, public agencies will normally not allow you to find your own birth mother, either on your own or through an attorney, then have the agency perform the home study and needed services. This is true even if the placement happened accidentally, not through any effort on your part. For example, if you were waiting with your local public agency in good faith for an adoptive placement, and before it occurred you were approached about a voluntary adoption, the agency will usually decline to have any role. This is because, as was alluded to before, their role is to find homes for the waiting children they are dedicated to serve. They will normally refer you to a private agency or attorney to complete that adoption, and terminate your pending public agency application.

Post-Placement Procedures. Private and public agencies handle post-placement procedures (after the child is placed with you) differently. Historically, both operated similarly. Once the child was born, the agency would require the child to be placed in a foster home until the birth parents had irrevocably relinquished the child, or the child is freed for adoption through a court action. The reason for the delayed placement was to eliminate any risk to adoptive parents of the child being reclaimed. This was a worthy goal, but the downside was it meant the child had to stay with foster parents, instead of bonding with his or her future parents. This foster home period could be days, weeks or even months, depending upon the circumstances. Adoptive parents did not like this policy. Birth parents didn't like it. Most child welfare professionals didn't like it.

As a result, over the last few decades more and more private agencies began to change their policy and agree to place newborns with the adoptive parents immediately upon the child's discharge from the hospital. In so doing, the adoptive parents were agreeing to a trade-off. Some would be taking a child into their home before the consent was irrevocable, but having the benefit of bonding with the child from birth. (To see how soon the consent becomes irrevocable in the states of interest to you, see the state-by-state review.) Presently, most all private agencies agree to immediate placements.

Public agencies have been slower to follow this trend and many continue to follow the more old-fashioned, conservative path. It remains common for them to delay the adoptive placement until the child is irrevocably free for adoption. With older children this is less of an issue, as usually they have been legally free for a long time, allowing an immediate placement once adoptive parents are located. For newborns, however, the issue remains one of conflict.

Luckily, an increasing number of public agencies have started to make placements before the child is irrevocably free for adoption. They usually term these placements *fost-adopt*. A fost-adopt placement is one where a child is placed with the intended adoptive parents, but technically designates them initially as "foster parents." Then, when the child is irrevocably free for adoption via a consent or court action, their official status is altered to "adoptive parents."

Some agencies prefer to term these placements "at risk" placements, rather than fost-adopt. Regardless of the labels used, however, the bottom line is that this allows you to have the baby in your home immediately, usually right from the hospital. Because the potential benefit outweighs the risk, most adoptive parents prefer such placements rather than having the child in foster care for the interim period.

Once a child is placed with you, whether through a public or private agency, there will be several post-placement home visits by the agency social worker to monitor the child's progress in your home. The number varies by state, but most range from two to four. Usually about six months after the child's placement with you (depending upon the laws of your state), the agency will be ready to recommend the adoption be granted, allowing the court to finalize the adoption.

Many agencies will require you to retain an attorney to prepare the necessary legal documents and appear with you in court, as legal proceedings are usually outside the scope of most adoption agency and are not covered by agency fees. Because the attorney is only handling a small part of the adoption, the cost is usually a small fraction of their usual "full adoption" fee. Some agencies have an in-house attorney, however, and he or she will prepare your needed documents, and appear with you in court, as part of the agency fee. Chapter 12 discusses what happens in court when the adoption is formally granted.

Placements via Foster Parenting. Adoptive placements resulting from traditional foster parenting are different from the fost-adopt situations discussed above. Each county or state licenses foster parents to care for children for whom the government has temporary legal custody. Generally, these children have been removed from their families by Child Protective Services due to parental abandonment, abuse or neglect. These children range from infants to older children.

The purpose of placing these children in foster homes is to provide a safe environment for the child, while allowing the child's parents an opportunity to put their lives in order and prove they can provide appropriate parental care. Depending upon the law of the state you live in, the birth parents may be granted from six to eighteen months to establish their ability to be adequate parents. Failing to do so, the court may terminate their parental rights and request the county or state adoption agency to find an adoptive home for the child.

Some states wisely recognize the emotional bonds which can form between foster parents and their foster children, thus give special consideration to foster parents wishing to adopt the children they've been caring for. In such cases, they are given priority status over other adoptive parents and can adopt the child they have been caring for. Other states do not provide much special treatment or many rights to foster parents. In fact, some foster parents are asked to sign a document promising they will not try to adopt their foster children. This might seem unfair, and often is, but the rationale is that the county or state desperately needs foster parents, and doesn't want to lose any. (Some adoptive parents have successfully challenged such restrictions by court action.)

As you can see, foster parenting is not a guaranteed route to adoption. For this reason, foster parenting should not be done with adoption as the only, or even the primary, goal. This will only lead to your disappointment, and perhaps failure to effectively meet the child's needs. However, for those families who would enjoy caring for a child and knowing they are providing much needed affection and stability in a child's time of need, it can be a rewarding option. It can also be a learning experience for those individuals who are considering whether adopting an older child is right for them. Both you and the child can benefit from the temporary living arrangements, and if it ends up turning into an adoption situation, you all benefit.

Foster parents are paid by the county or the state an amount deemed sufficient to care for the child's needs, ranging from a low of $250 monthly in some states to more than $800 in others. Most average about $500. Almost every state provides for a one-time reimbursement of expenses to purchase needed items for the child, such as clothes, etc. Most states set this amount at approximately $1,500.

Adoption Exchanges and Special-Needs Children. Because of the importance and difficulty of finding homes for hard-to-place children, special adoption exchanges and photo-listing books have been created to assist both public and private agencies in placing these children. An exchange is simply a means by which to get information about as many children as possible to as many adoptive parents as possible. Every state has it's own exchange (each is listed in the state-by-state review), made up of the waiting children within the state. Normally the state exchanges have almost all the waiting children in the state available for adoption, virtually all of them presently in foster care under the county's care. Most of the state exchanges have websites with photos and information about all these children. Some states prefer that the adoptive parents be from the same state when the feel it will serve the child's best interests. For example, the child might have extended family in the area and it would be detrimental to loose those extended family bonds. In many cases, however, adoptive parents from other states will be welcomed, giving you fifty data bases to consult.

There are also regional exchanges, each covering the territory of many states. These exchanges do not list all the children available from every state, however, only some. Typically, most states will only submit children to their regional exchange when they are having difficulty, or anticipate difficulty, in finding an adoptive home locally and need to expand their search. You do not need to live in one of the states covered by a particular regional exchange to be considered for the children listed. The regional exchanges are:

- National Adoption Center
- The CAP Book (Children Awaiting Parents)
- Northwest Adoption Exchange
- The Adoption Exchange

There is also a national exchange, established by the federal government (Department of Health and Human Services), found at adoptUSkids.org. This is the nation's largest photo-listing of available children, usually totaling approximately 5,000 children. As with the regional exchanges, however, many of the children in the state exchanges are not submitted, as they do not anticipate the need for a national search for adoptive parents, or the child may simply be new to the system and his or her caseworker has not taken the time to submit them. In fact, the 5,000 children on the national exchange is only a small fraction of the total children available when adding all the individual state exchanges. Appendix A gives contact information for the national and regional exchanges.

Ideally, the sharing of information via the state, regional and national – and you - will allow an adoptive parent who is working with a public or private agency in San Francisco to learn of a waiting or special-needs child available for adoption through an agency in New Orleans. The two agencies, with the assistance of the exchange, then work together to make the placement. Initially, only public agencies were involved in the placement of waiting and special-needs children via registries, but more recently many private agencies have become involved as well. Not all private agencies handle these adoptions as part of their services, however.

Adoption exchanges will normally speak directly with you about a particular child, but for any real advancement to be made in a possible placement, they will want to speak to a caseworker at your agency and who can provide your home study and further information about you. When a placement seems appropriate, a "go slow" approach is advised to make a smooth transition for the child. Moving to a new home, into a new family, is as major a change in a child's life as can occur. Often the adoptive parents will travel to see the child on multiple occasions, then the child might visit with them in their home. When both you and the child feel comfortable, the child can move in with you and the adoption can formally begin.

Your search for a waiting child will usually start on a local level, as each individual public adoption agency has its own children to serve as its first duty. So if you live in Orange County, California, Orange County Social Services may begin by showing you the local children in their care awaiting homes. The next step would be to visit the California state registry and see which children are available statewide. Next, the national and regional exchanges, and individual state registries, could be explored.

There are normally no fees charged to you by the exchanges. You will be required to have a home study, however. If you obtained this through your local public adoption agency, it was likely provided to you for free, or at a minimal cost (such as $500 or less). Some states will require you to hire an attorney for the final court appearance and any needed legal work. This can cost from several hundred dollars to more than a thousand. Other states arrange for the public agency to prepare your final court papers for you, eliminating that cost.

If you have a home study from a private adoption agency, then later elect to adopt a child in the county system, or via one of the exchanges, in most states you can use your existing home study. There is normally no need to do the home study process all over via the public agency. Sometimes, however, the public agency or exchange may require you to take special parenting classes dealing with adopting a waiting child and how best to meet that child's needs, if your private agency did not include that training as part of your preparation to parent.

To offset the financial expenses of adopting a special-needs child (future medical care, possible counseling for some children, et cetera), the federal government has created an *Adoption Subsidy* program (technically called the *Adoption Assistance Program,* or *AAP*) for eligible children. The subsidy gives the adoptive parents monthly support to offset the child's expenses, even after the child is adopted, until the child reaches age 18 (some states go as high as age 21). Additionally, the child can be deemed eligible for Medi-Caid, regardless of the adoptive parents' income, covering most medical costs. If your child is found to not have sufficient special needs to be eligible for the federal subsidy, or is ineligible for another reason, some states have their own subsidy programs to encourage special-needs adoption. The reasoning behind the subsidy, in part, is that the government will be paying foster parents anyway, so why not pay an equal or slightly lesser amount, and encourage the child's existing foster parents, or other adoptive parents, to adopt the child. This benefits the child by having a permanent family via adoption, as opposed to him or her remaining until adulthood under county supervision in foster care.

It is the job of your agency to help you with these subsidy options and your child's eligibility. Not all children will be eligible for the federal or state adoption subsidy. Just because a child is a *waiting* child (such as a young, completely healthy child) does not make him or her a *special-needs* child. Additionally, there is a highly respected national organization, the North American Council of Adoptable Children (NACAC) which offers information and assistance to adoptive parents, or prospective adoptive parents, about adopting a waiting child, and subsidy availability. Information about NACAC is provided in Appendix B.

There is also a tremendous tax benefit in adopting a special-needs child. A 2012 federal Adoption Tax Credit of $12,650 is available for adoptive parents whose adjusted gross income is $189,710 or less in the year in which the adoption is completed. The income can actually go up to $229,710, but the credit is proportionally reduced when income exceeds $189,710. This is not a *deduction* (like a mortgage payment). A *credit* is much better. It is a dollar for dollar elimination of tax owed, virtually giving you up to $12,650. In the adoption of a child who is not deemed to have special needs, you can only take the credit to the extent you had actual adoption expenses. In other words, if you did an independent adoption and paid $2,000 for a home study, $4,000 for an attorney and the birth mother had $1,500 in medical costs, you could take a credit of that amount, $7,500. If your adoption expenses were $15,000, you would be permitted to take the credit of $12,650 as the maximum amount.

You might be thinking that it appears there may be no expenses in a special-needs adoption, as public agencies and exchanges generally charge no fees. That means there are no expenses, so no tax credit, right? Wrong. When the adoption is of a child confirmed to be special needs (talk to both your agency and tax preparer to confirm that your child will apply), you are eligible for the entire $12,650 tax credit, *even if you had no adoption expenses*, assuming your income is not over $189,710. Your income can actually go up to $229,710, but the tax credit decreases proportionally when the income exceeds $189,710. Be aware that Congress normally renews the tax credit each year, and slightly alters the credit amount and the income eligibility levels.

In addition to the federal tax credit, some states offer special tax credits or incentives to adoptive parents adopting a special-needs child. The federal Adoption Tax Credit is discussed in more detail in Chapter 12. Be aware that the federal lawmakers tinker with the terms of the credit almost every year, so it may have changed after the publishing of this book.

Adopting a waiting or special-needs child can be a wonderful opportunity to bring a child into your home who desperately wants, and needs, a family. Every child deserves a family, but the reality is many won't ever get to be a part of one. It takes special preparation and education to be sure you are ready to meet the needs of these special children, however. In addition to the classes and educational opportunities which your local agency or exchange should make available to you, there are many great books to help you determine if such a child is right for you, and you for the child, and how to meet the needs of these children now, and throughout their lives. For some real "hands on" learning, you might consider talking to other adoptive parents who have adopted waiting and special-needs children. In addition to meeting them through your local agency, the North American Council for Adoptable Children lists adoptive parent support groups on its website, nacac.org. These families have adopted waiting and special-needs children so may be an excellent resource for you. More information about the North American Council for Adoptable Children is provided in Appendix B.

The Openness of the Adoption. Years ago most private and public agencies arranged only closed adoptions, while independent adoption was viewed as the "open" adoption alternative. A closed adoption is one where the adoptive parents and birth mother would never meet and identities were not disclosed. Although some private agencies still do closed adoptions, many now arrange open adoptions, typically in newborn placements. Although the term "open adoption" can mean many things (some agencies call it "cooperative adoption"), normally it refers to an adoption where the birth mother and adoptive parents personally meet and exchange personal information before the birth to be sure each wishes to go forward.

Depending upon the policy of the agency and the desires of the birth and adoptive parents, full identities may, or may not, be disclosed. The openness may continue after the birth in a variety of ways. In many cases the adoptive parents and birth mother maintain contact by sending pictures and letters once or twice a year up to the child reaching age eighteen, often using the agency as an intermediary. In a small number of adoptions the adoptive parents, birth mother and the child maintain face-to-face contact as mutually desired. This is found in about five to ten percent of recent adoptions.

Some birth mothers prefer the other extreme and want no post-birth contact at all.

Many adoptive parents have a knee-jerk reaction against open adoption, often thinking it will "complicate" their lives, or undermine their role as parents. Although you as parents have the right to select the kind of adoption you prefer, you might want to ask yourself the following questions:

- If our child ever needs bone marrow, or something like a kidney transplant, who will we be contacting?
- We will be raising our child from birth with the knowledge that he or she was adopted, and that adoption was a loving act by his or her birth parents. Won't it be natural that at some point our child will want to meet this person?
- If the birth parents' rights have been terminated and the adoption is finalized, and we are our child's only legal parents, do we really need to feel worried and insecure about the continuing existence of a birth parent?
- We have a lot of distant relatives who we see once or twice a year. They are part of our family, but have no right to interfere in our child-raising decisions. Is there a reason that a birth mother (or father) can't have a similar role?
- Can a child have too many people who love them?
- We know as our child grows, we won't be able to fill every need our child has. Sometimes he or she will turn to a teacher or a friend. Maybe at some point only a birth parent can address a particular issue. Do we want a relationship where we can call a birth parent if ever needed to fill a unique need that no one else can fill?
- We believe the birth mother placed her child for adoption with us because she wanted us to be his or her permanent parents, and she only wants the best for us and our child, so is there any reason to fear her?

Although private agency adoptions have become quite open, those through public agencies still tend to be completely closed. This is often due to the fact that a high number of the children they assist in placing for adoption were freed through court action due to inadequate or improper parenting and continued contact would not be deemed to serve the best interests of the child. Furthermore, the selection of the adoptive parents, and the placement of the child with them, was done completely by the agency. The birth parent had no role, as usually their rights were completely terminated by that time. Even in the small number of voluntary newborn adoptions which a public agency may handle, traditionally these adoptions remain closed as well.

Working with out-of-state adoption agencies. Most adoptive parents will do every aspect of the adoption in the state in which they live. They will hire an agency there, the birth mother will live and give birth there, and the adoption will be finalized there, in your local court. If you live in a state with great agencies from which to choose, good adoption laws making you feel secure, and a sufficient number of birth mothers in your region or state, why leave your own state?

Many adoptive parents aren't so lucky. What if you don't like what the local agencies have to offer? Or you want to work with them, but you don't meet their eligibility requirements. Perhaps there are few adoptive placements in your region or state. Maybe you are concerned that your state has laws which give birth parents an excessively long period in which to change their mind. Or could it be that your state is fine, but you want to expand your options to increase the likelihood of being picked for an adoptive placement quickly. There are many reasons to either do your adoption out of state, or work in both your home state and another state. You have several ways to do this.

Interstate Adoption. Let's say you've found a great agency but it is located in another state. No problem. You can hire the out-of-state agency to help you find a birth mother, offer counseling to her, help with her signing her relinquishment of parental rights, and arrange for the child to be physically placed in your care. Very shortly after birth, when the initial paperwork is done and you get interstate approval to bring the child across state lines (discussed in Chapter 12), you return home with your child. A local in-state agency that you've selected does both the pre and post-placement home study, and writes the final report to the court to complete the adoption. You complete the adoption in your local court, primarily under your home state's laws. (Sometimes the out-of-state's laws can apply, as discussed in Chapter 12.)

A twist on the above is that the out-of-state agency finds a birth mother for you and creates the planned placement, but perhaps the birth mother has no place to stay or has recently lost her job. She has no reason to stay in that region and would welcome the chance to get to know you better, and have you close for the moment the birth occurs. You agree, and you like the chance to go to doctor appointments with her, and not risk missing the birth due to living so far away. The answer? She can relocate to your home state, where you can find her someplace to stay (assuming your state permits assistance with living costs, as discussed in the state-by-state review). After the birth she may return to her original state, relocate elsewhere, or decide she likes what your state has to offer and stay. Regardless, in this scenario, your local agency would be performing all the needed agency functions, other than creating the adoptive match. They, rather than the out-of-state agency, would counsel the birth mother (or share in that duty with the other agency, at different points of the pregnancy), assist with her signing her relinquishment of rights, as well as do their usual home study duties.

You might fear using two agencies would double the cost, but that is usually not true. As discussed in more detail in Chapter 6 and 9, many agencies will only charge for the services they perform. Accordingly, if they are dividing their duties, their fees should be proportionally less. Not every agency will work that way, but most will.

Non-resident adoption. How about if we take all the reasons why you might be considering an out-of-state agency from the section above, and add one thing? What if the state in which you hired the out-of-state agency allowed non-residents to adopt, assuming the baby is born there? Perhaps you might want to finalize the adoption under that state's laws. Why? Maybe your state allows a birth mother thirty days to change her mind and the out-of-state agency's laws only permit 72 hours? What if it typically takes a year or more after birth to finalized your adoption in your state, compared to the out-of-state agency's usual time of three months? There are many other legal comparisons to be made between each state regarding such issues as birth father's rights, permitted birth parent expenses paid by adoptive parents, the adoption being open or closed, et cetera.

States permitting agency non-resident adoption are: Alabama, Alaska, Arkansas, California, Colorado, Delaware, District of Columbia, Hawaii, Illinois, Indiana, Iowa, Kansas, Louisiana, Maine, Maryland, Massachusetts, Michigan, Missouri, New Hampshire, New Jersey, New Mexico, New York, North Dakota, Ohio, Oregon, Pennsylvania, South Carolina, Texas, Utah, Vermont, Virginia and Washington. You can learn more about each state's laws and the agencies and attorneys within that state in the state-by state review.

In a non-resident agency adoption you start with the exact same scenario as we discussed for interstate adoption. You selected an out-of-state agency to help match you with a birth mother and that agency continues to do virtually everything in the adoption. After creating the adoptive match, it provides counseling for the birth mother, assists with her relinquishment, arranges for the baby to be released into your care, and makes the arrangements for your adoption to be finalized in its local court. The agency in your home state will only need to do your pre and post-placement home study. Generally, only the laws of the birth state where the out-of-state agency is located, will apply, so there is less chance of a conflict of laws as compared to an interstate adoption. These potential conflicts are discussed in Chapter 12.

CHAPTER 6

SELECTING THE RIGHT AGENCY

Just as selecting an attorney is the central element of an independent adoption, choosing the right agency is the key ingredient in the success of an agency adoption. Despite the importance of this decision, the vast majority of adoptive parents give much less thought to this decision than they should. In most cases they call a few agencies in their region and select the best of those few. You can choose to be like everyone else, or you can choose to succeed.

Considering there are more than 1,200 private adoption agencies in the nation (this is not even counting the equally high number of public/county agencies), you are clearly cheating yourself if you don't thoroughly consider agencies beyond those in a small radius of your home. There are many supremely qualified agencies located all around the country. There are also many to be avoided that fall short of what a good agency should do for you.

Adoption agencies are no different than any other business. You will see the same differences in quality of service as with other professionals you've hired, some great, some barely competent. The good news is that you can easily find an excellent agency by following some basic steps:

1. Select between private or public agency adoption.
2. Narrow your list of possible agencies.
3. Is the agency licensed?

4. Is the agency able to perform the specific duties you need?
5. Do you meet the requirements of the agency?
6. Fine-tune your list.
7. Specific questions to ask the agency.
8. Test the agency's knowledge.
9. Determine if their personality and approach to adoption matches yours.

Select Between Private or Public Agency Adoption

Chapter 5 illustrated how different private and public agency adoption are. If you are planning a public agency adoption, you are normally restricted to working with your local county adoption office. In other words, you can't "shop around" like you can when selecting a private agency. That doesn't mean you are limited to your local region as far as eligible children are concerned, however, as your public agency can work with national registries and other public and or private agencies on placements (usually children in the *waiting* and *hard-to place* category).

The good news is that if you plan a public agency adoption, your search for an agency is already complete. All you do is find your county's public adoption agency and you're done. It's sort of a good news/bad news scenario as you've got a choice of one agency. No choices, no options. If you can't find your local county adoption office in your phone directory, you can find it on the federal government's adoption website (the Child Welfare Information Gateway), childwelfare.gov, or you can call the state adoption office as listed in the state-by-state review in Chapter 15, and that office can give you the needed contact information.

If you plan on adopting through a private agency, however, as you will likely be doing if you plan on adopting a newborn, or doing an intercountry adoption, your choices are staggering. The remainder of this chapter is for you.

Narrow Your List of Possible Agencies

How do you go from more than 1,200 private adoption agencies and end up with one? Sounds daunting, but it's not. Obviously, you won't be looking at a thousand-plus adoption agencies. It's helpful to know they are out there, however.

You may be looking only for an agency in your home state, or wish to consider out-of-state agencies. I'd recommend you start locally and expand from there as needed. Who knows, the right agency might be only twenty miles away. For others, it might be a county away, in a neighboring state, or even the other side of the country. The answer is dependent upon the region and state in which you live, the type of adoption you choose, the kind of child you hope to adopt, and the services you will require.

Compiling your list of agencies will be done in the opposite way as compared to compiling an attorney list. This is because we are *subtracting* in compiling an agency list, and *adding* to an attorney list. What do I mean? When you compile a list of attorneys, there is no complete list of every attorney doing adoptions. True, there is the American Academy of Adoption Attorneys, and that's an excellent place to start, but there are many attorneys doing adoptions besides those several hundred. This means you need to build your list, then whittle it down. Compare this to agencies, where childwelfare.gov and adoption101.com list every private adoption agency in the nation - more than 1,000. So your problem is narrowing down this list, and deciding which ones to contact. Let's explore how to do this.

- <u>Only consider agencies in your preferred geographical regions or states.</u> Your selected regions or states from which to adopt will be unique to you and different from other adoptive parents. You might live in a well-populated region in a state with advantageous adoption laws and a good percentage of birth mothers. If so, you will likely select an agency in your home region and state. Another adoptive family may live in a state with very poor adoption options, so they'll select several states they feel are best for them, and will consider agencies in those states. (To determine the right states for you, consider the many in-state and out-of-state options we discussed in Chapter 2, and the information provided in the state-by-state review. Depending upon where you live, and the kind of adoption you want, different states will be best for each adoptive family. It is within only these states that you need focus your search for the best agency.)

- Call adoption attorneys. You might think that most adoption attorney are "in competition" with agencies, so would not recommend any. In most cases, this isn't true. Most attorneys, even in states where independent adoption competes with agency adoption, work regularly with adoption agencies. Adoption is a small world and the good professionals in the same region usually know and associate with each other. (Although you might not succeed in directly reaching the attorney him or herself, usually speaking to a staff person is sufficient as they will know who the attorney commonly works with, or avoids. Some might have a relationship with one particular agency causing them to unjustly favor one over others, that's okay, since you are hoping for a consensus, hearing one or more agency names several times, from different sources.)
- Join or visit adoptive parent support groups. If you live in an area with a large enough population base, it is likely you have a local adoptive parent support group. These are valuable people for you to contact as they've completed the process you are just starting. They can talk to you about their experiences with local agencies. Not only can they tell you why they hired the one they did, but why they didn't hire the others. (There are several ways to find adoptive parents support groups. *Adoptive Families* magazine, has a very helpful website, adoptivefamilies.com. The Child Welfare Information Gateway (a federal government site, formerly known as the National Adoption Information Clearinghouse), also includes this information on their website, childwelfare.gov. Go to Appendix B for more information about these websites. You can also call local adoption agencies and attorneys and inquire if they know of any adoptive parent support groups. Some agencies have their own support groups. These might be valuable to attend, although not quite as unbiased as if the group was assembled by a neutral entity.)
- Join *Resolve,* or attend one of their meetings. Resolve is a very established and respected national infertility organization with regional chapters throughout the country. Part of their focus on infertility includes adoption. Many of their members are in the process of, or have completed, an adoption, and can talk about agencies they used. To find a Resolve chapter near you, visit

resolve.org. For more information about Resolve, please see Appendix B.

- <u>Talk to other adoptive parents.</u> The more you start talking about adoption, the more you will find that people you already know have adopted. Most of these families feel no need to volunteer personal information about their family being formed by adoption unless there is a reason to do so. In most cases, upon hearing you share that interest, they are happy to share their adoption experiences. There are millions of adoptive parents out there. You will find them everywhere. You can ask which adoption agency they used and how they would rate their services. Also, ask if they can put you in touch with other adoptive parents who might have information to share with you about their adoption experiences. You will find that adoptive parents tend to know a lot of other adoptive parents.
- <u>Talk to people you know in the health care industry.</u> Many adoption agencies work with doctors, counselors and hospitals regarding the care of the birth mothers they are working with. For this reason, some healthcare professionals may be able to tell you about agencies with whom they have had contact in prior adoption situations.

If you previously read Chapter 4 (Selecting the Right Attorney) you have likely noticed that some of the recommended steps in compiling a list of possible agencies are the same as when inquiring about adoption attorneys. If you are like many adoptive parents just starting the process, perhaps unsure at this point if you will be doing an independent or agency adoption, clearly it makes sense to concurrently inquire about *both* agencies and attorneys when you speak to the people and groups recommended above.

Don't forget that your inquiries about adoption agencies need to be in the region where the agency has its office. That means that if you are inquiring about a local agency, let's say in your hometown of Chicago, you would be contacting Chicago professionals and support groups to ask about them. But let's say you were considering an agency in another city and state, perhaps Los Angeles. You will need to inquire about it with its local entities. That means finding the appropriate professionals and organizations the same way you did as described above, but in Los Angeles, and see what they tell you.

Is the Agency Licensed?

What you are really asking here isn't so much if the agency is licensed, rather *is it an adoption agency at all*. In many states, if you start your search for an adoption agency by opening your local yellow pages, or turning on your computer and searching on the internet, many of the ads you will see are for what you will assume are adoption agencies. They have names with sound like agencies, and they do adoptions, so what could they be but a licensed adoption agency? Right?

Wrong. In the majority of states, these entities are not agencies but facilitators. A facilitator is a person or business which helps arrange adoptions for a fee, but is not licensed as an agency or attorney. They can't do home studies. They can't witness relinquishments. They can't prepare legal documents or give you legal advice. They can't write a court report approving the adoption. What *do* they do? They find birth mothers to make adoptive matches. Is this a bad thing? Not necessarily. Finding a birth mother is an important part of most newborn adoptions. Make that, finding the *right* birth mother. And therein is part of the problem in dealing with facilitators.

A good agency or attorney is educated, trained and licensed to do their job. Furthermore, they are monitored by a state office, and if they don't perform their services correctly, they risk losing their licenses. To be a facilitator, however, most states simply require getting a business license. How easy is that? Go spend $25 or so for your license, make up a name, let's say Baby Love USA, and presto! You're in business. Now you can run your ads proclaiming "#1 in adoptions!" Or, perhaps, "Christian adoptive parents waiting for your baby!" (Sadly, you will often see a religious theme used as what sometimes appears to be a marketing tool, as the business rarely has any official tie to any religion.)

I would have less problems with facilitators if their ads clearly stated: "We are not a licensed adoption agency or attorney." The reality, however, is most ads imply to adoptive parents, and especially to less sophisticated birth mothers, that they are an actual licensed agency, with the protections that brings. A good question to ask facilitators is, "If you are truly dedicated to the field of adoptions, why don't you become a licensed agency?" The answer in many cases is that either they would be deemed ineligible, or they wish to continue to operate without the legal restrictions placed on legitimate licensed agencies. And a good question for you, if you are considering hiring a facilitator, is if the ads of the facilitator are incomplete and misleading, what makes you think that they will be completely forthright in other matters with you.

Another example of providing misleading information is in the advertisements many facilitators use. Most of them advertising out of the state in which they are located will not provide any information about their actual whereabouts. They will provide a toll free number and no address. Why? To entice birth mother and adoptive parent calls from all around the country to "get them on the phone and plant their hook," and only later reveal that they are located in a different state. By then, they likely hope, they have convinced the person to work with them, when initially the birth mother or adoptive parent may have never made the call if it was known their office was so far away. The average facilitator charges large fees, often more than most agencies and attorneys, despite the fact agencies and attorneys provide more services. Despite this, some adoptive parents elect to hire facilitators. That's fine, I just want to make sure you know what you are getting for your money, and what you are not.

Facilitators are not the only entities which omit important information like their actual whereabouts from their ads. Some legitimate agencies and attorneys have also been known to do this, and I think caution should be exercised with them when they do as well. The practice seems to be most used by facilitators, however.

Is the Agency Able to Do the Specific Duties You Need?

Each adoption agency is licensed to perform particular functions, or chooses to limit itself. Some do domestic; others do international. A small number do both. Some are licensed in multiple states while most are licensed in only one. Even within a state, some might be licensed only in one county, while others are statewide. Of those doing domestic adoptions, some might be licensed only to perform home studies. Others are additionally licensed to make adoptive placements.

Among those who make adoptive placements, they are further distinguished by those that have outreach programs, networking for birth mothers to contact their agency to select adoptive parents. Other agencies are more passive, and do little or nothing to create adoptive matches, leaving that to you to do on your own or via an adoption attorney.

With this wide diversity in services, it is critical you find the right agency offering the services you need. If you are hoping to be matched up with a birth mother to adopt a newborn, you will want an agency that actively networks and places children for adoption in addition to doing home studies. If you will be using another source to find a birth mother, such as an attorney or your own networking efforts, you might only need an agency that does home studies. If you are planning an international adoption, does the agency only perform home studies which are accepted for international adoption? Does it have a program in the country from the specific country from which you plan to adopt? Because international adoptions involve such diverse procedures than domestic agency adoption, they are separately discussed in Chapter 7.

Do You Meet the Requirements of the Agency?

So far, we've talked about you choosing an agency. The reality, however, is that they are also choosing *you*. Private adoption agencies can set their own guidelines regarding which adoptive parents they will work with. Some agencies have a religious affiliation, usually obvious from their name, such as Jewish Family Services. Some of these religious-affiliated agencies will welcome adoptive parents of all religious backgrounds, but most will only work with adoptive parents of their designated faith. Others will set their own unique requirements regarding your age, the number of existing children you have, whether you are married or single, length of your marriage, existence and number of any prior marriages, if one spouse must be a full-time parent, and similar factors.

Public agency adoptions have fewer restrictions. For example, as a government institution they can't exclude you based upon your religion. (They could, however, give preference to those with a religion which match the pre-existing religion of a child to promote stability and the best interests of the child.)

The one thing both private and public agencies will have in common in their requirements is that you show you can provide a secure and loving home for a child. In this regard, the existence of any evidence of child abuse, criminal activity or consistent financial instability is grounds for denial with both private and public agencies.

Fine-Tune Your List

You've likely eliminated a large number of agencies on your list simply by determining they don't offer the services you want, or that you do not meet their eligibility requirements. You should still have a large list of possible agencies (and if you don't, maybe you should be expanding your list to include other regions in your state, or other states). How do we further eliminate the "wrong" agencies, and get the right one for you? Here are my recommended steps:

- Request each agency's written materials describing all their services, fees and requirements. Besides receiving the information in writing (which is more definitive than information over the phone), it also gives you a chance to see the quality of the materials they present. An adoption agency will be preparing and processing many important documents for you. If they can't put together a professional-looking informational packet, that tells you something about the quality of their work and attention to detail. When you receive their information, carefully read what they have sent you. Does it give you all the information you need about them? Be cautious if the information is nothing but baby pictures and fluff. Creating your family is an important decision and warrants thorough information. Good agencies recognize this.
- Visit their website. This is one more chance to learn about their services. I still recommend, however, that you ask for their written materials. That is because the website is likely the work of a web professional. You deserve the opportunity to see the work of the agency, which is more likely to be seen in their written materials.

- When you first called the agency, did you get a good feeling from the initial person who answered the phone? Was he or she professional and friendly? Was it a person employed by the agency or an answering service? Remember, this will be the same person a potential birth mother will likely get on the phone in her initial call. If the receptionist is not warm and friendly, why would a birth mother be interested in staying on the line to speak to a social worker? That would mean fewer birth mothers to be considering you as adoptive parents through that office.

You will likely be immediately impressed, or not, with the materials you receive, allowing you to quickly shorten your list. We still have a ways to go, however, to get down to the best agency for you.

Specific Questions to Ask the Agency

Some of the following questions may be answered by the written materials from the agencies, or their websites. If not, these are important questions to ask. Since most agencies offer periodic free seminars to learn more about their services, that would be an excellent, and free, chance to get your questions answered. Depending upon the type of adoption you are planning, not all the following questions may be required.

- *How many years has your agency been in business?* (You've already verified they are an actual licensed agency, as discussed earlier.) There is no real detriment if the agency you are calling has only been in business a few years, as long as they appear to be doing their job well. Generally, however, the stability of a long-established agency is impressive.
- *How many adoptions has your agency done in its existence?* An agency's extensive experience is impressive, but only as it relates to how many adoptions it has done. You can't ask for much more than the combination of an established reputation combined with a significant number of completed adoptions.
- *How many adoptions do you complete each year? How about last year?* This is particularly important to you if you are hiring an agency to not just do your home study and assist with the

birth mother's relinquishment, but to help match you with a birth mother. Some agencies might only complete a couple dozen a year, while others complete hundreds. (Generally, those doing in excess of fifty are usually found in high population areas.) A high number of adoptions each year is impressive. As you will see in the next few questions, however, that information by itself can be misleading.

- *How many adoptive parents do you work with at one time waiting to be matched by a birth mother? Is there a maximum number you work with at one time? How many do you have at this moment?* These questions are what really put things in perspective. If an agency completes one hundred adoptions, but has three hundred waiting families, that means only one in every three couples are being picked in a year. An agency completing fifty adoptions with fifty waiting adoptive families being shown to each birth mother may only be completing half as many adoptions, but they appear to be making placements three times faster.

- *What is the average wait of your clients for an adoptive placement?For what kind of placements? What is a soonest versus longest estimate for a placement based upon prior clients?* When you ask these questions, you need to be clear about the type of adoption you want. For example, if you want to adopt a Caucasian or African-American newborn, then ask that specifically. It won't help you any to find out the average wait for a placement is fourteen months, and ninety percent of those were Hispanic toddlers. Obviously that sounds like the perfect agency for those seeking a Hispanic toddler adoption, but not if that isn't your choice of placement.

- *Are most of your adoptions "open" or "closed?"* Although each state has different laws and customs regarding how open or closed an adoption may be, often this is an area where the agency asserts its discretion, as they may elect to make adoptions more closed than independent adoptions in the same state. Assuming you want to adopt a newborn, find out if you meet the birth mother in person. If so, at what point of the pregnancy? Do you share first names? Last names? Can you be at the hospital for the birth? Hold the baby? What about post-birth contact with the birth family? If so, will it be pictures and letters one or two times a year, or face-to-face get-togethers? There is no right or wrong answer here. Adoptions are like marriages. They can all be different and yet work wonderfully. You simply want to make sure that your view of the degree of openness or closeness matches the agency's expectations.

• *Who selects us as the child's adoptive parents, the agency or the birth mother?* Some states, and the agencies within those states, continue to do adoptions as they were done fifty years ago, with no contact at all between the birth mother and adoptive parents. Overall, in the United States, this is becoming rarer and rarer in newborn placements. You might be one of the small number of adoptive parents who desire that degree of closeness, however.

• *Do some adoptive parents who hire you never get an adoptive placement, or have to wait several years? Do you find these adoptive parents have any ethnic, religious or other qualities in common?* You want to know if the agency is creating adoptive placements that match your goals, for people with the qualities you offer. For example, if you are a member of an ethnic group seeing to adopt a child of that same ethnic group, why retain an agency located in a geographical area where that ethnicity is not represented. The same holds true of issues like religion, as some states, such as Utah, have a disproportionate degree of Mormons, meaning less of other religions.

• *Do you have an outreach program to find birth mothers to select us as adoptive parents, or do you just help us do it ourselves?* Some agencies are active in networking and create many matches for their waiting adoptive parents. Others do little or none, focusing on preparing home studies for adoptive parents who have found their own birth mother, or who are adopting older children already freed for adoption. Chapters 8 and 9 are dedicated to teaching you strategies to find a birth mother and proceed with a newborn adoption. It is helpful, however, if your agency is working toward this goal as well.

• *What percentage of the birth mothers you find are in-state, as compared to coming from another state?* You may not care if your birth mother lives in, or out of, your home state, as you just want to get picked. Other families want to stay in-state, perhaps worrying about travel costs, easy access to the birth mother pre-birth and at birth, and the laws of the state where the birth will occur. If you want a birth mother from a particular state, there is no reason to hire an agency who appears to find birth mothers from other states.

- *When birth mothers contact you, how are we and other adoptive parents you are working with shown to her, giving us a chance to be selected?* Few agencies use waiting lists where they would only be showing the longest waiting families to each birth mother. Still, agency procedures can differ. Some show all their waiting adoptive parents, while others only show a few adoptive parents, selected to match characteristics of the birth mother which the agency feels is important. (Other than cases where a birth mother has characteristics not desired by the adoptive parents - ethnicity, drug usage, open or closed adoption, et cetera - you want to make sure you will be shown often and without delay, with the birth mother given a broad choice in adoptive parents. Why do you want her to have a "broad choice," rather than just you and one or two other adoptive families? A couple reasons. One is that if they only show a few adoptive parents each time, think of all the times you are *not* being shown. The birth mother destined to pick you never got to even see you. The other is that even when you are shown to her, you want her decision to be solid. The more adoptive families she has to choose from, the more likely she can be truly happy with her decision. If she had only two or three families from which to choose, she might be choosing the best family available, but without a diverse enough group to be truly excited about who she is selecting. This will be one of the toughest decisions of her life. She needs to be truly impressed and emotionally attracted to the family she chooses.)

- *What percentage of your clients find a birth mother through your efforts, as compared to your clients finding a birth mother on their own?* If one of the key things you hope to accomplish in hiring an agency is to have them help you find a birth mother, you will want to know how effective their efforts are. For example, an agency may complete forty adoptions a year, but if ninety percent of the adoptive parents found their own birth mother, it is not as impressive as an agency completing only twenty-five, all of which resulted from their own birth mother networking efforts.

- *Does your fee include your networking efforts to help us get picked by a birth mother, or is it a separate fee?* If the agency is networking for birth mothers, leading them to contact the agency to in turn select one of the waiting adoptive families, a lot of money is being spent by the agency in that outreach effort. This might include yellow page advertising and internet promotion of their website geared to birthmothers, contributions of time and/or money to organizations which indirectly leads to referrals, et cetera. Just like with their other expenses, these costs are passed on to you as the client benefiting from those efforts. The question is if it is part of their standard fee, which includes their agency services, or a separate fee specifically designated for networking efforts. (Either payment option is fine, as long as you know what you are paying for. Just like with attorneys, you can often expect to pay several thousand dollars or more for an effective networking campaign.)

- *What about if we want to adopt a toddler, older child, or a child with special-needs? Do you work with other agencies and exchanges in other states to help make a placement?* Some agencies primarily focus on the children relinquished through them, but many will work with agencies from all around the nation, as well as registries, to find the right child for you. If you want a child in this category, it is really essential that the agency takes full advantage of the information-sharing between agencies and states, or your options will be severely limited.

- *If we adopt a toddler, older child or a child with special-needs, is there any special funding programs to assist us with future costs?* You want to find out if these children are available for an Adoption Subsidy Program, and/or other benefits which might be unique to your state, if that is important to you.

- *Can we be listed with attorneys or other private agencies while we are working with you, and proceed with whichever attorney or agency finds an adoptive placement first?* The goal of every adoption agency and attorney should be to help you adopt. To that end, if you wish to hire more than one agency to obtain your goal as quickly as possible, you need agencies and attorneys who will work within that philosophy. Most all will be agreeable. Some agencies, however, require you to only work with them. I believe this is wrong, as the agency is making itself the key figure in the adoption. In reality, the adoption is about you, and the child you will be adopting, not the agency.

- *Do we pay for your services as we work through the adoption, or do we pay it all in advance?* A few agencies charge their entire fee in advance, but this is quite rare. That's because their services are usually clearly divided, as it makes little sense to charge fees before each stage of service is reached. For example, all agencies will require a pre-placement home study. That's one fee. When an adoptive placement is made there will need to be services provided to the birth mother, such as counseling and assisting with her relinquishment. There will be a fee for that. Then there will be a post-placement home study, and a fee for that. Why would they charge that in advance when it is not known when, or if, that post-placement home study will even be needed. Furthermore, why charge some of these fees if another agency (perhaps out-of-state) or an attorney, is providing some of those services? With these facts in mind, you should be very cautious in working with an agency requiring full payment for the entire adoption in advance.

- *What are typical birth mother expenses we will be expected to pay?* Almost all states allow adoptive parents to help with the adoption and birth expenses, although some states make different rules for independent or agency adoption. Standard costs may include medical bills and the birth mother's living costs while she is incapacitated due to the pregnancy. Some agencies have, or are affiliated with, unwed mothers' homes. This is often an inexpensive way to meet a birth mother's food and rent needs (often about half what an apartment would cost), but many birth mothers don't like living in a group setting and are used to living on their own. (Some birth mothers have few, or no, expenses - they have insurance and are employed, or live at home), while others may have significant expenses. If your birth mother will have any expenses, you want to know in advance what they are, and for how long. As a general rule, expenses for birth mother needing full assistance will range from $600 - $1,200 per month for food and rent. Much is dependent upon where the birth mother lives. When you get into high living costs, however, it is a sign for potential caution. For example, if an agency improperly encourages birth mothers to work with them by offering them a luxury apartment at several times the rent of a typical apartment, or similar gratuitous inducements, it borders on bribery. And bribery is not conducive to a successful adoption, or finding the right kind of birth mother. To learn more about permitted living expenses, see the state-by-state review and Chapter 12.)

- *Do you provide counseling for birth mothers?* Placing a child for adoption will be one of the most emotional moments of a birth mother's life. The more prepared she is, the more likely she can make the placement as planned. Counseling is one major tool to help prepare her for the birth, and the emotions to follow. Both she, and you, deserve the benefits she will receive from pregnancy/adoption counseling. Some state laws require counseling, and some do not. If an agency feels counseling is not important, or in any way discourages birth mothers from receiving it, I believe it indicates a lack of not only empathy, but a basic understanding of the emotions at work, and the making of a successful adoption.

By the time you have received answers to these questions, you will have a definite "yes" and "no" pile of agencies. However, we still need to whittle down your list at bit to find the best agency for you.

Test the Agency's Knowledge

Just as I recommended in the independent adoption chapter that you "test" an attorney's knowledge, I recommend you do the same regarding agencies. The problem is that this is harder to do with an agency. This is because with an attorney, you have one person - the attorney - who will be doing all the work, and you know who to question. With an agency, however, there are different people involved. Perhaps one social worker will be doing your pre-placement home study. Another will be doing your post-placement home study. Yet another might be working with the birth mother, providing counseling and assisting with her relinquishment. It is possible none of these social workers deal with the procedural and legal side of the adoption. It could be the director, an in-house attorney, or a private practice attorney hired as needed for legal work.

Regardless, just as the agency will need to be aware of these issues when a birth mother calls and they begin processing the adoption, someone should be prepared to answer your questions about important issues such as interstate adoption requirements, permitted expenses for birth mothers, the Indian Child Welfare Act, birth father's rights, et cetera. If the social worker answering your questions says such issues are not in her or his area of responsibility, ask to speak to the person who *does* have that responsibility. Asking hypothetical questions about how problems are solved is not at all unreasonable as if they can't answer those questions now, how can they solve them when they occur? As with attorneys, you will quickly see some agencies really "know their business," while others struggle.

Here are some recommended questions:

- *I've heard about something called the Indian Child Welfare Act. Can you explain what that is?* As we will discuss later in Chapter 12, this is a federal law, normally superseding state law, which says if a child is a member of an Indian tribe, or eligible to be a member, the tribe must be given notice and certain procedures followed. If the agency is unfamiliar with the Indian Child Welfare Act, or says it never applies in their state, beware. More and more adoptions are at least potentially touched by the Indian Child Welfare Act, such as where the birth mother has a small degree of tribal heritage which could make the child a member. Noncompliance with the Indian Child Welfare Act can potentially invalidate an adoption, a high cost to pay for an agency's ignorance.
- *We may do an interstate adoption. Can you explain to me how the Interstate Compact works?* As we will discuss in Chapter 12, more and more adoptions are interstate, where you live in a different state than the state in which the child is born. The Interstate Compact provides that prior to a child being transported across state lines by adoptive parents, certain procedures will apply, such as a pre-placement home study of the adoptive parents, and approval from both states' Interstate Compact administrators. In many states, however, the Interstate Compact administrator is not involved, and approval is given directly agency to agency. This is fundamental knowledge every agency should have regarding their own state procedure.

- *What are the birth mother and birth father's rights? Can they change their minds, and if so, for how long?* These issues are the most basic and important of all, so the agency should know these issues frontward and backwards regarding their own state.
- *Is there a federal tax credit for adoptive parents?* The agency should certainly know about the federal tax credit. For 2012, if the adoptive parents have a modified adjusted gross income of $189,710 or less in the year in which the adoption is completed, they are eligible for a tax credit of $12,650 per child adopted. Your income can actually go up to $229,710, but the tax credit decreases proportionally when the income exceeds $189,710. It is not reasonable to expect an adoption agency to know the detailed tax repercussions of adoption, but they should know the existence and basics of the tax credit.

There is much more to an agency adoption than the above questions, but they are diverse enough to give you an idea of an agency's knowledge. Those particular questions may not even be applicable to your individual adoption, but it doesn't matter. The questions are an excellent indicator of what your agency knows, or doesn't know. If they are ignorant about these issues, the same is likely true regarding other important adoption issues, and you know to look elsewhere.

Determine if the Agency Staff's Personality and Approach to Adoption Matches Yours

Deciding if an agency's "personality" matches yours is more difficult than with an attorney. That's because with an attorney you will be working almost exclusively with one person. True, he or she will have a secretary or paralegal, but the attorney has the primary responsibility for everything. For better or worse, most agency adoptions are more of a "by committee" undertaking. As mentioned earlier, there might be different social workers for the pre and post-home study, yet another one for birth mother counseling, and perhaps even an attorney hired by the agency for legal work. Some small agencies may have one person do virtually all the work. All you can do is your best to get a feel for the staff's personality and approach to adoption.

CHAPTER 7

INTERNATIONAL ADOPTION

An international adoption is one where you adopt a child who is born outside the United States to a citizen of another country. International adoptions have long been a popular method of adoptions. However, they are potentially much more legally complex than domestic adoptions, as an international adoption involves three sets of laws, not just one as would be the case if you were doing a domestic in-state adoption: 1) the laws and procedures of your home state; 2) our federal government's adoption and immigration requirements; and 3) the laws of the country from which you adopt.

Does this mean an international adoption is three times more complicated? No. To the contrary, in ideal circumstances, they are sometimes simpler than a domestic adoption due to the fact the path to many countries is so established that the process becomes almost automatic. The potential exists, however, for more complications and costs, and this demonstrates the importance of working with a quality international adoption program with an excellent support staff overseas.

To give you the full picture of how international adoption works, and how to find the right program and country for you, I'm going to do the following:

- Provide an overview of international adoption.
- Discuss the pros and cons compared to domestic adoption.

- Walk you through the entire process step-by-step.
- Give statistics regarding the most popular countries from which to adopt.
- Discuss keys to finding the best international agency.

Overview

The procedures you must follow in an international adoption will be determined by many factors: the eligibility restrictions on the adoptive parents set by the adoption program you select and the child's country of origin (your age, marital status, etc.); the laws of the child's country governing adoption; the adoption laws of your state governing international adoption; and the USCIS's (United States Citizenship and Immigration Service) requirements concerning the admission of the child into the United States and eventual citizenship. (The USCIS was previously known as the INS - the Immigration and Naturalization Service.)

All international adoptions require a pre-placement home study by an agency licensed by the state in which it is located to do international home studies. In that sense, every international adoption is an "agency adoption." However, the home study requirement is only a very small part of what makes up a completed international adoption. The critical part is the completion of the adoption itself overseas, and the country you select from which to adopt.

Not every country permits their children to be adopted by foreign citizens. Why do some countries allow it, even welcome it, while many don't? The answer lies in a mixture of cultural, political and financial factors. The bottom line is that some countries have an inability to care for its parentless children, or lack the ability to create adoptive homes for them within their nation. As a country, we should be grateful for the opportunity to adopt these children, fulfilling a need that our own county can't fully satisfy.

There is actually no shortage of waiting children within the United States, as discussed in previous chapters. Specifically, the United States has approximately half a million children in foster care, many of them free for adoption. It would be far simpler for adoptive parents to adopt these domestically-waiting children, rather than travel 10,000 miles away. But the majority of the adopting parents adopting overseas feel America's waiting children do not meet their criteria (often citing issues like age, ethnicity and freedom from concerns over possible birth parent objections).

The countries from which Americans most frequently adopt changes year to year. For example, recently Guatemala was a popular country, prior to being "shut down." (And it will likely be reopened when the problems leading to its closure are solved.) For a time this has occurred with other counties, many of whom re-opened their doors to American adopting parents after months or years of closure, such as Russia and Ukraine. According to the U.S. Department of State, the most popular countries from which Americans adopted in 2010, and the number of adoptions from each country are:

- China: 3,401
- Ethiopia: 2,513
- Russia: 1,082
- South Korea: 863
- Ukraine: 445
- Taiwan: 285
- India: 243
- Colombia: 230

You might be wondering why countries such Canada, Australia and England are not listed. After all, it would be easier to travel to a country where English is spoken by everyone, and which is more "tourist friendly." The reality, however, is that most industrialized nations all face the same problem as America - there are more couples waiting to adopt than there are children (or at least newborns) free for adoption. For that reason, if you travel overseas to adopt, you can expect to meet other adoptive parents who have traveled there from countries like Canada, France, Germany, Italy, England and Sweden, to name just a few.

Most of the countries with children free for adoption are countries undergoing economic problems or social conditions leading to some women being unable to parent, and countries unable to provide adoptive homes. Unlike America, where foster homes are used, almost all foreign nations place children in orphanages, and their countries recognize that is not the best way to raise and nurture a child for an extended time. Things are changing overseas, however, and the landscape of international adoption is slowly changing, with dramatic effects upon prospective adoptive parents in America.

For years, international adoptions increased more and more each year, up to almost 23,000 adoptions in 2004. Over the last few years, however, the number of intercountry adoptions have actually declined every year. Most people attribute this to increased regulations and costs due to the implementation of an international treaty called the Hague Adoption Convention, increased bureaucracy and delays in foreign countries, and the fact many countries which previously were a good source of international placements now offer mainly special-needs children. As can be seen below, international adoptions by Americans have decreased by more than half in the last seven years:

- 2004: 22,990 children adopted
- 2005: 22,734 children adopted
- 2006: 20,680 children adopted
- 2007: 19,609 children adopted
- 2008: 17,475 children adopted
- 2009: 12,753 children adopted
- 2010: 11,059 children adopted

This huge reduction in international adoptions does not mean intercountry adoption is not a viable means of adoption. Eleven thousand children is still a significant number. However, it is an indication that you will want to seriously examine the pros and cons of international adoption before you go that route, and be particularly careful regarding the country from which you adopt, and the agency or attorney you will employ to assist you.

But let's explore why international adoption has decreased by more than 50% in the last seven years. One reason has been touched on already: increased costs and bureaucracy required by the Hague Treaty. This is not to say the Hague Treaty is bad for adoptions. To the contrary, it has helped provide increased security and less fraudulent practices by certain agencies, attorneys and facilitators, both in the United States and abroad. Still, it has reduced the number of approved international adoption agencies and attorneys, and added bureaucracy, which increases costs.

But this is likely not the main reason why international adoptions have decreased so dramatically. The main reason is that the type of children available overseas has changed, not meeting the goals of many adoptive parents. In prior years, there were a significant number of children deemed "adoptable" by the majority of the Americans seeking to adopt; the children were relatively young and healthy and in the same ethnic group as the adopting parents. (Not all adoptive parents have these goals, but a significant number do.)

Recently, however, the countries from which many adoptions traditionally took place either stopped allowing their children to leave their country for adoption, or they dramatically reduced the number of children available. In some cases, the reason for this is actually good for the children. For example, some nations were previously forced to offer their children for adoption due to insufficient funding to care for orphaned children, and existing social stigmas in their nation about adoption. As those situations have improved, and adoption is becoming more common in their countries, the need for adoptive parents from America and other nations has been reduced.

The result is that in many countries, particularly in Eastern Europe, the children most Americans deem "adoptable" are being adopted in their own counties. The need for international adoption (and the need for a child to change languages, culture, citizenship, et cetera) often no longer exists. Frequently the children left available for adoption are older, or have special needs. Just like in the United States, it is often these children waiting for an adoptive home. Even in China, where its unique culture dictates the increased familial value placed on a son over a daughter, leading to the adoption of many female children, the situation is slowly changing. So the question many adoptive parents end up asking myself is this: "If I end up adopting an older child, or a child with special needs, perhaps not matching my own ethnic group, why travel to a foreign country, spend approximately $25,000 to $50,000, worry about a child adapting to a new language and culture, when I could adopt a waiting child in my own country, for about no cost?" The waiting children of the world need homes, whether they be in Moscow... or Cleveland.

Hague v. Non-Hague Countries

There are two types of international adoptions: Hague and Non-Hague. Over the last few years more and more countries have signed an international treaty called the Hague Adoption Convention. It is simply an agreement between nations to follow certain rules and procedures to protect both children being adopted, and the adoptive parents. To see the list, go to the U.S. Department of State's website, adoption.state.gov. More and more countries are constantly becoming "Hague signatories," meaning the special terms of the Hague treaty apply to them. About 80 countries have signed to date, including recently the United States. As will be seen, however, international adoptions by Americans can be Hague or non-Hague, depending upon if the country from which they adopt is a Hague country or not.

Hague Adoptions

The vast majority of countries from which international adoptions occur have signed the Hague Treaty. This means that if your country of citizenship (America) *and* the country from which you adopt, are both Hague countries, you must follow the provisions of the Hague Treaty. If the other country is not a "Hague country," it is a non-Hague adoption (discussed below), despite the fact America is a Hague country. Here's how a typical Hague adoption works:

- Select an "accredited adoption agency" or "approved person," referred to as an *ASP* (Adoption Service Provider)(not to be confused with the same term used uniquely in California for social workers handling independent adoptions). In most cases the ASP will be an adoption agency, but in some cases attorneys are also approved (they are referred to an an "approved person"). The job of the ASP will be to: 1) identify a child available for adoption; 2) make sure the child is properly free for adoption (consents signed or parent rights terminated); 3) do your home study (or approve another agency's home study, such as where an attorney is the ASP, or you live in a state different from the state in which the international adoption is located; 4) evaluate the potential placement and make sure the child's best interests will be served; 5) continue to evaluate the placement to be sure the child and adoptive family are doing appropriately; and 6) take custody of the child if an unforeseen problem occurred requiring a new placement.

114

- The United States Citizenship and Immigration Services (USCIS), must determine that you are deemed eligible to adopt. To do this you complete a form called the *Application for Determination of Suitability to Adopt a Child from a Convention Country* (USCIS form I-800A). This is a form your selected international agency will assist you with.
- The I-800A must be approved by the USCIS. Then your ASP can prepare your *dossier* (your home study and other forms required by the child's country), translate your dossier, and send it to the foreign country's Hague-approved central adoption authority. When a child is identified for you by the adoption authorities, your ASP is given a report on the child's medical, psychological and social history (called an Article 16 report) and also provides the child's name and birth date. It will be verified by the foreign country's central adoption authority that the child is fully free for adoption. An English translation of all information about the child should be prepared for you and given to you by your ASP. This is the child's *referral* to you.
- You travel to the child's country and meet the child. Sometimes two or even three visits are required, but one or two is the norm. It is not unusual to have "in country" time of about 3 weeks if only one visit is required, but slightly shorter visits if multiple visits are required. Most all international adoption programs arrange most everything for you while you are in the foreign country. They recommend or book a hotel, have a translator and driver for you, and provide an attorney if one is needed for court. Usually your translator goes almost everywhere with you, and certainly to the orphanage to help you interact with the orphanage staff and child. Your "child time" is critical, as this is when you make the determination this is the right child for you, and you for him or her, and that you feel the information presented regarding emotional and physical health is accurate. Even with the greater security of a Hague adoption, it is not unheard of that some of the information provided about the child might be inaccurate (e.g. subjective assessments of the child's emotional or psychological state).
- Once you have accepted the child's referral, you will request USCIS's provisional approval to adopt that child (or in some cases multiple children) via a form called *Petition to Classify*

Convention Adoptee as an Immediate Relative (USCIS form I-800). Your ASP assists you with this. The USCIS will determine that the child meets certain legal requirements to be what it terms a "Convention adoptee," then you or your agency will submit a visa application for the child. When it is determined that the child appears eligible to immigrate to the U.S., the U.S. Consular Office will issue an "Article 5" letter.

- You finalize your adoption, usually done in the child's country. Every country has different laws and procedures to finalize an adoption. You will want your ASP to fully educate you on your selected country's procedures prior to formalizing an adoption plan with that country. Sometimes this can all be done on your one and only visit overseas, while sometimes it is a completely separate visit, after meeting the child previously. Just as in the United States, the finalization of the adoption will be in court (or administrative hearing), and your ASP will normally arrange for a translator to be present, as well as needed parties, like an attorney.

- With your adoption now finalized overseas, you are legal parents of the child, but you still need to get your child home. The foreign country which just granted the adoption will issue a new birth certificate. Normally this will list you as lawful parents, and show the child's new name, as was changed due to the adoption. The child is not yet a U.S. citizen, however, so the foreign country will issue a passport. Once you have the amended birth certificate and a passport, you can apply for a U.S. visa. The child must first be examined by a physician in the foreign country designated by the U.S. government (called a "panel physician"). The primary purpose is to be sure the child does not have a contagious disease or disability that may be a bar to visa issuance. The visa will be issued by the U.S. embassy or consulate in the country from which you adopted. An immigrant visa is issued, allowing the child to enter the U.S.

Non-Hague Adoptions

Even though the United States is a Hague country, if the country you are adopting from is not a signatory to the Hague Treaty (a "non-

Hague country"), the provisions of the Hague do not apply and different procedures apply. The adoption will be done basically as international adoptions were done before the implementation of the Hague Treaty. To see which countries are "Hague countries" and which are not, visit adoption.state.gov. Let's explore how step-by-step how a non-Hague adoption works:

- Start off by selecting your international adoption agency or attorney. Since the U.S. government is not screening these entities under Hague requirements, you will want to exercise even more caution and investigate any agency or attorney you are considering hiring. In most countries you will be adopting from, the adoption will be arranged via a licensed U.S. adoption agency. In a small number of countries, however, American attorneys assume this role. (Regardless, you will always need an agency to at least conduct your home study.) It is wise to make sure the agency or attorney you work with is licensed as an agency or attorney, and is not just a facilitator (a business, usually employing a name that sounds like an agency, but is not licensed as an agency or attorney). Many states have laws making facilitators (referred to by some as "paid child finders") illegal, but some states permit them. To confirm the agency is actually licensed and competent, follow the same steps as outlined in Chapter 6 for domestic agencies. For attorneys, check their licensing with the state bar and follow the guidelines in Chapter 4.
- Just as in Hague adoptions, you will be working with the USCIS, and it needs to verify you are eligible to adopt. You complete a different form for non-Hague adoptions, however, an *Application for Advance Processing of Orphan Petition* (USCIS form I-600A). You will need to complete a home study prior to submitting this form, along with other documents (like a marriage certificate if married). Your agency or attorney will help you with this. At the time the I-600A is filed, you notify the USCIS of the country from which you plan to adopt, so that they can notify the U.S. embassy or consulate in that country of your approval. Your agency or attorney will prepare your *dossier* (your home study and other forms required by the child's

country), translate your dossier, and send it to the appropriate authority in the foreign country.

- Your agency or attorney will notify you when they have found a child deemed appropriate for you. This means the foreign authority has reviewed your dossier and selected a child for you. Since this is a non-Hague country, the country may have no central adoption authority making the placement determination (required by Hague countries). Instead, your agency or attorney may be working with a regional authority or even a specific orphanage. There is no specified transmittal of information about the child, as in Hague adoptions, but you will want to make sure you receive as much information as you feel you need prior to commencing further in the adoption plan, such as traveling to the child's country to meet him or her. Some countries do not identify a specific child, rather approve you and you learn about specific children when you arrive and meet with the adoption authority of that country.

- You normally adopt the child in their home country. Most countries require one or both of the adoptive parents to travel to the foreign county to finalize the adoption, while a few nations allow the child to be transported to the U.S. for the adoption to occur there. Regardless, the adoptive parents will want to spend time with the child prior to the adoption being finalized to make sure the placement feels right to them, and to learn more about the child and verify prior information provided to them about him or her.

- You apply for the child to be deemed eligible for immigration to the U.S. Just because a foreign country permits you to adopt a child there does not mean that child will be granted permission to enter the U.S. Only children who meet certain qualifications are eligible. Accordingly, it is critical, prior to adopting a child, that he or she will be considered what the U.S. State Department defines as "an orphan." This is a more restrictive test than exists in Hague adoptions. Just because you can adopt a child overseas does not mean that he or she legally qualifies as "an orphan" to be permitted a visa to enter the U.S. and gain citizenship. The term "orphan" as used for this legal purpose is broader than the traditional meaning of a child whose parents have died. (For example, it can include a child relinquished to an orphanage or whose parents have had their rights terminated by a foreign court.) This "orphan" determination is made by the USCIS when the adoptive parents file a *Petition to Classify Orphan as Immediate Relative* (USCIS form I-600). This is normally done at the U.S. embassy or consulate in the child's foreign country. Included with the Petition will be required documents, such as the child's birth certificate, court order of adoption, proof of orphan status, and more.

- When the USCIS has approved the I-600, you must obtain an immigrant visa at the local U.S. embassy or consulate so the child can accompany you home to the U.S. As discussed above for Hague country adoptions, the child will need to be examined by a panel physician as part of the visa process. The child's country will issue a passport for the child, as the child is not yet a U.S. citizen.

All the above referenced forms, I-600A, I-600, I-800A and I-800, can be viewed and downloaded at adoption.state.gov as well as at adoption101.com (Thanks to adoption101.com for granting permission to paraphrase much of the above international adoption from their website.)

Citizenship

Thanks to the Citizenship Act of 2000, a child is generally automatically granted U.S. citizenship upon their entry in the United States, provided: 1) the child is under the age of 18; 2) lives in the custody of the American adoptive parent; and 3) the child lawfully entered the U.S. (e.g. with a visa); and 3) the adoption was finalized overseas, or is properly finalized in the U.S. If the adoption was finalized in the U.S. rather than overseas, citizenship begins when the adoption is granted, not when the child enters the U.S.

Pros and Cons

Domestic and international adoptions have tremendous differences, both in the way the adoptions are completed, and the characteristics of the children being adopted. What is a "pro" for one family might be a "con" for another. Why might you prefer international adoption over domestic? There are several reasons:

- You do not want to adopt a newborn, and feel the waiting children available in the U.S. are not right for you. (Some countries make children under age one available for adoption, but even in these nations, you can't have custody of a baby from the moment of birth, as can occur in a domestic adoption.) In most cases, China offers the youngest children, about one year of age, while other countries average several years of age older, from 2 to 6, or older.

- You might worry that you will be ineligible or unable to adopt domestically due to various factors (age, marital status, etc.), which are frequently not issues internationally (although some countries do have requirements).

- You may be worried that even if you are eligible for a domestic adoption, you may wait a long time for a birth mother to select you. You want a more definite timetable to have a child in your home, which may be more likely in international adoption than in domestic.

- You wish to adopt a child of a specific ethnic group and believe (rightly or wrongly) such a child might be difficult to adopt locally.

- You might be of an ethnic group where there are few adoptive placements locally, yet you wish a child of your same ethnic group. China is an example (although the majority of adoptive parents going there are Caucasian).

- You have humanitarian concerns for the children living overseas in orphanages who desperately need homes, and this is more compelling for you than the domestic scenario, with many adoptive parents vying for the babies available. Be aware, however, as was discussed in Chapter 1, that adopting to "save a child" by itself is actually seen as an inadvisable reason to adopt. Also, don't forget there are about half a million children here in the U.S. in foster homes, either free for adoption, or able to be freed upon someone's desire to adopt them.

- You may not be comfortable with the typical open nature of many domestic adoptions. Not everyone feels comfortable in working closely with a birth mother and possibly having continued contact. You may prefer to work with a foreign government which has already severed the parental rights to a child, and complete a closed adoption.

- You may have extreme anxiety about the fact most birth mothers in most domestic newborn adoptions have a certain time in which to change their minds, often even after the child has gone home with you, and you refuse to take that risk (even though the percentage of failed adoptions is quite low).

There are also potential disadvantages to international adoption:

- Most countries require you to travel to the child's country (usually once or twice). Although some countries bring the child to the U.S. via an escort, the norm for most countries is to require you to go to their country and finalize the adoption in their court.
- You will be traveling to a country where you will most likely not speak their language, and where few people speak English.
- Winters in some countries popular for intercountry adoptions can be quite severe (such as all the Eastern European nations).
- Although many of the countries from which you can do international adoptions are not third-world nations, they are still going to be quite a bit more primitive than you are used to.
- Depending upon the country you adopt from, your out-of-country time may range from two weeks to two months, usually with both adoptive parents present for some or all of the process.
- Things can still go wrong just as in domestic adoption. Some adoptive parents complain they arrived in the foreign country only to find the child was not yet free for adoption, or that other adoptive parents were promised that child, although the Hague treaty has helped tremendously with that. Sometimes adoptive parents discover the child's photos they were shown may have

been years old. Luckily, both these occurrences are rare, particularly with well-established programs.

- You will be dependent upon a translator and guide, and in some cases a foreign attorney, to navigate the complicated legal system in the child's country. They will be speaking a foreign language and you are trusting them to accurately relay important information about the child's health history, the procedures and problems, et cetera.

- Health histories may not be available, or guaranteed to be accurate.

- Most children are raised in orphanages and many of these institutions lack the resources and staff to fully emotionally and physically nurture a child, meaning the longer a child stays there, the more likely he or she is to be negatively affected by their environment. Orphanages can range from excellent to terrible, with most falling in the middle. Some countries, however, have reputations for more nurturing orphanages.

- Even in the best orphanages, where children are loved and nurtured, the care can't equal the one-on-one attention and love of a traditional parent-child relationship. For this reason it is not unusual for some children to initially be slightly to moderately underweight and physically underdeveloped compared to other children their age raised in traditional families. The good news is that most of these children physically "catch up" quite soon.

- Children raised in orphanages are more likely to suffer from "attachment disorder," sometimes more severe the longer they stay in the orphanage. In basic terms, attachment disorder is when a child has difficulty bonding with you as parents due to never having a loving and trusting parent-child relationship previously. He or she has simply never learned through experience and observation that "it is natural to get love and give it back." Instead, if a child was neglected or abused, he or she can become distrustful of adults, hampering the ability to fully bond with you, no matter how loving you are. Not all children suffer from severe attachment disorder simply because they lived in an orphanage, however. Many adoptive parents report they see little or no sign of it once the child has adjusted to their new home. This can be due to the fact some orphanages are staffed by loving and dedicated people with nurturing one-on-one relationships with their children, and that each child is unique and affected differently by their surroundings. Not all countries use orphanages due to concerns over these issues. A small number of countries are like America and use foster homes, allowing them to try to duplicate a more traditional family and a smoother transition into an adoptive home.

- There is always the risk the country you are adopting from will change its requirements in the middle of your adoption, requiring you to redo extensive paperwork and applications, or shut down entirely.

- Some countries have traditions we as Americans find distasteful and which would be illegal in our country, but are customary there. "Expediting fees" or gifts are sometimes demanded by officials who know that without their assistance, you can't complete your adoption. Fortunately, your adoption program can tell you in advance if such expectations will occur in the country you are adopting from, and if so, how it is handled. When we are faced with such improper conduct here in America, we have a legal system in place to demand justice. In some countries, however, it is the justice system itself that sometimes demands the very fees or gifts that we believe to be improper. Often these costs are handled by the international program and are built into your pre-paid program fee.

You can see there are both good and bad elements to an international adoption, and that those elements are completely different from domestic adoption. Most adoptive parents instinctively know right from the beginning if domestic or international adoption is right for them. Some of the negative issues can be avoided by carefully choosing the international program you will work with. This means not just choosing the right agency or attorney operating a top quality international program, but the right country from which to adopt.

The good news, however, is that virtually all of the above detailed steps are the job of your international adoption program. So, your first job is to find a program. A good program will know the "ins and outs" of working with the USCIS and foreign governmental officials. The program should also know the exact eligibility requirements of the country with which they are working and what, if anything, you would be required to do in the child's country to legally complete the adoption and bring the child home.

Fees can vary in international adoptions as much as in domestic adoptions. Most programs charge between $15,000-$30,000. Adoptive parents must be very careful to find out what is covered in the program fee. Some programs do not cover the cost of your home study, your translator/guide overseas, car and driver while you are overseas, the translation and authentication of your dossier, or the orphanage donation. These services can each cost thousands of dollars. Most programs estimate you should plan spending $150 per day while in country for your hotel and meals, although country costs vary.

Keys to Finding the Best International Program

As was discussed in Chapter 2, you are not limited to agencies and attorneys with international programs in your home state. *You want to find the best program, not the closest.* A significant number of adoptive parents retain an international program located in another county, or even another state. This opens a lot of doors. To find potential international adoption programs, and learn about different countries and what they have to offer, you can do the following:

- Go to adoption.state.gov and review the list of Hague approved agencies and attorneys. Although you may end up electing to adopt from a non-Hague country, it is helpful to see those agencies which are approved, and those which were denied accreditation.

- Talk to everyone you know who has adopted, including those who did domestic adoptions. Adoptive parents share information with each other, and tend to have a wide informational net. They can either tell you about their own experiences with one or more international programs, or tell you about other adoptive parents they know who can. Don't just ask for a list of international adoption programs; try to meet people who have adopted from different countries to learn more about what the children and procedures are like from that country. Only you know what is most important to you. For some adoptive parents the key question is where do they go to adopt the youngest possible child. For others it is where do they find the healthiest and most nurtured children.

- Call local agencies and attorneys, even if they only do domestic adoptions, and ask for recommendations. They can often point you to a good intercountry program.

- Join or visit adoptive parent groups. Some of those participating have done international adoption. To find them, visit the websites of *Adoptive Families* magazine and the federal government's Child Welfare Information Gateway, provided in Appendix B.

- Join or visit Resolve and attend their adoption support groups. To learn more about Resolve, see Appendix B.

- Read *Adoptive Families* magazine and peruse their advertisements..

- Visit childwelfare.gov or adoption101.com, which provide listings of each state's adoption agencies, and contact those agencies indicated who either have international adoption programs, or perform international adoption home studies, as well as attorneys who have international programs.

Once you have your list of potential international programs, consider the following questions to help find the best agency or attorney:

- *Are you a licensed agency or attorney?* As discussed previously, some entities which have names like adoption agencies are actually facilitators - not licensed agencies or attorneys - and are viewed with suspicion by many in the adoption field. This is particularly true in international adoptions. I suggest you only work with an international adoption program which is operated by a licensed agency or an attorney who is a member of the American Academy of Adoption Attorneys.

- *Are you Hague accredited?* If not, why not?

- *With which country or countries do your work?* Some agencies or attorneys work with a dozen or so countries, while others specialize in just one country. You might want to be a bit cautious with programs that list a very large number of countries from which they do adoptions. Sometimes working with an excessive number of countries indicates the agency or attorney does not have their own staff in those countries, rather subcontracting from another agency. (More on this below.)

- *Does your overseas staff work directly for you, or are they contracted through another agency or attorney's program?* If you learn they subcontract another agency's labor overseas, it is not necessarily a reason to stop working with that program. However, you do want to be extra cautious when checking out other aspects of the agency, and inquire why, if they have a viable program in that country, they have not invested the time and money to hire their own staff there.

- *We are interested in hiring your agency/law office, but you are located in a different state than the one we live in. Will that cause any problems or extra costs?* Often the answer is "no." You will need a home study by a local agency, but that will be required regardless of the state where the intercountry program is located, so that is not an extra cost. And unlike domestic interstate adoptions, where you either finalize the adoption in the child's state of birth or your home state, most all international adoptions are finalized in the child's country, having nothing to do with the state in which you live, or where the agency or attorney is located. Even if you do not complete your adoption overseas, and instead have your child brought to the United States, you will usually finalize the adoption in your home state.

- *How many adoptions has your program done with the country we want to adopt from this year? How about last year?* You want to see a record of reasonable success. However, you may wish to be cautions of those programs which boast of completing hundreds of adoptions a year. An adoption is not an assembly-line function. Bigger is not always better.

- *What are the children like which that country has available for adoption (age, ethnicity, health, gender, etc.)?* You want to make sure before you start a program if the children available in a particular country meet your goals. Some vary tremendously in age and health issues. You can also learn about a particular country by calling the U.S. embassy which processes Orphan Petitions in that country. Ask what most children are like who are being adopted by Americans over the last year.

- *What specific health tests are given to the child before we consider them for adoption so we are fully informed? HIV? Hepatitis B? Syphilis?* Some countries have good orphanages and this includes regular physical check ups, and checking for various health problems. Other countries do much less, and it will be up to you when you arrive to either have a private physician do it (which can be difficult if a child is in an orphanage), or wait until the *panel physician* does the exam as required by the U.S. embassy before your child enters America.

- *Are there children waiting for immediate placement? What is the average time to complete an adoption, measured from the very start of the process, to bringing a child home?* Although your first goal should be to find the right child, from the right country, you will want to know what your possible timetable looks like. Some countries have children waiting and you are invited over quickly after receipt of your dossier. Other countries have more applications than they have children, meaning a backlog exists.

- *What are the procedures to adopt from the country we will be working with? Do we go to the country to bring the child home or does an escort transport the child to us? How many visits do we make? Both of us, or just one? How long will each visit be?* Some adoptive parents look at their visit, or visits, to the child's country as a great adventure, and look forward to it. Others, whether because of limitations in how much time they can take off from their jobs, difficulty in leaving home due to having an existing child to care for, or simply the costs of repeated trips overseas, have limits on how many times they can leave the country, how long they will stay there, and if one or both adoptive parents need to go each time.

- *What is the full program fee? Does it include the authentication and translation of our dossier? The home study? A translator, car and driver to meet us at the airport and bring us to all our official meetings? The translator and driver's food and lodging?*

Are we expected to give the orphanage a donation to help the remaining children there, and if so, how much is it? What about the translation of the foreign court documents for our embassy overseas? The cost of a lawyer doing our child's re-adoption for us when we get back? If it's not included, what will those fees be? Intercountry adoption program fees can be very misleading. Knowing all the required elements of your intercountry adoption in advance, as you are now learning, will allow you to figure out the true total program fee. An intercountry program which looks like a bargain at $15,000 may soon become overly expensive when you add several thousand dollars each for your dossier, your translator and guide overseas, in-country car and driver fees, the orphanage donation, expediting fees, overseas court costs, and attorney costs in your re-adoption at home. A program which is significantly more expensive – let's say $25,000, but which includes all of those fees might actually be less expensive. The key is avoiding any programs that attempt to mislead you with a "low" fee, glossing over the extra costs to come later. Remember, just like in domestic adoption, bigger is not always better, nor is the most expensive necessarily the best.

- *Is the adoption completed and approved by the court in the child's country or are we only given guardianship?* Some countries will only grant guardianship, thus requiring you to adopt the child under your state law when you return home.

- *Do you have get-togethers of adoptive parents who have already adopted, so we can meet them and their children? If not, can you give me the names of at least six adoptive families who used your program in the last year whom we can call to ask about their experiences?* Meeting other adoptive parents who have been where you are going, assisted by the same people who will be assisting you, is very important. They can give you the lowdown of what it was like from their perspective.

These questions, coupled with the general questions regarding attorneys and agencies provided in Chapters 4 and 6, should help you find an excellent program, whether in, or outside, your state. Remember, last year more than 11,000 international adoptions are completed by Americans. There is no reason you can't be one of them.

CHAPTER 8

STRATEGIES TO
FIND A BABY TO ADOPT

This chapter is dedicated to one thing - finding a birth mother to choose you as the adoptive parents for the child she is expecting. According to the National Center of Health Statistics, there are more than three million unplanned pregnancies in the United States each year. Three *million*. Of these, more than a million will elect to terminate their pregnancies. About 130,000 will plan adoption. The others will parent the child or place with a relative. So the question is how do you find these women, to get information about you in front of them so they will not only choose adoption, but pick you?

In previous chapters we've discussed the most important action: hiring an adoption attorney or agency, either in or outside your state, whose services include showing you to birth mothers contacting their office to start adoption planning. Often hiring the right adoption professional is enough in itself to result in creating your adoptive match. My advice, though, is don't stop there. The more you do, and the better you do it, the higher your chances of success. Plus, we don't want just *any* adoptive placement, we want the right one for you – the right birth mother placing for the right reasons – so wouldn't it be nice to have a *choice* of adoptive placements? Not just one? If you want to achieve that, be prepared to use some originality and effort to obtain it. I'll provide the originality if you'll provide the effort. Deal?

While your attorney and/or agency is doing their best to match you with a birth mother, you are doing the same. Here's a key difference, however, and why you want to be active on your own behalf in various networking strategies. When your attorney or agency is contacted by a birth mother seeking the right adoptive parents for her expected baby, she will be shown the many waiting families your adoption professional represents. This means your chances might be one in ten, one in forty, whatever. But when you find your own birth mother, and then have your attorney or agency get involved to make sure it looks like an appropriate and safe placement, you are normally the only considered adoptive parents. After all, your hard work should pay off for *you*, not other waiting adoptive parents.

I'm going to suggest some tried and true networking methods, and some ones you have not heard of before. The key is to exhaust these methods. Don't look for an excuse to do nothing and go after your adoption half-heartedly. Do it with double the intensity you did for other important aspects of your life: getting an academic degree; finding the right job; choosing your dream house; battling infertility.

Before I list these networking strategies, let me say one thing:

It only takes one.

I know from personal experience in working with more than nine hundred adoptive families that they are quick to disparage certain methods, saying "too many people already do that," or "if I send my photo-resume letter to doctors, they will just throw it away."

It only takes one.

You may be right. Of the letters you send out, the calls you make, the people you talk to, ninety-nine percent of that effort may be wasted. Actually, let's be brutally honest. Ninety-nine percent *will* be wasted. Doctors will toss away your photo-resume letters without a glance, as will most health-care professionals when given to them in the traditional way. Even your friends, without the right approach, will not know what to do with them.

So what.

You only need one letter to be passed on to a birth mother to be successful at adoption.

It only takes one.

But to find that *one*, you need to get in the game, and use every opportunity to get yourself out there, waiting to be discovered by a birth mother. And more than that, you've got to do everything in the most effective manner, using original techniques.

Prepare a Photo-Resume Letter

This is the foundation of your search for a birth mother. For a birth mother to seriously consider you, she will want to initially see what you look like, and read what your life is like. This is the heart of a photo-resume letter. Because we are going to use it for so many things, and because most are prepared poorly, I want you to recognize the importance of creating the best possible letter. It is the essence of your quest. A typical photo-resume letter will have a photo of you, and a letter describing what your life is like, giving a birth mother a chance to visualize what a child's life will be like with you.

Your photo. Nothing is more important than your picture. You could have the most eloquent letter accompanying it, but if the birth mother does not find the photo attractive, she won't even bother reading the letter. That's just reality. Take it from someone who has sat next to hundreds of birth mothers and watched them go through a stack of photo-resume letters.

Let me digress here for a moment, because it is just about here that most adoptive parents go into a panic, fearing they don't have the "right" look. I've heard it all: I'm overweight, we're too old, my husband is balding, etc. The reality is all of us are insecure about some aspects of our lives, particularly our appearance, and for some reason most adoptive parents assume every other adoptive parent in the world looks like Julia Roberts and a young Paul Newman, and that every birth mother will end up with them.

The reality, however, is that adoptive parents come from all walks of life, duplicating the general population. They will be skinny or obese, tall or short, black or white, Christian, Jewish or agnostic, college educated with a fancy job or a high school graduate working in manual labor. You get the idea.

Here's the key thing to make you relax and stop worrying if you feel you will not be attractive to a birth mother. Rarely does a birth mother elect adoptive parents based upon physical attractiveness or professional job status. True, they want their child to be raised in a financially secure home and be presented with options in life, but that exists with most middle-income families.

Here is the reality of who birth mothers choose as adoptive parents: They select adoptive parents they can *identify* with. This means people they feel comfortable with, that make them feel good about themselves when they meet. Comments I frequently hear from birth mothers when explaining why they selected one family over a stack of others are:

- "The adoptive mom reminds me of my favorite aunt."
- "They look like they love to laugh."
- "I can tell they really love each other."
- "They like to do the same kind of things I do."

What I *don't* hear from birth mothers in choosing adoptive parents are such comments as:

- "She's the most beautiful woman I've ever seen!"
- "Wow, the adoptive dad has impressive muscles!"
- "I bet they're millionaires!"
- "With all those college degrees, they must be geniuses!"

Okay, I'm being a bit silly, but you get the point. But now you are thinking, if the above is true, then why did I say if a birth mother does not like the look of your photo, she will not read your letter? This sounds shallow, and seems to contradict what I've just said about why birth mothers pick certain families. However, it's not. Here's why.

When most birth mothers look at photo-resume letters, they will either get a spark, or they won't. A good example is when you are young and single, and you're walking across campus, or in the mall, and your eyes and mind are open to finding someone special. Maybe your head would be turned by a few people, but the rest go by unnoticed. Even you might be unable to explain why one person caught your eye and you hoped to engage them in conversation. It was just a gut feeling. The reality is that everyone is interested, and attracted to, different types of people. Even we don't know why we are so attracted to someone. Just look how different all your friends' spouses are from each other. Everyone finds different things attractive. For some, it is finding someone who is our complete opposite. Or it may be someone who is just like ourselves. Birth mothers are no different. And because birth mothers come from all walks of life, as do adoptive parents, there is someone for everybody. An obese adoptive parent couple may worry their obesity may disinterest many birth mothers. This may be true for slender birth mothers, but they may be just the kind of couple an overweight birth mother identifies with and will select.

Now that we've tossed away your insecurities, let's discuss preparing your photo for your photo-resume letter:

- Take an accurate picture. Making yourself look like a fashion model, then walking in the door for your meeting with a birth mother looking completely different serves no purpose. If you are not who she thought you would be, the meeting will likely go for naught. Just as bad, another birth mother who would have picked you if you looked "normal" didn't, because she wasn't interested in someone looking like a fashion diva.
- Don't hire a professional photographer. Many will disagree with me, but I recommend you have a friend take your picture, or use a timer, using a good quality camera. Why? Studio photos tend to look artificial, plus they look like you are trying too hard. Plus, since you will be duplicating your photo for many, many photo-resume letters, most professional photographers copyright their photos and won't give up their negative, charging you an exorbitant fee for duplicates. Better to get copies at your discount drug store for a fraction of the cost. (The biggest reason for not using a professional photographer is that you want to emphasize the personal aspect of your presentation. You want it to smell of *home* and *family*, not slick commercialism. You want the picture to be a casual one, emphasizing the fact you will be a fun and loving family.)
- Some adoptive parents use just one photo of themselves, while others use five or six and make a collage. Neither is better than the other, assuming that if a single picture is used, it is a great picture. The only time I think it is definitely advantageous to use a collage is when the adoptive parents already have one or more children. It can be difficult to get a young child to cooperate and get that one "perfect" picture with all of you, and a collage lets you mix and match to give an accurate view of your family. If

you do elect to use a collage approach, don't use multiple pictures of the same thing: you standing in front of the fireplace; you standing in front of your house; you standing in front of your fountain in the backyard. Instead, use the collage to show a full view of your family: A picture of both of you; a picture of the extended family (so a birth mother can see beaming future grandparents, aunts and uncles et cetera, at a family event), one or both of you doing one of your favorite activities, such as hiking in the mountains, on a ride at Disneyland with your existing child or a favorite niece or nephew. By the time she sees all the pictures, a birth mother should feel she really knows you.

- Smile! I can't tell you how many times I look at my clients' possible photos and see picture after picture with the wife showing her glowing smile, and next to her a husband with a toothless version of a smile. For some reason, even the happiest and most motivated husbands have a tough time showing a nice, toothy smile. I'm not saying to show a false smile, but I am saying that if you are not smiling in your photo, why would a birth mother pick you? She will assume if you can't smile to be picked for adoption, you never smile.

- Inside or outside? I recommend outside photos. Inside pictures are usually filled with distraction, the backgrounds containing the corner of a doorway, the corner of a painting, et cetera. If you are outside you can select a bright and beautiful background. This might be the beach, the mountains, a local park with beautiful flowering shrubs, a local restaurant with a gorgeous Mexican tile fountain, an historic building, etc. One caution with outside pictures, though. Avoid bright sunlight. You don't want to be squinting in your pictures, and you definitely don't want your eyes hidden behind sunglasses. (Whether inside or outside, I'd avoid using holiday pictures. For example, a photo of you standing in front of a Christmas tree is nice for December, but untimely when a birth mother sees it in July.)

- Wearing casual clothes is preferable to something formal like a suit and tie. This is not an Easter picture to give to your parents. This is to show a birth mother what you are like. Successful but casual clothes, like a polo shirt and slacks for men, is perfect. For women, a casual dress or pants is fine.

- Make sure your faces are easily recognizable. For example, you might have a great picture of you on vacation standing in front of a volcano in Hawaii, but if you are so tiny that your bodies are an inch tall in the picture, with your face a fraction of that, no one can see what you look like. Instead, either have your faces fill the picture, or go with a full-body shot (sitting on a bench, standing arm-in-arm, et cetera).
- Choosing the right picture is the key. How do you do it? Start by taking *lots* of pictures. Don't just go through your existing pictures and use one of those. You might be lucky and find a perfect, recent picture, but I find this to be rare when looking for that single, great photo. Instead, most adoptive parents take pictures specifically for their photo-resume letter. Because it is hard to create the photo which best personifies you, and because so much is riding on it, I recommend you take three or four rolls of film, about 72 exposures. Take a dozen in one location in one position, then another dozen in another position. Then off to yet another location. Maybe some with pets, some without. Try a few clothing changes. Play "model for a day." Don't be shy about showing affection in your picture. Arms around each other, or hands held, only emphasizes your affection for each other. (If you are a single person your main picture will be of you alone, but a collage is the perfect chance to show the significant others in your life. This visual demonstration of the support of family and friends is important for birth mothers to see. The odds are, even after taking all these pictures, you will only find one or two which satisfy you. In fact, it is not uncommon for adoptive parents to not like any of the pictures and use the first round of photos as a learning experience, and do better the next time around. Perhaps you notice you are squinting in the sun, framed the pictures poorly, the clothes you selected did not photograph well and distract the viewer from your faces, the background was not attractive, et cetera. In your second go-round you can correct any such mistakes. In addition to the fact that your photo is the most important part of your being selected by a birth mother, it is also the least expensive part of the process. Even if you repeated the process three straight weekends to come up with the perfect picture, what

would the cost be? A few hours of your time and fifty dollars? Accordingly, it is time and money well spent.

- If you are using just one picture, the size is usually 3 X 5 or 4 X 6. You can scan the picture into the letter, use a color copier, or have prints made and staple one to each letter. Any of these three options are acceptable. If you are using a collage approach, most of the photos will likely be quite a bit smaller, and will almost certainly be scanned or copied onto the resume letter, as trimming and stapling multiple photos would be too time-consuming and not very visually appealing. (In deciding on issues like the size of the picture, and whether to staple an actual snapshot (which has a nice homey and personal aspect to it), or go with the more convenient scanned photo or color copy, it is best to decide in advance how you will be using the letters. For example, if your preference is to give out your letters in person, or mail several at a time in one large oversized envelope, there is no problem with using letters with a snapshot of any size stapled to your letter. But if you are going to be mailing individual letters folded in a traditional business-sized #10 envelope, if your picture is 4 X 6, or if it is positioned vertically, you will have to fold the snapshot in every letter. You would not have this problem with scanned or color-copied resume letters, or an attached 3 X 5 snapshot positioned horizontally at the top, or exact center of the page. Below I will be discussing different networking techniques in using your letters, and if you know which methods you plan to use in advance, you can make the mailing of your photo-resume letter more convenient and economical. One warning: if you are attaching a photo to letter, don't paperclip it. Pictures have a habit of becoming separated from letters, and when they get reattached, your face might be on someone else's letter. A staple or glue gun is usually best - glue sticks seem to loose their adhesiveness quickly.)
- If you scan the photo into your letter, or use a color copier, it is critical to use top quality equipment. Nothing is worse than blurred or distorted photos. Before paying your local copy store to make a large quantity of your letter, have them print one and check out the quality.
- If you already have a child, or children, feature them in your photos. This may sound obvious, but some adoption

"strategists" advise you to hide the fact you have children, and present yourselves as childless. Their reasoning is that some birth mothers are less likely to select you if you already have one or more children. While there is some truth to this statement, to hide the existence of your children is not a good strategy. You want to honestly represent yourselves to a birth mother. Either she will like you for who you are, or she won't. (Hiding the existence of your existing children is doubly ridiculous as at some point the birth mother will be told about important facts about you: your profession, length of time married, number of children if any, et cetera. So what is gained by hiding the fact initially? What viable birth mother will be attracted to childless adoptive parents, then discover they didn't bother to mention what should be the most important part of their lives - their children - and still want to select them? And the birth mothers who may have liked the fact that the adoptive parents had children because they wanted their child to be raised with siblings didn't consider them because they appeared to be childless. So not only is this dishonesty unfair and offensive to birth mothers, but it actually potentially hurts your chances of success by losing possible birth mothers.)

The resume letter. I think the ideal resume letter should be long enough to describe yourselves, but not so long as to start boring the reader. Remember, the photo-resume letter is just a first look at you. It is not expected to tell a birth mother every fact about you. It is to have a birth mother say, "I like what I see and I want to learn more." Let's talk about what to include and what to leave out.

- How do you start out your letter? Many times I see the salutation "Dear Birth Mother." I'd suggest you don't use it. I believe it is so impersonal that it strikes the wrong tone right from the start. But decide for yourself. When you get mail addressed "Dear Homeowner," is it greeted with enthusiasm and anticipation? No, I didn't think so. I believe starting out "Dear Friend," "Hi," "Hello," or a similar greeting is better. Actually, there is no need to even have a salutation at all. Why not just start out your letter getting right to the point: "We are Carol and Mike and we are hoping to adopt."

- Your names. Depending upon the custom in your state, and on the advice of your agency or attorney, you will list either only your first names, or your last name as well. (If you are going to use your photo-resume on the internet, I strongly suggest omitting your last name. (Networking via the internet is discussed later in this chapter.)
- Just as with your picture, you want to show a birth mother that a child will be loved in your home, and that you have a life filled with activities of interest. For one couple it might be quiet activities: reading the Sunday paper in bed together with a box of donuts; Friday nights spent renting old movies and popping popcorn. Others might be active and like hiking, scuba diving and skiing. Just like we discussed above about appearances, birth mothers are all different in what attracts them to certain adoptive parents. Some birth mothers will identify with quiet couples, while others are into active people and sports. Or music. Whatever. The point is, you don't need to be anything but yourself, as there is no perfect description in the eyes of most birth mothers, beyond wanting a loving and secure home for their child.
- Talk about your jobs, or if one of you will be a stay-at-home parent, but keep it brief. For example, writing that you have been a 4th grade teacher for five years is sufficient. You don't need to add that you were voted teacher of the year, have guaranteed job security based upon seniority, and are the only teacher in your district with a Ph.D. in childhood psychology. I'm not saying a birth mother is not interested in those impressive facts, but save them for later, and not risk boring her when initially reading perhaps a large number of photo-resume letters.
- Your hobbies and interests are what define you in many ways, and what a birth mother will identify with. Either she has the same hobbies, or dreamed of doing them but never had the opportunity, and wants her child to have the chance to experience them. I think you can't list too many hobbies, as long as they are genuine interests. Such activities might be scrapbooking, gourmet cooking, church, aerobics, movies, softball, tennis, reading, and countless more. More is not always better. Just be honest and describe yourselves.

- Where you live is important to birth mothers. You may choose to list the city and state, or just the general area. Some birth mothers like the idea of doing the adoption in the same state where she lives, so will prefer in-state couples, while others might visualize a family on a distant coast as the best place to for a child to be raised. When you mention where you live, talk about why you like it: "We go to Dodger games every weekend and love the museums the city has to offer;" "We like the mountains so we can hike in the summer and ski in the winter," "We really enjoy our house in the suburbs. We have a lot of kids on our street and a great park just around the corner. It's very safe and all the kids ride their bikes to school."
- Your pets are part of your family; don't forget to mention them. When describing dogs, particularly large breeds, it is a good idea to mention their gentleness and experience around children.
- Your letter should be typed, not handwritten, in an easy-to-read font. I recommend the length, including the photos, should be one page, or one double-sided page. That's my recommended maximum length. The last thing you want is for a birth mother to get a short, well-written letter from every other couple, and yours is a long rambling treatise. She is likely to put it on the bottom to be read last, and find someone she falls in love with before she gets to it.
- The paper you use is important. This is not a job resume. You aren't going to use plain, boring paper. Your target audience of this letter is female, and young females at that. You want your letter to be *pretty*. Either choose a nice color, or perhaps stationary with a nice border. Alternatively, you might dress it up with some stamped images, or punch holes and intertwine a ribbon. You are showing the birth mother receiving it that you care about what you are doing and have invested time and emotion into it.
- There is no need to volunteer something negative in the letter. For example, you may be concerned that you have several prior marriages, a bankruptcy many years ago, or one or both of you are older than you look. In most all states, a birth mother is entitled to know these facts prior to consenting to the adoption (and I find almost all are very open-minded about such information), so you know she needs to be told these things. The

question is if you put it in your photo-resume letter, which is perhaps seen by her when she is alone, and no one is present to give extra information or immediately answer a question. (To me this situation is different from the wrongness of initially omitting that you have existing children. Having one or more children is something you should be proud of and be shouting from the rooftops. A fact which some might see as negative is different as a birth mother might unfairly dismiss you when a little more knowledge might keep her interested. I think that what is important is that whoever gets the birth mother's initial call about her interest in your letter, whether that is you, or more likely your adoption attorney or agency, that he or she *immediately* tells a birth mother inquiring about you of those negative facts before she invests the time and emotional commitment to meet you. This gives you, or your attorney or agency, the chance to give extra needed facts to put the fact or incident in perspective, which would have taken too much space in a short photo-resume letter. Upon knowing the extra information, she can decide for herself if she wants to take the next step and meet you or not.)

- Be yourselves. There is no need to strike a false chord in your letter. If you are funny, great, be funny. I've even had couples make funny "Top Ten" lists why they'd make great parents. If you are a quiet, thoughtful couple, that's fine too, and your letter should reflect that in its style and tone. Birth mothers come in all sizes and personalities, just like you.

- Don't dwell on your infertility or personal heartbreak in trying to conceive a child. Birth mothers are facing their own personal crisis with the pregnancy and don't want to read letters from people sharing their heartbreak. Mentioning you are adopting due to infertility is fine, but don't try to gain a birth mother's sympathy. Keep your letter positive and uplifting and fun to read.

- Mentioning, or not mentioning, your religion is a difficult decision. A birth mother is entitled to know it, but do you want to put it in your letter? For Christian adoptive parents, there is usually no downside to mentioning it. In fact, in most cases it will be beneficial. For adoptive parents who have no religious affiliation, writing "we have no religion," strikes a potentially negative chord to what is supposed to be a positively toned letter. And what if you are in a non-mainstream religion, such as Seventh Day Adventist. Perhaps reading that would cause a birth mother to unfairly dismiss you from consideration, knowing nothing about the religion due to her young age and lack of exposure to many faiths. Instead, if you, or your attorney or agency, immediately tells her about your religion when she expresses an interest in you, immediately followed by giving her some information about it, she is much more likely to be open-minded and consider you.

- Your letter must to have a contact phone number. It can be your number, or that of your attorney or agency. If you are networking with your photo-resume letter outside of your region, a toll free number is helpful, and most attorneys and agencies have one for that purpose. As mentioned before, I recommend if you are dispersing your letter on the internet, don't use your home number. If you want to use your own number, rather than your attorney or agency's, consider a temporary extra phone line or cell phone.

- Each letter should be hand signed so it looks personal, not mass-produced. After the letter has been photocopied, sign your first names as the bottom of each letter.

Okay, you've got your photo-resume letter. Now the question is how many copies to make. The answer will depend upon how you use it. If your attorney or agency is networking for you, they will want some copies - from dozens to hundreds - depending upon how they plan to use them. To maximize the exposure you will get from them, however, the largest distribution of the letters should be through your own networking efforts, supplementing your attorney or agency's efforts.

We will start with the most basic strategies, and advance to some lesser-known techniques. It is not necessary to do all of them. You will likely find that some methods appeal to you more than others. The more you do, however, the wider your outreach and the better your chances of quickly finding the right birth mother. (In the next chapter, we will continue with strategies for success, as I explain *The Power of Three*.)

Traditional Networking

There is no limit to how broad your networking attempts will be through *traditional networking* with your photo-resume letter. Traditional networking involves compiling lists of people in the health care industry, who may come into contact with a woman with an unplanned pregnancy, and give them your photo-resume letter, perhaps leading that birth mother to you. This will include obstetricians, gynecologists, family practice doctors (as many women start their pregnancy care with a general practitioner before transferring to an OB/GYN), counselors and psychologists (as unplanned pregnancies lead many to counseling to deal with their decisions), and abortion and pregnancy planning clinics.

You can elect to send these out to local professionals in these categories, throughout your state, or in other states. A small traditional networking campaign would be 1,000 letters, and a large one closer to 3,000.

If a letter costs you thirty cents to duplicate (assuming you buy nice paper, and are using a computer to print the letter and photo), and the envelope and postage (assuming you fold your letter into a traditional #10 envelope) is another fifty cents, the total is eighty cents. This means a general networking effort of 1,000 photo-resume letters will cost approximately $800, not counting the cost of the mailing list itself, which I'll discuss in a moment.

I hear three reasons from adoptive parents why they don't do general networking:

1. *My letter will just get thrown away.* True, most of them will be immediately discarded. But remember, it only takes one letter reaching one birth mother to make the entire campaign a success. The more letters you send, the better your odds of success.
2. *Everyone sends out letters to healthcare professionals, so even if my letter is kept by the doctor or counselor receiving it, it will just be lost in the mass of other letters.* Actually the overwhelming majority of adoptive parents *don't* do traditional networking. Either they don't know about it, or they convince themselves it will be a waste of time. And even among those

who do it, not everyone is networking in the same regions you
will select.

3. *I don't know how to compile a list of names and addresses to
send the letters to.* The best way to prepare a networking
mailing list is to buy it pre-printed on mailing labels. You just
peel and stick. True, this may make the recipient mentally
lump it into the "junk mail" category before opening it, but the
only alternative is to handwrite all the names and addresses,
and that is just too time-consuming a task when talking about
a minimum of 1,000 envelopes. There are two ways to
counteract the impersonal appearance of an envelope bearing
an address label. One is to use a personalized return address
sticker or rubber stamp, like you likely already use for
personal correspondence. The other is to make the label less
obvious by using clear labels tending towards invisibility on
the envelope, rather than the traditional white labels. (If you
don't have return mail address stickers, you can find them on
the internet by searching under the term "return address
stickers" and purchase them for about fifteen dollars per
thousand. Finding mailing lists for health care professionals,
especially pre-printed on peel-off labels is more difficult. To
find them you can search on the internet under "mailing lists."
This will lead you to companies which sell this information by
any guidelines you request: homeowners, shoe repair stores, et
cetera. Accordingly, you can buy a doctor list, but be aware
that a general "doctor list" will be of little assistance, as it will
include dermatologists, podiatrists, et cetera, which is of no
value to you. You want primarily obstetricians, gynecologists,
and to a lesser degree, family practitioners, as well as other
healthcare professionals (hospitals, counselors, abortion
clinics), so if you go this route, specifically request those. As
I'll explain momentarily, you may also want beauty and nail
salons. Some companies can provide you with the categories
you want for only the states you want, while others can't. Also
remember that you don't want just the mailing *addresses*
printed on mere sheets of paper, as that would require you to
write all those addresses on the envelopes. You want them *pre-
printed on mailing labels and ready to use*, so ask if they can
ship them that way. If they can't, another option for you is to

have them email you the names and addresses, with instructions how to use Microsoft Word's "merge mail" features, allowing you to format the information so that you can print them yourselves onto blank sheets of labels you've purchased. This is only recommended for those truly computer savvy.

Non-Traditional Networking

The healthcare industry is the obvious place to start for networking. It is not the only place, however. A much less known category in which to network, but one I've found to be very successful, is hair and nail salons. These are female-dominated industries, and discussing other people's business seems to be the order of the day when getting a hair cut, or your nails done. A customer's best friend's daughter's pregnancy would not be an uncommon topic of conversation. Getting your photo-resume letter into the right hands can in turn get it to birth mothers.

There are other reasons why including beauticians in your networking campaign is a good idea. One is that there are a lot of them. If a mid-sized city has ten obstetricians and gynecologists, don't be surprised if it has ten or twenty times as many hair and nail salons. This allows you to focus on a particular geographical area and not run out of appropriate recipients. Another reason is that even among adoptive parents who do elect to network, many don't think to include beauticians. This makes them an underused group of people, and few have received photo-resume letters.

If you are networking in your own region, you may want to personally deliver some or all of your photo-resume letters. In a hair salon, for example, you'd give one to each person working in the store, taking a moment to tell them how you hope they will help you: simply keep the letter on hand until they hear of an unplanned pregnancy situation, then to pass it along. If they like you, most will be excited to do it and be part of the creation of your family, much more so than a physician's office where you have no relationship with that office.

Besides personally delivering them, you can also purchase mailing lists of hair and nail salons, just as with healthcare professionals, as discussed earlier. If you are mailing the letters, I'd advise a basic cover letter, so the recipient knows why they are receiving the letter. This can be as simple as stating:

Hi,

We are hoping to adopt and are sending you our photo-resume letter in the hope you will pass it along if you hear of a woman facing an unplanned pregnancy who would like to learn about us.

Thanks!

When you create your cover letters, you could even print four "cover letters" to a page, and cut them horizontally, to reduce copying costs and give the recipient a simpler, smaller packet to review. Using a partial page for your cover letter would also allow you to staple it to your photo-resume letter in a place allowing your photo to show through behind the cover letter. Sample cover letters for traditional and non-traditional networking are provided in Appendix C.

Here's a checklist for traditional and non-traditional networking:

1. Prepare your photo-resume letters.
2. Copy the number of photo-resume letters you will need.
3. Prepare a cover letter.
4. Copy the cover letters you will need.
5. Buy or share a mailing list of healthcare professionals, and other groups you think will be helpful (like beauticians), in the region you wish to network, making sure you purchase them on pre-printed mailing labels (or have the ability to create them yourself on your computer from the data provided).
6. Buy #10 business sized envelopes.
7. Buy return address mailing labels.
8. Mail (or in rare cases, hand deliver) one cover letter stapled on top of one photo-resume letter, to each professional on your list.

Personal Networking

Traditional networking can be effective, and I recommend you do it. I'll admit, however, my favorite kind of networking is what I call *personal networking*. It requires no purchase of mailing lists, no huge mailings of one, two or three thousand letters, and no direct mailings to healthcare professionals where the risk is higher your letter will be tossed.

The heart of personal networking is to ask people you know to *personally* give their healthcare professionals, or other helpful individuals, your photo-resume letter. The biggest advantage to this method is that because they (the doctor or other selected recipient) are getting it personally from someone they have a relationship with (their patient or customer), so they are much more likely to take it seriously and keep it.

Here's how you mount an effective personal networking campaign:

1. *Make a list of friends and family.* When I say make a list, I mean make a *big* list. You are not just listing your best friends; you are listing *everyone you know*. This means your friends from work, from your college days, your neighbors, people you exercise or work out with, who go to your place of worship, et cetera. You get the idea. Start with your Christmas or Hanukkah list and try to triple it. Try to compile a list of at least a hundred people if you can. For some, based upon where they work, this is easy. For others it is impossible. Just do your best. Some brave souls will open their church directory and presto, they've got three hundred names. You may be thinking that, sure, friends will help, but why would mere acquaintances do so. Keep reading, and I believe you will see why they will participate, and how effective this can be.

2. *Write a "Dear Friends" cover letter.* Unlike the cover letter used for healthcare professionals or beauticians, this cover letter takes a different approach. It will be a short, typed letter stating you are hoping to adopt, and ask for the help of your friends and acquaintances by doing several *specific* things: the next time they go to their family doctor, *personally* give him or her your photo-resume letter, and mention they know you;

the next time they go to their gynecologist or obstetrician, *personally* give him or her your photo-resume letter, and mention they know you. The same with their minister or rabbi. And the person who cuts their hair, does their nails, and so on. A sample "Dear Friends" cover letter is provided in Appendix D.

3. *Mail each person on your networking list five copies of your photo-resume letter (with a traditional networking cover letter – provided in Appendix C - stapled to each one), with a single cover letter paper-clipped to the top of the stack, explaining why you are enclosing the letters, and what to do with them.* Now, your friends, who'd like to help you adopt but don't know how without specific guidance, know exactly what to do. So the next time they go to their family doctor, they bring along a letter. Their next OB/GYN appointment, they bring a letter. The next time they go to church, they bring a letter. If they can think of friends in other healthcare fields working with pregnant women, such as counselors, they give him or her a letter. (Personal networking is primarily a local means of networking, as most of the people you know will live in the region where you live and work. But don't forget about friends and family out of state. Send them a packet as well.)

4. *Be confident your letters will be handed out as you are hoping.* Let me ask you something. If you received a letter like this from an acquaintance, maybe not a best friend, but someone you know and thought well of, wouldn't you enjoy the chance of helping and maybe being the person who created the link which lead to the creation of your family? I find most people are thrilled to do this. True, most husbands getting the letters won't run out to hand them out, but most of the wives, a definite yes.

5. *Let the numbers work for you.* If you have one hundred people on your list, and each one gives out the five photo-resume letters you included in your envelope to them, you have now reached 500 key people. And a high percentage are likely to keep the letter, because they personally got it from someone they know.

I believe personal networking is *a must* in an effective adoption campaign. You may be shy about telling others you hope to adopt, but I encourage you to get past that. Your friends and relatives likely know many people who have adopted and are very comfortable with the subject. In fact, you will be amazed how may calls you will get from acquaintances receiving your letter who have personal experience with adoption they never had reason to share before, not knowing of your interest in adoption.

Here is a checklist for personal networking:

1. Prepare your photo-resume letters
2. Prepare a "Dear Friends" cover letter for your friends who will receive them (Appendix D).
3. Prepare (if not already done for traditional networking) a traditional networking cover letter (Appendix C) and staple one cover letter to each of the photo-resume letters.
4. Paperclip one "Dear Friends" cover letter on top of a stack of five photo-resume letters (each of which already has a traditional cover letter stapled to it).
5. Buy large 9 X 12 inch envelopes so you won't have to fold the photo-resume letters, and place one packet of five photo-resume letters inside.
6. Mail, or hand-deliver, your packet to each person on your list containing one cover letter and five photo-resume letters.

Advertising. Placing a classified ad in local newspapers has been a popular way to reach birth mothers for decades. About half the states permit adoption ads (the state-by-state review tells you which states permit and which don't). Personally, I've never been a big fan of newspaper advertising, but to be fair, I must say I know many adoption professionals who have used the method with viable results.

Usually an advertisement, or "announcement" if that sounds better, is a small ad placed in the personals or classified section of a newspaper. Even when it is permitted in a state, the individual newspaper may have its own requirements, such as a letter from your attorney or agency to be sure the adoption will be done correctly.

If you elect to place an ad, as with all types of networking, you might elect to only do it locally, or go into other states. The newspapers can range from being major papers with huge circulations to small town weeklies. Although most will be "general circulation" newspapers, the newspapers of college, special interest and religiously-oriented entities are possibilities too. Those who employ advertising as one of their prime networking methods usually advertise in several dozen papers, and expect to do so for several months.

Typical ads might be:

ADOPTION. LOVING COUPLE IN OREGON HOPES TO ADOPT INFANT. MEDICAL BILLS PAID. 1 (800) 555-1234

ADOPTION NOT ABORTION. WE ARE A CHRISTIAN COUPLE HOPING TO ADOPT. CAN HELP WITH LIVING AND MEDICAL COSTS. CONFIDENTIAL. CALL COLLECT: 1 (212) 555-1234

PREGNANT? WE HOPE TO ADOPT AND CAN OFFER A LOVING HOME AND A WONDERFUL LIFE IN THE COUNTRY. WE HAVE A COMPLETED HOME STUDY. WE CAN COME TO MEET YOU. 1 (800) 555-1234

Newspaper advertising has been popular over the years for one simple reason. It's easy. You can reach a large number of people by simply phoning in an ad, rather than compiling mailing lists and stuffing envelopes. The cost is about the same, as running a large number of ads in fifteen newspapers for two months each often equals the cost of a networking campaign of about 2,000 letters ($25 per ad per week times eight weeks is $200, times fifteen newspapers is $3,000). Of course, you could elect to do a smaller campaign. The primary disadvantage of newspaper advertising is its impersonal nature and lack of any control over who sees the ads. With a networking campaign, you are directing your photo-resume letters toward people in the healthcare industry, or specific people like beauticians. Contrarily, your ad can be seen by anyone, including people who are not even pregnant and think they see an opportunity to manipulate someone.

If you feel advertising is an outreach method you wish to employ, I strongly recommend you have an adoption attorney or agency to receive any calls, and have them heavily screen any callers before passing them through to any contact with you. Good adoption situations can come out of adoption advertisements, but extra caution is needed at the early stages to be sure you are working with a legitimate person sincere about adoption planning. As a general rule, however, I find the high cost of extensive advertising to not be as cost effective, or beneficial over a longer period of time, than both traditional and personal networking.

The internet. The internet has become our new yellow pages and educational resource rolled into one. For this reason, some birth mothers, just like some adoptive parents, will make going online their first step toward adoption.

There are several routes to being seen by birth mothers searching online. One is to retain one of the adoption professionals who advertise heavily on the internet (some spend hundreds of thousands of dollars annually, telling you how high their fees to you need to be to offset those expenses). By hiring those agencies, attorneys or facilitators, when a birth mother contacts them, one would assume she would be shown your photo-resume letter if you are a client. You might find, however, that when using the guidelines provided in Chapters 4 and 6 regarding how to select the best attorney or agency, that these entities don't measure up to your scrutiny. As a general rule, I don't have the highest opinion of adoption entities advertising widely and forcefully on a national basis, whether they be agencies, attorneys or facilitators. Many seem more concerned with making a large profit than serving a limited number of people.

The other way to be exposed to birth mothers who go online is to work with one or more of the services which showcase adoptive parent photo-resume letters. They charge you a fee to offset their costs of internet advertising. Sites generating a fair amount of birth mother traffic will usually charge from $100 to $300 per month for a featured spot on their site.

But how do you find a good site? I won't list any, as the internet world changes quickly and a valid URL today sometimes doesn't exist tomorrow. That's one good reason to not invest money in long term exposure on the internet. Better to pay for one month or so at a time.

Remember that being visible on an internet site is only helpful if birth mothers are actually visiting the site. So how do you know if it generates a lot of traffic? Many sites brag of high "hit" totals on their sites, but that information is hard to verify, or to know if the site visitors are even birth mothers, not other adoptive parents. As a result, my advice is this: *in your mind pretend you are a birth mother looking for adoptive parents.* Sit at your computer and go on your favorite search engines, likely Google (which handles the lion's share of internet searches), and type in search terms just like a birth mother would. Clearly you will start with something basic like "adoption," and perhaps expand into other words or phrases, or a geographical search like "Adoption, Illinois."

What comes up on your screen will be the same thing birth mothers will see. You want to go where she would go. So click on the URLs offered, perhaps starting on the top few which usually get the most interest, or even on one of those hated pop-ups. You will find several sites which list adoptive parent resumes for birth mothers to see and contact. With a little digging into the site, you will find out how to have your photo-resume letter listed and what the cost is.

Another option is if you are a computer savvy person, you can create your own website, and do just like the adoption listing services do, by paying listing fees to search engines like Google and Yahoo and compete for a top spot with chosen search terms. This is quite an endeavor, however, and is not suggested unless you already have experience in both website construction and working with search engine companies, and understand how to bid for "pay per click" exposure.

Just as with newspaper advertising, the advantage to internet exposure is a lot of potential exposure with little work. No mailing lists or envelope stuffing. The disadvantages are that you can't control where people are who access your photo-resume letter. Of course, that's fine if you don't care if your birth mother lives in California, Idaho or Massachusetts. One advantage it has over newspaper advertising, however, is that it is a directed medium. For example, with a newspaper ad, anyone looking at the paper will see your ad, not just those with an interest in adoption. On the internet, only those searching for adoption sites should find it. This reduces the likelihood of wasted calls or potential scams. Still, birth mothers found through the internet, just like via the newspaper, require careful initial screening to be sure all is bona fide before getting involved. The use of a skilled adoption attorney or agency to handle these initial calls is critical.

One big disadvantage to an extensive posting of your resume online is that you will likely get calls from less than reputable adoption agencies, attorneys and facilitators, stating they represent a birth mother who saw your letter and wants to meet you. Of course, the request for money, usually to be wired to them, before your attorney or agency can fully investigate the situation, will be a part of their call. Think about it. If they were a legitimate entity – the kind adoptive parents want to work with - they would have their own adoptive parents from whom the birth mother could choose. Right? The fact they need to troll the internet for paying customers tells you all you need to know.

Adoption "Business Cards." Think how often you stumble across someone's business card, perhaps left in a restaurant, or on the seat of a cab, et cetera. Often it is for a realtor or mortgage broker, or other professions where people sometimes have to be aggressive to get noticed. Clearly they leave their cards everywhere to be found. Sometimes adoptive parents do the same thing. A typical adoption business card (the same size as a regular business card) might have your picture, with the caption, "Hoping to adopt!" in large letters next to it. On the other side might be a very short bio, providing your first names, some bare bones information, and a contact phone number. An example may be:

> *We are Glen and Carrie. Our dream is to start our family through adoption. We are both teachers. We can help with pregnancy-related costs. Please call to learn more about us! 1-800-555-1234.*

You then give a card to each person you interact with each day, or leave them in public places where they are likely to be found. Like with newspaper and internet advertising, I recommend you don't use your home phone number and having an attorney or agency screen the initial calls is a good idea.

Facilitators. A facilitator is a person or business that is not an attorney or an agency, rather and entity which finds birth mothers, usually for a fee. Usually for a large fee. Many, in fact, charge as much or more than agencies or attorneys, despite the fact they can provide only a small portion of the needed services. As a general rule, I caution adoptive parents against using facilitators as they can't perform any of the functions attorneys or agencies can. They can't give legal advice, do legal work or make court appearances. They can't do home studies, place children in an adoptive home or write court reports. Some states make facilitating an adoption for a fee a crime, while most states have no legislation on the issue. Those caveats being said, however, if you are aware of what a facilitator is, and still want to use one to help you find a birth mother, it is an additional option for you.

Just like attorneys and agencies, facilitators find birth mothers in many different ways. Many facilitators rely heavily on large yellow page ads and the internet. Some birth mothers will decline to work with a facilitator when they learn their true nature as a non-agency or attorney (although it is tough for anyone, especially young birth mothers, to know their true status, as facilitators usually employ names which sound like agencies). Other birth mothers, however, may prefer a facilitator as they wish to go outside of what may see as normal adoption channels to make an adoptive placement. Of course, that may be the very reason to avoid such a birth mother.

Despite the questionable issue of the high fees facilitators charge in relation to their limited services, the bottom line is that some do produce results. Because they are unlicensed and untrained, however, unlike attorneys and agencies, they are less able to effectively determine a good from a bad adoption. For this reason, it is particularly important when working with a facilitator that you have an experienced attorney or agency to screen any birth mothers located by the facilitator, and help you make sure you have a viable adoption.

Complicating the issue is that unlike attorneys and agencies, there is no formal data base for facilitators in most states. This is because it is a largely unregulated industry, without the strict licensing laws affecting attorneys and agencies. The simplest way to determine if the entity you are considering is a facilitator or not is to just ask if they are a licensed agency, and if so, in what state. If the answer is no, they usually fall into the general category of facilitator. To verify what they tell you, you can call the state social services office (provided in the state-by-state review) for the state in which they are located and ask the agency licensing office if they are a listed agency.

How do you spot a good facilitator from a bad one? This is a difficult question. For example, with an attorney, a prospective client could call the state bar and inquire about any disciplinary actions against the attorney, and learn where they went to law school and how long they'd been in practice. With an agency you can call the state social services office and verify their status and ask about how long they've been in business. Such questions about facilitators to a similar independent government office are generally impossible. My only advice in this area is to read my advice for selecting a good attorney in Chapter 4 and ask the same questions. In addition, here are some specific recommendations if you are determined to hire a facilitator:

1. Ask for the full contract you will be expected to sign in advance of arranging a meeting or paying any initial fees. Have your attorney look it over to be sure it seems appropriate.
2. Don't pay a large portion of your fee in advance. I give this same advice when hiring an attorney or agency, so I'm certainly going to give it regarding facilitators. I believe you should pay for services as you go through the process. Why pay their entire fee, or a significant portion of it, before you even know if they can indeed find you a birth mother, and if they do, if you will want to work with that birth mother.
3. Ask what methods they use to find birth mothers and make sure you agree with the methods used.
4. Ask what region or state the birth mothers typically come from. This may not matter to you, but if you only want a local birth mother in your home state, that is unlikely to happen if they rely solely on national internet advertising, leading to most placements being out of state.
5. Ask the attorney or agency you will be working with if they agree to work with facilitators. Some work regularly with facilitators and have a good relationship. Others may view them as infantpreneurs using questionable taste in networking techniques and a reputation for arranging risky and expensive adoptions, and will decline to work with them.

6. Ask the facilitator for a list of past adoptive parent clients. Don't accept referrals to adoptive parents simply "matched up" with a birth mother, or who just received a baby but the adoption is not finalized by the court. Those are adoptions "in progress" where things can still go wrong. You want to insist to speak to recent adoptive parents who have *completed* their adoptions in court. They can report on the entire gamut of working with the facilitator, from beginning to end. I'd also recommend you ask for a significant number of referrals, not just three or four. Even the worst professional in any business will please *some* of their clients. You want to be sure they please *most* of them. Accordingly, I'd ask for at least ten. And recent ones too. Most facilitators I've encountered boast of helping with a very large number of adoptive placements every year. If this is true, there should be no problem giving you a large number of referrals.

When you speak to their prior adoptive parent clients, ask:

1. How long did you wait to be selected by your birth mother?
2. What was she like? (See if the typical birth mother located by the facilitator is of the ethnic group you hope to adopt from, has a health and drug history you feel is appropriate, et cetera). Remember that you are talking about the birth mother of the child the adoptive parents adopted, so you want to be respectful in your questions, but thorough enough you feel confident in the information you obtain.
3. Did you have any false leads prior to the placement that worked?
4. What were the fees you paid the facilitator?
5. Where there any fees you didn't expect?
6. Did you get the chance to meet the birth mother before the birth?
7. Were you given complete birth mother (and birth father, if available) health histories?
8. Did the facilitator cooperate with your attorney or agency?

There are some good facilitators performing a valid service, for a fee commensurate with the limited services they are able to provide.

Unfortunately for the adoption field as a whole, however, many are profiteers with little adoption training, and adoptive parents have little recourse when the adoption is handled improperly.

*   *   *   *   *

So there you have it, a wide selection of networking techniques and strategies to help match you with a birth mother. Let's review what we have so far:

- You are going to not only select a skilled adoption attorney or agency, but one whose services includes networking for birth mothers, helping to lead to an adoptive match, or alternatively advise you on your own networking campaign.
- You are not going to sit and wait to see when, or if, your attorney or agency will be successful in creating an adoptive match. You are going to mount your own networking campaign.
- You are going to put great effort into the best photo and resume letter you can do, and duplicate it as needed to effectively network.
- You are going to choose not one, but several, networking strategies. These include, in my personal order of preference:

1. Personal networking (mandatory for an effective campaign).
2. Non-traditional networking (mandatory, at least 1,000 letters).
3. Traditional networking (mandatory, at least 1,000 letters) if not doing non-traditional networking,
4. Internet advertising.
5. Adoption business cards.
6. Newspaper advertising.
7. Facilitators.

Do you think we are done strategizing? Not a chance! Maybe the biggest part of guaranteeing you a fast, newborn adoption is in the next chapter, *The Power of Three.*

CHAPTER 9

THE POWER OF THREE

The routine way to do a newborn adoption is to select an adoption attorney or agency, and wait for them to tell you that you've been selected by a birth mother. That's the norm across America. It's just the way it has always been done. There is certainly nothing wrong with that, particularly if you maximize your odds of success by hiring a great attorney or agency, and are diligent in your networking.

Even when doing everything right, you might still find that you wait longer than you want for your adoptive match to occur. Part of the reason for this is that no matter how active you are in your adoption efforts, the bottom line is that you still have to wait for a birth mother to pick you for the process to begin. Adoption is a game of "hurry up and wait." You diligently hire the right professional, energetically prepare your photo-resume letter, get your networking efforts going, but then the reality is that you sit and wait to be picked. You might be lucky and get picked in the fraction of the time you expected. It happens. But for every adoptive parent who gets picked in a week, there is someone else at the other extreme, perhaps waiting years. This can be true even for adoptive parents in the same geographical area, with the same personal characteristics and lifestyle to present to birth mothers. It's much like dating, and like dating, it is not always a fair process. Why does one person find the perfect spouse at age twenty-five, and another person, equal in every way, never finds that special partner? Adoption has the same dynamics. Thus, the issue becomes beating the odds, and doing so quickly.

This is how you do it. As we've discussed, the key element of being matched with a birth mother is to hire an attorney or agency that includes birth mother networking in their services. But who says you only have to hire one? Tradition?

Forget tradition.

I want to encourage you to hire *three* attorneys and/or agencies. That's right, three, not one. And I recommend you will hire them all *simultaneously,* not wait to hire someone new only if you become disappointed with how long the process might be taking with the first one you hire.

Your first thought will be "I can't afford that." Wrong. You are probably assuming that hiring three adoption professionals will triple the cost. To the contrary, although it will increase the cost of your adoption, it will not even double it. Here's why. You are not hiring three adoption professionals to do the *entire* adoption for you. Instead, you are hiring them to perform the initial stage of their services: advise you of adoption laws and procedures in their region or state, and to show you to birth mothers contacting their office to select adoptive parents. As we discussed in Chapters 4 and 6 regarding selecting the right attorney or agency, those with the fairest payment schedules charge as they work through the different stages of the adoption. Only a portion of that will be due initially, until you are matched with a birth mother.

So you pay each of the selected professional their initial fee, then when one of them comes up with an adoptive match you wish to accept, you can kindly thank the other two for their services and let them know their services are no longer needed. The only fees you have thereafter will be for the attorney or agency who created your adoptive match. (If you are doing an interstate adoption, you will still need one attorney/agency in each state.)

Doing the math is simple. If the average time to be picked by a birth mother in a particular region when working with competent attorneys or agencies is fifteen months (averaging those lucky enough to be picked in days, and others waiting years), by hiring three you've mathematically reduced your average to five months. Of course, the average waiting time in one region might be more or less, but you get the idea. Because you've tripled your exposure to birth mothers, you have tripled your chances. It's that simple. It's that obvious.

By the way, the extra money you paid to start with to the extra professionals whom you will not end up using is not necessarily wasted. If you are like many adoptive parents, particularly if you are adopting your first child, you will likely be considering starting another adoption a few years after completing the first one. Often the retainer agreement with the "dismissed" attorneys or agencies who did not create the first match will provide that you can become "active" again with them, as you paid the initial fee and are entitled to return to that stage with no additional initial fees. This gives you the chance to start a new adoption later with virtually no money out-of-pocket, as you've paid most of if with two "unused" adoption professionals. In other words, you're pre-paid for adoption number two.

So how do you put such a plan into action? Think back to when we discussed finding the best attorney and/or agency, looking in both your home region and other states you wanted to consider. Likely you found several well-qualified attorneys and agencies and had a hard time narrowing it down to just one, particularly if you did a broad search in more than one state. Now you don't need to limit yourself to just one.

Not every attorney or agency is right for this strategy, however. Some will have fee structures which require an unreasonably large percentage of their fee up front. These attorneys or agencies are not for you, but I already recommended against hiring such a professional in those chapters even when hiring just one. You also need to be honest with whomever you are hiring that you plan to take this approach of hiring several adoption professionals and continue only with the one who first helps create a good adoptive match. There are some adoption professionals who do not like this multi-professional strategy, and will insist on being the only entity involved in your adoption. Fine, that attorney or agency is not right for you.

The vast majority will be happy to work with other adoption professionals, knowing you will proceed only with the one creating your adoptive match. In fact, you are creating a healthy unspoken competition between the entities you hired. This can only be to your benefit. Each wants to look good and produce results. Each wants to do the entire adoption and earn their fee. It's simply human nature. They know you are going to be telling people, *"I hired one attorney,*

Joe Smith, and an agency, Children's Family Services, both in our home state, and an attorney out-of-state, Jane Doe. . . and it was Joe who came through for us first."

The key question for you when employing this strategy is whether to focus your efforts in one region, or to spread out into other states. As you know from Chapter 2, there are fourteen different types of adoption available to you. If you are like most adoptive parents, several options seemed attractive. In fact, it was likely tough for you to choose between doing everything in-state, doing an interstate adoption, an identified adoption, or a non-resident adoption. Now you don't need to choose just one. You can open the door to several types, and see which comes through for you first.

Here is some specific advice. Let's say you live in a large metropolitan area (Los Angeles, Chicago, et cetera). in a state with good adoption laws, good adoption attorneys and agencies from which to choose and a significant number of birth mothers making placements within the state. With all that going for you, you might prefer an in-state adoption using only local professionals. Therefore, you might want to hire all three of your professionals in your state, but spread out over different counties.

If you are open to an out-of-state adoption, either interstate or non-resident, this opens up unlimited doors for you, as you are not considering just attorneys and agencies in one state, but several. Perhaps the entire nation. Now you can really analyze the state-by-state review and determine which states appear attractive when them, and consider a non-resident or interstate adoption.

I think the best utilization of The Power of Three strategy is to mix attorneys and agencies, selecting one of one type and two of the other. Depending upon your state, either attorneys or agencies will be the primary way in which adoptive matches are created. Also, even if your local agencies do not create as many adoptive matches as attorneys, if your state requires a pre-placement home study from a private agency (as compared to some states which only require a post-placement home study), why not use the agency for the double duty of the required home study, and also trying to create an adoptive match? Due to the fact laws and procedures vary so much from state to state, it is impossible to provide one perfect strategy for everyone. However, by the time you have finished this book, and spoken to some local professionals, you will find that the routes best for you will become immediately clear. It is just up to you to act on them.

Also, there is no reason you can't hire one or two attorneys or agencies to start a domestic adoption, and (and if you are considering international adoption) start an international adoption as well. If you are selected by a birth mother before a child is available for you overseas, you can put the intercountry adoption on hold (perhaps until you are ready for your next child) and complete your domestic adoption. If you are not picked by a birth mother and you get the word there is a child now available to you through intercountry adoption, you can complete that adoption and put the domestic one on hold. The only thing to be aware of in this example is that the costs of intercountry adoption can often be more front-loaded due to the costs of preparing a dossier and submitting it overseas. Also, some intercountry programs will want a commitment from you to not start another adoption once your dossier has been submitted overseas. (This is a reasonable issue as the intercountry agency or attorney would not look good in the eyes of the foreign country if its adoptive parents continuously withdraw from the process after time and energy has been expended by the foreign country.)

Here are some sample scenarios, and how to perhaps best use The Power of Three:

- *You live in a state with unfair adoption laws and few or no adoption options.* Hire all three attorneys or agencies in states permitting non-resident adoption, and do virtually everything in the state of birth. (You will still need a local agency for your home study, so you might want to consider that as one of the three).

- *You might be moving to another state and hesitate to hire local attorneys or agencies.* If your present state permits non-residents to adopt, and the adoption laws are fair, there is no detriment to hiring local attorneys or agencies as they can continue to fully serve you if you move. However, if your present state does not allow non-residents to adopt, you should consider adoption professionals in states allowing non-resident adoption, so they can assist you regardless of where you live. Alternatively, the adoption professionals you hired before you moved can continue to network for a birth mother, and do the adoption as an interstate adoption, to be finalized in your new home state.

- *You live in Connecticut, Georgia, Illinois, Maryland, Minnesota, New Jersey or New York which bar attorneys from finding birth mothers to create adoptive matches, or doing so for a fee.* Hire a skilled adoption attorney in your home state, but hire two out-of-state attorneys or agencies who can network as part of their services to you. Or, you can retain an in-state agency, which unlike attorneys *can* network under the states' laws, to meet your in-state needs, *if* you feel the agency and their in-house attorney can meet your legal needs as well as an independent attorney.

- *You live in a region with good adoption attorneys and/or agencies, and in a state with fair adoption laws, so you'd like to finalize the adoption in your home state, but there appear to be few birth mother matches created locally.* Hire a local attorney or agency to handle the in-state work and court finalization, but concurrently hire two out-of-state attorneys or agencies experienced in creating adoptive matches. You can then do an interstate adoption from virtually any state, where the child will be born, but you will be completing it in your home state.

- *You just want a child as soon as possible and don't care if you adopt a newborn or older child, via domestic or international adoption.* Hire two domestic adoption attorneys or agencies to start networking for a birth mother, and one international agency or attorney to start the overseas adoption. Since both domestic and international adoption require home studies, sometimes you can use the pre-placement home study prepared for an international adoption, for a domestic adoption, avoiding a waste of those costs.

Well, you can't say you don't have options! You might even complain you have too many. That's a nice problem to have. Best of all, The Power of Three strategy triples your chances of success, cuts by sixty-seven percent the likely time of that success, and opens the door to hundreds of supremely qualified attorneys and more than a thousand agencies throughout the nation. The only limits you have are those you choose to set on yourself.

CHAPTER 10

RED FLAGS TO A RISKY ADOPTION

I firmly believe the surest way to avoid a failed adoption is to never start a risky one. Just because you are selected by a birth mother as adoptive parents doesn't mean that you will want to accept the placement and work with that birth mother. You want to make sure she is the right person for you, doing it for the right reasons. Hard as it may be to believe, sometimes that means passing on an adoption opportunity.

How do you spot a risky adoption? It is not mystical at all. No fortuneteller is required. Looking at specific characteristics of the birth family and the motivations for adoption will give you the answer. That, and your gut instincts - the same instincts which safely guide you through life - will separate the "right" from the "wrong" placements.

The Birth Mother's Age

Many people wrongly assume that most adoptions are started by high school girls facing unplanned pregnancies. Although there is a high number of unplanned pregnancies in the high school years, fewer of these pregnancies result in adoption than those of older women, usually aged 18 to 26. What happens to all those high school

163

pregnancies? Most of these young women will terminate their pregnancies, or raise the children themselves.

Generally speaking, the younger the birth mother is (as well as the birth father), the riskier the adoption is. There are several reasons for this. The biggest one is the lack of life experience and maturity that a young girl will have, as compared to someone more mature. A young birth mother doesn't yet know what it means to face the obligations of parenthood and life as an adult. All her needs have been met by her family. An older birth mother, however, has faced issues such as having to earn money for rent, what it feels like to be hungry because your paycheck wasn't as much as needed, coming home from work tired and having no energy to do anything, much less care for a child as a single parent. Also, a young birth mother is subjected to the peer pressure of her equally young and inexperienced friends who think it would be "fun" to have a baby, or who perhaps are young single moms themselves and want their friend to share the experience.

The biggest reason working with young birth mothers is risky is simply the narcissistic nature of most teenagers. Most care about themselves, and their life at this moment in time, and little else. This may sound simplistic, but talk to any parent of the vast majority of teenagers, and you will be convinced it is true. An example we can all associate with is the first time someone breaks your heart, the girl or guy who you were sure - at let's say age sixteen - was the person you wanted to spend your life with, and your heart aches when you lose them. At the moment of that break-up, you believe that pain you are feeling will never heal, and your life is over. As adults we all know that feeling will pass, and we will grow up to fall in love again. But when you were sixteen you would have done *anything* to make that pain go away if you had it within your power.

So, let's compare this to adoption. Imagine you are a very young birth mother giving birth for the first time. You face more emotions than you ever though possible, and the pain of losing your child is unimaginable, despite common sense and parents telling you that you are too young to parent. You know adoption is the right thing, but it hurts to say goodbye to the child you just gave birth to. Hurts more than you thought it would. More than you thought possible.

What do you do if you are that young birth mother if the law grants you the right to change your mind? Unlike with failed love, you *do* have the power to relieve your pain. So do you eliminate your pain by stopping the adoption? Some will, and that is the danger of young birth mothers. Of course, any birth mother can change her mind, teenager or adult, but the younger she is, chances are the more she will be unable to deny her emotions.

Does this mean you should never ever work with a birth mother under a certain age? And if so, what is that age? Fourteen? Sixteen? Eighteen? No, it does not mean that. I've worked with birth mothers as young as twelve (I'm sad to say) and have seen those adoptions work out fine. So what is the answer?

I think the key is not focusing specifically on a numerical age, rather the birth mother's maturity. Although, generally speaking, the older a person, the more mature he or she is. This is not always the case, however. There might be cases where a fifteen year old birth mother is more mature, and therefore more likely to make the placement, than some twenty-year olds. Her maturity is going to depend on many factors: her life experiences, or lack of them, to date; how she was raised; her degree of intestinal fortitude, and similar factors. The only way to determine this is to personally get to know the birth mother, and encourage her to receive professional counseling (discussed momentarily) to help prepare her for the emotions ahead.

The Influence of Family and Friends

We are all influenced by those around us, particularly the people most important to us. Our family. Our friends. For this reason if a birth mother is surrounded by negativity, where her closest friends and family members are trying to dissuade her about placing her child for adoption, it creates a significant risk. Remember that her family and friends are only doing what they feel is right for her and themselves. Don't take it personally, as rarely does it have anything to do with you as the adoptive parents. It is simply their hope that she will keep the child in the family.

Sadly, often it is clear to an impartial person that the birth parent should not be listening to this negative advice, as anyone could see the future for the birth mother and child would be bleak. There are millions of people in the United States, however, and hundreds of millions around the world, who live in similar, or worse, situations than she does. They face poverty, lack of education, single parenthood and other challenges, yet they survive. We have to understand that not every decision has to make sense to us. Some families and friends will just be against adoption, despite all the reasons to the contrary.

So what do you do when that happens? One important consideration is the birth mother's age. If she is young she is much more likely to give in to family pressure. This is particularly true if she is a minor living with her parents. In most states a birth mother under age eighteen does not need parental consent to place a child for adoption (see the state-by-state review), but she is dependent upon them for everything. She would be hesitant, as would any of us, to alienate those she is dependent upon. Also, if her family says they will take care of the baby and do all the work required, the birth mother is more inclined to say "yes."

Situations involving negative input from family members is entirely different when a birth mother is an adult and no longer lives at home, and is not financially dependent upon them. A disagreement over the pregnancy and how to deal with it is likely not the first time she has had disagreements with her family about how she should live. Since she is already on her own she is much less likely to be controlled by their desires. If her parents do not live locally, she may not even share the fact she is pregnant, preferring to not admit the unplanned pregnancy to her parents.

Luckily, few adoptions involve a great deal of anti-adoption sentiment by a birth mother's family and friends. Most want what is best for her and know raising a child under difficult circumstances will cause both her and the child to suffer. Actually, in the vast majority of adoptions I've handled, most involve overwhelming support for adoption from the birth mother's parents and family. That is why it is a significant concern when that support does not exist. It is not unusual for a birth mother to have one or two people against the adoption, but if this is just a small percentage of the people impacting her life, you can feel good about the fact she is receiving emotional support from most of her key people.

The Due Date

Birth mothers can start adoption at any time in the pregnancy. Some will call an adoption attorney or agency the minute they discover they

are pregnant, perhaps only two months along. Others ignore the fact they are pregnant, wait until the last minute, and finally contact someone when they give birth. This brings up a question: Is there a good or bad time to start adoption planning?

The answer is that yes, there are times when adoption planning should be avoided, or at least delayed. Starting an adoption with birth mother early in her pregnancy, such as in the first trimester, has several risks. Let's look at the practical reasons first. There is a 15% chance that a pregnancy will be miscarried during the first trimester. Do you want to incur the financial and emotional costs of an adoption only to have it result in a miscarriage? You may have already gone through that heartbreak as part of your infertility which brought you to adoption. The last thing you want to do is go through it again, even indirectly via adoption, if it can be avoided.

The other reason is that when a birth mother is so early in her pregnancy, it is generally too soon for her to make a complete emotional commitment to adoption. She can *intellectually* determine it is the best decision for herself and the baby. *Emotionally*, however, she can't anticipate how she will feel about the pregnancy until she *feels* pregnant. Until she is far enough along to feel a baby inside her, and perhaps even start "showing" enough for people around her to remark on the pregnancy, she can't truly emotionally come to grips with the pregnancy. So what happens if she made a commitment to you as adoptive parents when only two months pregnant, then by the eighth month is asking herself how she got herself into this situation, and wants a way out without hurting you? The likely answer is a failed adoption.

This doesn't mean you can't start an adoption with a birth mother two or three months along, but it does mean you acknowledge extra risk in doing so. The safest course is to work with birth mothers who are at least halfway through their pregnancy. Even better, in their last trimester. If a birth mother contacts your attorney or agency and she is too early to intelligently start adoption planning, the smart professional won't immediately match her up with adoptive parents, nor will he or she turn the birth mother away. Instead, he or she should begin to work with her, perhaps start counseling and get her started on paperwork which will later be necessary in the adoption (health history forms, et cetera.). This allows the birth mother to feel she is accomplishing something and know she has a plan in place, yet slows

down the start of the adoption. Soon, a month or two will have passed and she is far enough along to start adoption planning.

There is usually no such thing as starting "too late." Some birth mothers will even wait until they are at the hospital and they have already given birth. They may have been in denial about the pregnancy, been embarrassed, or simply not known who to call. Amazingly, I've actually had some birth mothers tell me they hesitated to call someone but they were afraid there would be a legal fee for them to pay to place a baby for adoption. Last minute "after-birth" placements can often be the most secure, as the birth mother has gone through the one emotional moment most adoptive parents fear the most - the birth - and wants to plan an adoption. The only detriment to starting an adoption when the birth has already occurred is that you don't have the usual time to gather information, get full medical records, try and find birth fathers, et cetera. This means that sometimes there can be unsolved legal risks there was no time to solve before you bring the baby home.

Health History

Your agency or attorney should have the birth mother (and birth father if he is available) complete detailed health history forms. It is my belief that the adoptive parents should be given this information prior to even meeting a birth mother. This is because some health issues, such as extensive drug usage during the pregnancy or extended family members with congenital health problems or psychological disabilities, could be so severe that they may influence your desire to even start the adoption. Even if there are no such serious conditions in the birth family, you will want to know as much information as possible to share with your pediatrician.

Knowing as much about your child's biological history is tremendously important. When your child's pediatrician asks you if anyone in the family is allergic to a particular medicine, right handed or left, or do people in your family start needing eye glasses at a particular age, not to mention more serious questions, the birth mother will not be standing next to you to answer. You need and deserve complete written health histories. If you are adopting a not-yet-born baby, the health history you receive will likely be exclusively from the

birth mother (and sometimes the birth father) based upon their family knowledge, and any relatives they contact for more information. If you are adopting an older child, you should additionally have the child's existing medical records.

It is unreasonable to expect an adopted child to have a perfect health history. Every family - likely yours included - has a grandparent who had a heart attack, an aunt who battled obesity, an uncle with diabetes and other maladies. Such things are just part of life. Those problems don't make everyone in *your* genetic circle unadoptable, so why think of others that way? However, if there are potential health concerns of a major nature, you owe it to yourselves and the child to be sure you are prepared for the challenges that might lie ahead.

Adoptive parents often ask if the child they plan to adopt is born with a medical problem which they did not anticipate and feel they can't handle, do they have to complete the adoption? This question might sound hard-hearted and cruel, but it is a fair question. The answer is no. You are not the legal parents until the adoption is granted by a court. This means, as tragic as it would be, that adoptive parents have the right to abandon a placement should they feel they need to do so. Although this may sound wrong, remember that birth mothers have the same right to change *their* mind after the birth, so to some extent it is fair, as each can back away from the other.

In addition to the completion of birth parent history forms, an important part of obtaining health information is via the birth mother's doctor. It is common for the birth mother to sign an *Authorization to Release Medical Information*. This form waives the doctor-patient privilege and allows the medical office to release records and information about the pregnancy and fetus to the attorney or agency, or directly to the adoptive parents. In many open adoptions, the adoptive parents are accompanying the birth mother to some of her doctor appointments, so they are right there next to her to hear what is said, ask questions to the doctor, and stay up to date. This may seem to make the need of an information release form unnecessary, but there may be instances where the adoptive parents do not accompany the birth mother to the doctor, or want to discuss information not addressed at the medical appointment.

Here's a final thought on health histories which, depending upon your mindset, will make you feel better or worse about health issues.

In many cases, the birth father is unfindable. This is due to the fact that a significant number of adoption situations arise out of one-night stands and casual relationships, meaning last names and contact information was not exchanged. Or, perhaps he is known but he does not wish to be contacted, perhaps being fearful of child support obligations if she were to keep the baby, and he ignores efforts to contact him. The result of these common situations is that sometimes there is no birth father health history available, besides the cursory information the birth mother will know, such as his ethnicity and general appearance.

So how is this lack of birth father information in many adoptions going to make you feel better or worse? Well, some adoptive parents worry so much over a birth *mother's* health issues that they realize the futility of such worries when the other half of the gene pool is unknown, other than ethnicity and appearance. For other adoptive parents, this only serves to double their potential anxiety. The same issues exist in international adoption, but even more so, as sometimes there is even little or no information about the birth mother.

Drug or Alcohol Usage

Sadly, drugs are becoming more and more common in our culture, so they are a reality we have to deal with in adoption. Does this mean that all birth mothers use drugs? No. Does it mean *most* birth mothers use drugs? Again, no. There is no way to definitively state the percentage of birth mothers who use drugs, but it is fair to say it is a small amount, but sizable enough that you may face the issue. (When I say this I am referring to voluntary adoptions, not county adoptions where the child was taken from the birth parents due to drug problems. In those cases, drug usage is much higher.)

Naturally, you want a drug-free pregnancy. Every adoptive parent does. But does that mean you should decline a birth mother who has selected you if she used drugs or alcohol during the pregnancy? Obviously, you can decline such placements, but you may be passing on what might be an excellent adoption without the risks that you believe exist.

First of all, you need to decide where you draw the line in drug usage, and that requires that you educate yourself. In addition to the assistance of your family doctor and gynecologist, and your attorney or agency, an excellent resource to learn more about the potential effects of drugs on a fetus is the Organization of Teratology Information Specialists. They have access to studies on all types of fetal drug exposure and the potential consequences and can answer hypothetical questions. "If a woman used crystal methamphetamine a few times in the first trimester, then stopped, but smoked marijuana twice a week in the last trimester to help stop nausea, what is the likelihood that could affect the baby, and if so, how?" No one can give a definitive answer, but they can tell you what is know. Their website is otispregnancy.org Their toll free number is (866) 626-OTIS.

You will be surprised that some drugs do not cross the placenta, meaning they usually don't directly affect the fetus. What about drugs that *can* affect the child? Every adoptive parent will view the situation with a different comfort level. Would you consider working with a birth mother who only smoked marijuana a few times early in the pregnancy, then stopped when she learned she was pregnant? Most adoptive parents would accept that placement with no hesitation. What if the drug was crystal methamphetamine, but again only a few times early in the pregnancy? At this point some adoptive parents are backing away, while some are still on board. What if it was consistent usage of methamphetamine throughout the pregnancy, and she tested positive for drugs at birth? Or daily alcohol? Now most adoptive parents are abandoning ship right and left, leaving only a few families interested in the placement. These are personal decisions for adoptive parents and everyone's feelings and interpretation of available research will vary.

Whatever you decide, it is important to make your decisions based upon actual research, not knee-jerk reactions. Here's an example. Let's say you are presented with a birth mother who consumed a single glass of alcohol of daily, perhaps more on the weekends, throughout the pregnancy. And let's also say she smoked multiple packs of cigarettes throughout the pregnancy too. You are probably ready to bail on this adoption already. You are thinking of such things as fetal alcohol syndrome and the carcinogens from the tobacco. I won't even try to dispute those concerns, but here is a question for you. Ask everyone you know who is in their late 40s or older if their mothers smoked several packs of cigarettes a day, and had alcohol on a daily basis when their mothers were pregnant with them. In fact, ask yourself about *your* mother's pregnancy if you are in this age range. The answer will be that a large number will answer "yes" to both questions. No one knew any better back then, so many women drank wine every night, perhaps cocktails on the weekend, and smoked while pregnant. Now ask yourself, are all those people who just answered "yes" fetal alcohol syndrome suffering individuals? Are they in terrible health due to their mothers smoking? Probably the answer is no, and your friends in that age group are normal people, not a generation of unadoptable men and women.

Don't get me wrong. I'm not encouraging you to ignore issues like drugs and alcohol. They are indeed important and you need to talk to your family doctor, your obstetrician/gynecologist, et cetera. What I am encouraging you is to not pass on a placement due to what might be incorrect assumptions on your part, perhaps losing a placement which was actually the best one you could have asked for.

The birth mother's honesty. Many worry that a birth mother may lie on important issues like her health history and drug usage. This is true; they could lie. But then, so can adoptive parents lie to a birth mother. Luckily, I find that few birth mothers lie. The reason is that most are planning adoption for one simple reason: they want a wonderful life for their child. They are hardly doing that if they lie about important facts, hurting the child later by having hidden that information. After all, she could have terminated the pregnancy - in some ways an easier option for her - but instead she went through a 40 week pregnancy, the painful and potentially life-threatening experience of childbirth, just to give that child to you. Such sacrifices do not normally gel with lying.

Still, there will always be some birth mothers who do lie, and if so, usually it will be about embarrassment over drug usage. This is where your attorney or agency's approach is critical. If he or she is very non-judgmental with the birth mother, and from the very beginning makes clear to her that there are adoptive families waiting out there regardless of whether there was drug usage or not, she is much more likely to be honest.

Drug testing. Fears over a birth mother using drugs may lead you to request drug testing. This is a possible option, but has disadvantages. For example, if you are working on having the kind of open, trusting relationship many newborn adoptions start with, and she tells you she has never used drugs, and you reply, "of course we believe you, but take a monthly drug test anyway," her opinion of you is likely damaged. She may agree to what you want and not complain, but a bit of the unequivocal trust she needs to see in - you to be her child's parents - is perhaps gone. A good example might be if your spouse required you before marriage to take a polygraph test, fearing you were lying about things in your past. You might agree to do so, but you'd be deeply hurt over the request and your relationship may suffer.

Another reason drug testing is not as beneficial as you might think is that they are not infallible. Certain drugs only show up for certain periods of time after usage (some only days, and some, like marijuana, usually longer), and tests can sometimes be tricked or have false readings. Blood tests generally show positive results longer than urine tests, so if you elect drug testing, doing so by blood is usually more reliable. If a birth mother is a savvy drug user, however, she likely knows exactly how long a particular drug will be in her system, and know when she'd be clean for a test.

Of course, the reverse could be true as well. It's conceivable that a birth mother inclined to take drugs could be dissuaded from doing so if she knows she'll soon be tested. I don't find this very persuasive, however, because if she used and then tested positive, and you declined to work with her anymore, she'd just find another adoptive family. So there goes the dissuasion theory; there's no real penalty for her if that's her true inclination. I think usually the best route is to decline to work with a birth mother you don't believe in, and work with one you trust. That may sound absurdly simple, and I will admit it is not foolproof, but then neither are the above "safeguards" of drug testing. Each option has its pros and cons. I think selecting the right birth mother, then showing faith and trust in her, offers the most "pros" and the least "cons."

Goals and Future Plans

A birth mother who has future goals and plans is more likely to place than those who don't. Those that have no interest in getting a job, pursuing an education, finding the right man and marrying, improving her lifestyle, et cetera, is more likely to look at the baby right after birth and think that he or she can fill the void and make her life complete. Compare this to a birth mother who has dreams and goals, and can recognize that raising a child at this time, under these circumstances, will ruin or delay the goals she has for her future. This latter type of birth mother is more aware of the child's future as well, and how those future opportunities and lifestyle will be diminished is she were to try to parent under her present difficult circumstances.

Feelings of the Birth Father

I consistently talk about birth mothers within this book, but don't mention birth fathers nearly as often. This is no disrespect to birth fathers, rather a reflection of the reality that very few of them elect to get involved in adoption planning. Every adoption has a birth father, however, whether they are findable or not, and that makes them potentially an important part of the adoption.

When the birth father is unknown or can't be found, or is findable but has no interest in the pregnancy, this is probably one of many factors leading many birth mothers to consider adoption. A pregnancy is viewed completely differently, however, when it results from a caring relationship with a loving partner. If he wants to raise the baby, either alone or with her, this is potentially a major disruption in the adoption on two fronts. One is that he could seek to object to the adoption on legal grounds (discussed in Chapter 12). The other is that, even if he has no plans to object in court, if he prefers that she keep the baby, he may try to influence her to change her mind. If their relationship is, or was, a solid one, this will make his feelings a significant influence upon her.

Luckily for adoptive parents, a very small percentage of non-marital birth fathers elect to object to adoption planning. Most of the pregnancies they are involved in leading to adoption were one-night stands, casual encounters or terminated relationships. This makes both birth mother and father unlikely to want to be linked to each other for life through the child, and is one more reason for adoption.

Regardless of the birth father's initial feelings when he is first contacted, the surest way to get him to cooperate in adoption planning is to treat him with respect. Acknowledging that he is an important part of the child's creation, asking him for a personal and health history, and extending a similar offer as to the birth mother regarding sending pictures and updating letters about the child if he is interested, are important courtesies. This is particularly true with birth fathers who are initially unsure if they want to parent the baby or not, and are confused. Sometimes, just like a birth mother, they need time and counseling to see the benefits of adoption and see it as a loving, unselfish act. Some wrongly initially see it as abandoning their duties as a man. The more understanding they have about the true nature of adoption, the less likely any anti-adoption sentiments will persist.

Legal Risks

An important consideration in starting any adoption is if there will be any legal risks. To some degree, every adoption has risk, such as the chance the birth mother will change her mind. I'm referring to avoidable issues, however. For example, are you aware in advance of a legal challenge that will be filed in the adoption? This could be by an objecting birth father, an Indian tribe's intervention pursuant to the Indian Child Welfare Act, or other problem. (There are several potential trouble spots in every adoption and these potential issues are discussed in Chapter 12).

It is critical is to analyze every possible complication in the adoption based upon the unique facts in your adoption. You may elect to proceed despite the possibility of a known problem, but if you do, you want to know the full extent of the risk. Will you have to go to court? How long will the court action take? How much will it cost? How likely are you to win? Have you considered the affect on you and the child if you bond, then have to give up custody after protracted litigation? Fortunately, litigated adoptions are rare. One reason for this, however, is that many cases destined to be litigated are abandoned before getting to that point.

Motivation for Adoption

There are many reasons for a birth mother to start an adoption. In a nutshell, the "good" reasons are a combination of either not wanting to parent a child, or recognizing they are not ready to be a mom, usually combined with factors like insufficient income, inadequate employment, having one or more other existing children to raise, the goals of college or a career, or lack of an appropriate relationship with the birth father. We need to be on the lookout, however, for the "wrong" reasons.

Sometimes a birth mother will either consciously or subconsciously start adoption planning as a way to spur the birth father into action. Perhaps he greeted her disclosure of the pregnancy with apathy, and he is a man she had hoped – and still hopes - to have a relationship with. She may think adoption will get his attention and nudge him into action, to mature and solidify their relationship. The only way to determine if this is her motivation is to get to know her and learn more about her feelings and changing emotions toward the birth father. Some giveaways can be that the birth mother and father had a long relationship, or are only very recently broken up. Usually it is fairly clear when she is not "over him."

Another improper motivation is if she is placating someone important to her, doing the adoption to get their approval, when it is really not what she wants. This could be the birth father who is telling her he will continue being her boyfriend, but not if she keeps the baby, or her parents who are already raising one or more of her children (and know this one will soon become their responsibility as well). In these situations, the birth mother is trying to please *them*. But if it's not what *she* really wants and feels in her heart is the right thing, she is likely to change her mind when the baby is born and her true emotions come out.

The greatest concern regarding improper motivation is monetary. It is understandable that a birth mother needs a safe and comfortable place to live, and food to eat, both during the pregnancy and while she recovers. For this reason, most all states permit adoptive parents to provide pregnancy-related assistance. There are two areas of concern, however, in these financial arrangements. Some birth mothers will want improper financial benefits, literally wanting to be "paid" for their baby. Not only is this illegal, but demonstrates a birth mother placing a child for the wrong reasons and who is trouble in every way. These situations are easy to spot and avoid. (See Chapter 12 regarding permitted financial assistance, and the state-by-state review.)

Questionable financial situations that are more difficult to spot are those where the birth mother is seeking assistance in categories that are legally permitted, but are grossly excessive. For example, a birth mother may need to rent an apartment. Accordingly, a standard apartment, likely one she could afford on her own when she starts working again after the pregnancy, is reasonable. Some birth mothers may insist on an apartment which might be double or triple what they would normally stay in, and could not afford to live in afterward. With this kind of birth mother, you will usually see other pregnancy-related costs be enhanced as well, such as food, maternity clothing and transportation. Even if these expenses could be considered lawful as they fall within appropriate categories for pregnancy-related expenses, it is clear the birth mother is seeking to grossly escalate her lifestyle at your expense. When this becomes the motivation for adoption - turning a pregnancy into a luxury vacation - she is a risky birth mother to work with as her true motivations are suspect.

Will She Accept Counseling?

Counseling is often an important part of success in adoption. The problem is, however, that most birth mothers feel they don't need counseling, so don't embrace it when offered. (Although a few states make counseling mandatory, in many cases it is optional.) Birth mothers will often say they know what they want, and don't need counseling on the subject. It could be they are correct. They could also be wrong.

What they typically don't understand, due to their young age and inexperience, is that while their decision toward adoption seems obvious to them now, things can change dramatically at, and shortly after, the birth. The emotions of going through giving birth - likely for the first time - and seeing the baby, plus the effect of hormonal changes due to the pregnancy and child birth (you've likely heard of "baby blues" and postpartum depression), not to mention the reality that she may never see her child again, can hit her like an emotional sledgehammer.

The goal of counseling is two-fold. First, it is to help her explore her options and let her reaffirm to herself that adoption is the best option for her and the baby. Second, it is to prepare her for the likely

177

emotions of birth and separation, so she knows to expect them. Counseling can serve as "pause button." If she is feeling more emotional pain than she anticipated post-birth and is thinking the only way to stop that pain is to stop the adoption, she can remind herself that her counselor discussed these very emotions, and that her pain means she is a normal, loving human being, not that she is making a mistake. Rather than give in to those temporary emotions, she is more likely to look back to the decisions she made when she was more analytical.

Pressure To Go Forward

Earlier I discussed the dangers of pressure on a birth mother. Now I want to talk about pressure on *you*. It is possible that your photo-resume will fall into the hands of an adoption facilitator, agency or attorney who is less than ethical and will aggressively contact you (one more reason to put your attorney or agency's number on your photo-resume letter, not your own). These adoption businesses may have seen your photo-resume letter online, or received it indirectly from your networking. Many of these individuals have few or no waiting adoptive parent clients, but advertise for birth mothers. When they find one they show any available photo-resume letters (yours), then call you to say you've "been picked" by *their* birth mother. It likely does not surprise you to hear that this revelation is immediately followed by the need for you to send money to them, and/or the birth mother to "secure the placement." If you hesitate, they will say that they will have to call another family, one "the birth mother can count on."

It would be easy to recommend that you not bother speaking to businesses like these, even if they claim they are reputable because they are a licensed agency or attorney. (Yes, even some agencies and attorneys engage in such behavior, not just facilitators.) But I'm aware that is easier said than done when they are presenting you with what appears to be an excellent adoption situation. Admittedly, even "bad" agencies, attorneys or facilitators can be contacted by an excellent birth mother. This creates a difficult situation, when the birth mother is great, and the adoption entity is someone you'd normally never hire.

So if you want to consider going forward in such a situation, here are some things you want to do in every adoption, but in particular in those where you are contacted by an adoption entity you did not retain:

- Have your attorney or agency talk to the birth mother and make sure it appears to be an appropriate placement, with no legal impediments to success.
- Have your attorney or agency talk to the entity who found the birth mother and is requesting a fee to inquire about their legitimacy, fees and any information they have on the birth parents.
- Receive a full health history for the birth mother (and if he's available and willing, the birth father).
- Have her sign an Authorization to Release Medical Information so you can speak to her doctor to confirm the pregnancy and inquire about her medical condition.
- In most states (laws vary) it is wise to have your attorney or agency speak to the birth father to be sure he will not be opposing the adoption.
- Speak to the birth mother initially by phone, make sure she likes you and you feel confident in her. If the initial calls go well, arrange to quickly meet her in her region, or pay to have her come to you, so you can meet face-to-face to be sure the placement feels right.
- If your attorney or agency is in the same region where you will be meeting the birth mother, have him or her meet with the birth mother face-to-face as well to give you additional feedback.
- Only pay the intermediary when you are confident and ready to go forward with the placement. Also, ask yourself, why this business is calling you, a stranger to them, rather than making a placement with one of their own existing families. These types of questionable entities, even if they are a licensed agency or attorney, usually state they "can't keep up with so many birth mothers calling." The reality, however, with many such businesses is that the word is out on them, and they can't attract clients, so must troll for them, the adoption version of an ambulance chaser. Don't forget the advice from Chapters 4 and

6 regarding how to inquire about the legitimacy of an attorney or agency. Many of them will apply to situations like these.

As you can see, there are many red flags to a risky adoption. Does this mean you never do an adoption with a red flag? No, it does not. It would be nice if every adoption were perfect, but the fact is that many aren't. Birth mothers' lives are rarely neat and perfect. If they were, they wouldn't be doing an adoption. They'd be raising the child themselves, or have a family member do so. Accordingly, that does not mean you pass on an adoption if one aspect of it is not perfect. The pros and cons in each adoption must be weighed and analyzed, by both you and your adoption professional. Some red flags, such as a birth mother "selling" her baby, are so significant that the one such factor alone is enough to send you running away.

Other factors, however, are less significant and you might only want to pass on the adoption if there are multiple cautions. For example, let's say that a birth mother presents you with an excellent adoption situation but refuses to go to counseling, saying she "does not need it" (a common refrain). If she appears emotionally stable and her health history indicates no psychological disabilities, most adoptive parents would still do the adoption, and hope that they and their adoption professional can prepare her for the birth experience or later convince her to receive counseling. What if that same birth mother declining counseling also reports that her parents are divorced, and her mother supports the adoption but her father doesn't. You are disappointed her father is against the adoption, but unless the birth mother is young and living with him, making her dependent upon him, you are still likely going forward with the adoption. We have two red flags at this point, but likely not significant ones. But now let's add a relationship with the birth father which you fear is not over, with emotions still flowing between them, with reconciliation a possibility. Or perhaps the additional caution is high projected costs, or a possible legal problem such as the Indian Child Welfare Act (discussed in Chapter 12). Any one of those concerns, might be enough to push you to declining the placement. This is where the guidance of your adoption professional will be tremendously helpful. Likely he or she has met hundreds or thousands of birth mothers and has a good feel for what to expect. That, combined with your own gut instinct, usually results in successful adoptions.

CHAPTER 11

WORKING WITH
THE DOCTOR AND HOSPITAL

Adoptive parents often have a great deal of anxiety about being fully informed about their future child's health. This is understandable. When you are planning to adopt a not-yet-born baby, it is the birth parent's health history, and that of their extended families, which is sought. We've previously addressed the fact that this is accomplished by having birth parents complete detailed health histories.

But what about the records and information about the fetus, the birth mother while pregnant, and the baby at birth? You naturally want the latter information as well to be as sure as possible that there are no medical situations which could affect your ability and desire to go forward with the adoption, such as an unanticipated major medical problem or need.

Access to Medical Records

If you are like most adoptive parents, you understandably want to do more than look at health histories and review a doctor's notes (even assuming they could be deciphered, as doctors are somewhat infamous for their handwriting and usually need to be deciphered by his or her staff). You want to simply call the doctor or his or her staff and ask pre-birth questions like, "Is the baby okay?" "Does the ultrasound look normal?" "Is there anything we should know, or problems we should be prepared for?"

There are two ways to make this happen. Every birth mother should be asked to sign an Authorization to Disclose Medical Information. This form waives the doctor-patient privilege and allows the doctor's office to speak to those named on the form. Usually the form will list you as the adoptive parents, and either the agency or attorney. If it is a closed adoption and everything will be done through an adoption agency, they will usually be the ones having the direct contact and will forward the information to you.

If you live in a state where it is the norm to have an open pre-birth relationship, and you live close enough to make it feasible, it is not unusual for you to actually accompany your birth mother to several of her doctor appointments. This is great for both you and her. For you it is wonderful to share in the pre-natal care, get to know the doctor and personally ask questions, and have special moments like seeing the fetus in an ultrasound, or hearing his or her heartbeat. For a birth mother's perspective, these moments are also important. The chance for her to see your emotion at these times helps reassure her how much you want to be parents, and how excited you are about the baby. It can help forestall any subconscious doubts that you will not love the baby like your own.

Post-birth, the hospital is given the Authorization to Disclose Medical Information form, allowing you to have full access to medical information for both the birth mother and the baby. This applies to not only verbally asking questions, but having a copy of the birth records sent to the child's pediatrician whom you've selected.

The Hospital

While the child is at the hospital, many states allow you to have contact with the baby, including both holding and feeding. You can also have contact with the birth mother. In fact, in many open adoptions, the adoptive mother, sometimes the adoptive father as well, is asked by the birth mother to be her labor coach. Not only will sharing in the birth of your child be a wonderful moment for you, who better than you to take part in the birth in the eyes of the birth mother.

Of course, some birth mothers prefer that you wait outside until the birth is complete, and those feelings are to be respected.

When you interact with your birth mother at the hospital, it is important that she sees you care about *her* as a person, not just as a means to get a baby. That means spending time with her, not just the baby. It is also a great time, if she has elected to see the baby, to take pictures of all of you together. This is a great way to one day show your child it took all of you, loving him or her, to create your family. It also shows your birth mother that you value and appreciate her, and that you will be sharing the knowledge of her critical role in your child's birth and placement with you with your child.

Some birth mothers fear seeing the baby after the birth will be too difficult for them, and naturally those feelings should be respected. We never want to make a birth mother do something she is not comfortable with. Most birth mothers, however, want to see the child they created, and to have time for a personal goodbye. Many birth mothers refer to the time with the baby at the hospital as "their time," noting you have a lifetime thereafter. These options should be addressed in her pre-birth emotional counseling

Insurance and Medical Costs

Virtually every state allows you to pay your birth mother's medical costs, although some states require that it be paid through an agency or attorney, or obtain court approval first. It's nice, however, if you can avoid medical costs. It may surprise you, but it is very common in adoption that the adoptive parents don't have to pay *any* medical costs. Many birth mothers have insurance through their job. Others may be covered by their parents' policy, if she meets certain age and residency requirements. Regardless of which situation it might be, the coverage might be an HMO (health maintenance organization) with one hundred percent coverage, or a PPO (preferred provider organization) with only eighty percent. Still, paying only twenty percent is much better than one hundred percent.

Her insurance eligibility should not be affected in any way due to the fact the baby is being placed for adoption, other than coverage will usually not extend into nursery or pediatric care after you have custody. Of course, usually your health insurance coverage will pick up coverage from this point, leaving you with no uninsured period. You will want to discuss this with your health insurance provider in advance. Sometimes though, even when both you and the birth mother have insurance, there will be an interim period when neither insurer feels they should provide coverage. This is an issue your adoption professional can look into before the birth to avoid any surprises.

What about if she had no insurance? Can she use yours? The answer is virtually always no. This is because each policy holder is a determined risk by the insurer, and while they agreed to insure you, they did not agree to insure someone whose health history they know nothing about. You are the insured, not the birth mother, even if the baby is to be placed with you. That doesn't mean you are looking at paying medical bills, however.

Medi-Caid

Not all birth mothers will have insurance. In fact, most won't. That doesn't mean you are destined to pay medical bills, however. That is because most birth mothers, due to the fact likely unemployed, or have low income employment, are eligible for their state's version of Medi-Caid. Many birth mothers will already be on such a program when they start adoption planning, and if they aren't, you can often assist them to apply. Usually the only requirements are to show that she is a resident of a particular county and state, is pregnant, and is income eligible. Just as with insurance, the fact she is placing the child for adoption should not affect her eligibility. Usually Medi-Caid coverage will cover 100% of her medical costs, although not all doctors and hospitals will accept the coverage, as frequently the payment is less than paid through private insurance.

Each state has different insurance regulations determining when your insurance can cover the baby after the birth. Some will start as soon as the baby (or an older child) is placed with you for adoption. A few will not provide coverage until the adoption is finalized by a court, which might be six months or more away. Since no one wants to see a child without insurance, however, normally the birth mother's coverage (if any) will apply until your coverage will pick it up.

What if the birth mother has no insurance and is not eligible for Medi-Caid? Perhaps she makes too much money at her job, but insurance is not offered there. Well, this means you are probably paying medical bills, so you will want to know what they will be in advance. You will usually be paying a doctor for both prenatal care and to deliver the baby, and separately the hospital for using their facility. Sometimes other doctors are required, such as an anesthesiologist if she is having a caesarean birth, or an epidural. Also, a pediatrician will charge for examining the baby at the hospital.

Doctors usually charge a flat fee for both pre-natal care and the delivery. Usually there is one set fee for vaginal deliveries and a higher one for caesarean births. Some doctors, if they know a patient has no insurance, will offer you a pre-pay discount if you pay in advance. Many hospitals are the same way. They often have a special discount rate if you pay before the patient (the birth mother) is discharged. Sometimes these discounts are huge, particularly with hospitals, sometimes as much as fifty percent. Apparently their reasoning is that when someone comes in for medical care and has no insurance, the hospital may never receive any payment, so they'll gladly accept a lesser payment if it is timely.

Releasing the Baby from the Hospital

Each state has different procedures regarding releasing the baby to you from the hospital. This can also differ on whether you are planning an independent or agency adoption. Even within the same state individual hospitals may have different policies. As a general rule, however, in most independent adoptions the child will be released directly to you, usually requiring the written permission of the birth mother, or in some states, a judge. Either way, it will be the job of your attorney or agency to meet these requirements. But you and the birth mother should know them in advance so everyone is prepared for them, and be comfortable with the procedures.

There is almost never a foster home intermediary placement in independent adoptions. In most all agency adoptions, an immediate placement can also be made, but in some states the agency will keep the child in foster care for a short period until the child is legally free for adoption, which could take only a few days, or can take much longer.

The state-by-state review in Chapter 15 provides the typical hospital release procedure for both independent and agency adoption in each state.

CHAPTER 12

LEGAL ISSUES: STEP-BY-STEP

There are many legal steps on the road to a completed adoption. Some of them are routine steps. Others involve issues you hope to avoid that typically only arise in difficult or contested adoptions. The best way to avoid those issues, however, is to know about them from the start. That allows you to have a chance to solve the problem before becoming too involved emotionally or financially in an adoption, or avoid the adoption entirely. Let's look at the routine procedural steps in every adoption, as well as the legal issues which can come up along the way, in the order you are likely to encounter them.

The Petition for Adoption

Every adoption requires court approval to be granted. The start of the process to obtain approval is to file a *Petition for Adoption*. In most cases this is filed shortly after the child is placed in your custody. Some states will require that the birth mother first sign her consent, and others will allow that it be signed and filed later. In some agency adoptions, particularly public adoption agencies, the child may need to be in your home for a prescribed period before the Petition can be filed.

The Petition for Adoption will normally identify you as the adoptive parents and establish the court has jurisdiction to handle your case (based upon your residence, where the baby was born, et cetera). It will also name the birth mother and father (if known), the date and place of the child's birth, the name of the child on the initial birth certificate and how you would like it to be changed after the adoption is granted, and list what agency, social worker or state adoption office will be doing your home study.

Who prepares and files your Petition for Adoption? In an independent adoption it will be your attorney. In an agency adoption it will usually be either an attorney you have hired, or one on staff for the agency. The first issue is where you will file your Petition for Adoption. In most cases you will file it in the county and state in which you live. In fact, usually you have no choice and can only file in your local court. Some states, however, allow non-residents to adopt in their state, and permit you to file it in the county and state of the child's birth, the location of the placing adoption agency, or sometimes even the birth mother's residence.

Your Petition for Adoption, once filed, will be assigned a case number by the court and a file will be opened. Adoption files are normally confidential, so the only parties permitted access besides court personnel are you, your attorney, and the home study agency.

The Birth Mother's Consent to Adoption

As an adoptive parent, one of your primary concerns in your adoption is when will the birth mother sign her consent to adoption, and when does it become permanent and irrevocable. Every state is different, not only regarding what they call the consent, but also when it can be signed, who must act as a witness, and when it becomes permanent. The form used for a birth mother to give up her parental rights might be called a *consent*, a *relinquishment*, a *surrender* or a *voluntary termination of parental rights*.

Most states impose a waiting time after the birth before a consent can be signed. Many states make this period seventy-two hours, while others require a longer time. Each state will also designate a specific person who can witness the consent. This is usually a judge or a social worker, or sometimes an attorney. Even within a state, the laws regarding when a consent can be signed and before whom can vary between independent and agency adoption. Please refer to the state-by-state review in Chapter 15 to see the specific procedures in the states of interest to you.

If you live in one state, and your birth mother lives in another state, do you execute a consent under the birth state's laws, or those of the state where you live? The answer depends upon the states involved. Some states will accept the consent to adoption as prescribed under the laws of the state where the birth occurred. Other states you're your home state's consent forms and procedures be used, even if the birth occurred in another state. In many cases, you end up executing double consents, one under both states' laws. Even if this is not required, it is often a good idea. This is because sometimes a *conflict of laws* issue will arise. This is where each state has different laws, and there is a dispute regarding which should apply. The safest thing in many cases is to execute both consents, providing extra security for you. The last thing you want is to execute only state A's consent, then a dispute arises and it is determined state B's laws apply. If you did not have the birth mother sign state B's consent, it may be determined she never gave up her parental rights and you are powerless.

Some states require birth mothers to have their own attorney and advise them of their rights. Others require counseling or meetings with a social worker. The goal is the same: to protect a birth mother and make sure she knows her rights and options. In a very small number of states, if the birth mother is under eighteen, she must have the consent of a parent, or a court-appointed individual (sometimes called a guardian ad litem), to give up her parental rights. In the vast majority of states, however, birth mothers under eighteen do not require the consent of a parent or other person.

Can the Birth Mother Revoke Her Consent?

Every adoptive parent's worst nightmare is that their birth mother will place the child for adoption, then change her mind. Although some states make her signed consent permanent the moment it is signed, most give her a prescribed time in which to revoke the consent. This might be twenty-four hours, seventy-two hours, ten days or even a month or more.

Some states make this right to revoke the consent automatic, imposing no burden upon the birth mother, other than to perhaps fill out a form. Other states require a court hearing and require a birth mother to prove the child's best interests would be served by being with her rather than with you.

Once the revocation period is over, the birth mother has basically lost the right to change her mind and you can feel fairly secure. The principal exception would be cases where the birth mother can prove that fraud or duress was used to obtain her consent. Such a showing could invalidate a birth mother's consent after the usual revocation period has passed. Such situations are extremely rare, however, for the simple reason adoptive parents and the adoption professionals they work with are smart enough not to use fraud or duress. Fraud, by the way, is usually considered a significant deception, not simply a small misunderstanding. For example, situations involving sufficient fraud to perhaps invalidate a consent would be such situations as the post-birth discovery that you had a criminal history that you had tried to hide, not that she thought your eyes were blue when in fact they are green. It is almost unheard of for a birth mother to challenge an adoption on grounds of fraud, even more so for such a request to be granted.

Because each state is different regarding how long a birth mother has to change her mind and revoke her consent to adoption, and any burden she is required to prove, the state-by-state review provides each state's unique laws.

When The Birth Mother Does Not Consent

If the birth mother refuses to sign a consent, and wants to stop the adoption, normally she has the automatic right to stop the adoption and reclaim her baby. There are some circumstances, however, where an adoption can proceed without the birth mother's consent, although they are not commonly used. Such situations can arise when the birth mother disappears after placing the child with you but before signing her consent, or where she refuses to consent, yet does not seek custody and wants the child to stay with you.

Every state has some kind of provision to involuntarily terminate parental rights when called for to protect a child's best interests. One such action is *abandonment*. Typically, if a birth parent fails to fulfill her parental responsibilities, specifically not having any contact with the child, or provide financial support, a court can terminate their rights and allow those who have been caring for the child to adopt. The required length of time to constitute abandonment differs, but is usually six months. Abandonment situations are rare in independent or private agency adoptions, and are more common in the adoption of older children via public agency adoptions.

The Rights of the Birth Father

When a pregnancy results from an established, caring relationship, even outside of marriage, the mother and father of the expected baby usually elect to keep the baby. Adoptions, however, rarely come from these situations. Instead, they are usually the result of one-night stands, short relationships, or relationships which soured with news of the pregnancy, leading to the birth father to distance himself (often fearful of a lifetime of child support and parental obligations). For this reason, many birth fathers welcome the news of adoption and elect to cooperate.

Determining the rights of birth fathers, and the proper way for them to show their consent, can be a complicated legal issue. This is because not only does each state have different laws regarding birth fathers rights in adoption, but each state will also distinguish between different categories of birth fathers.

Escalated Fathers' Rights. Some birth fathers will have escalated rights due to a special relationship with the birth mother or the child. This usually includes a man who is married to the birth mother, or who has lived with or supported the child prior to the adoption. Usually for an adoption to proceed with a birth father in this category you will need to obtain his consent. If he refuses to give it, you may be unable to adopt the child, unless a situation such as abandonment exists. Sometimes this creates tragic results. For example, a birth mother may honestly tell you of fleeing her spouse due to his physical abuse of her. That birth father will be subject to both criminal and civil penalties for that behavior, but it will be almost impossible for you to use that as grounds to adopt his biological child without his consent.

Alleged or Putative Fathers. Most birth fathers do not fall into the escalated categories above. In fact, they are quite rare in adoptions. As you likely assume, most birth fathers in adoptive placements are one-night stands, casual encounters, or perhaps they were dating for some time but he has no desire to take responsibility for a child. Most states label this category of birth fathers as "putative" or "alleged." The overwhelming majority of men in this category not only support adoption, but are thrilled about it, as it will end their anxiety over potential child support obligations if the birth mother were to keep the child. We must be cautious, however, with the few birth fathers who may seek to challenge the adoption against with desires of the birth mother.

States fall into two general categories in determining the rights of these types of birth fathers. Some states are "notice" states, and put the burden on you as the adoptive parents and require your attorney or agency to give written notice to the birth father, informing him about the pregnancy and adoption. Usually he will have a set time in which to object, and if he doesn't, his rights can be terminated in a fairly simple court proceeding. Many states even allow alleged/putative birth fathers to waive their rights *before* the baby is born, usually by signing a simple form, and a court can usually terminate their rights shortly after the birth.

Sometimes the birth father can't be found to give him notice. He may have moved and not given the birth mother his new address, or their relationship was so short that phone numbers and addresses were never exchanged. He could even be hiding out of fear of his potential obligations and court proceedings. In these situations your attorney or agency will need to show it used due diligence in trying to find the birth father. This might include a property records check, a phone book search and a Motor Vehicles Bureau inquiry. Some states will require publishing the notice of paternity and adoption in a local newspaper, usually buried in the back with the classified ads.

If he can't be found with due diligence, typically the court can sever his rights and the adoption proceed without difficulty. Sometimes a birth mother will not even know the birth father's last name. In those cases, search efforts are usually impossible (you can't do a search for "John in Cleveland"), so his rights are terminated as an "unknown father."

What if an alleged/putative father receives his notice and is one of the few who wishes to object and seek custody? Each state will define his rights differently, but most will require a judge to examine his behavior and lifestyle and ask questions like: "Did he take responsibility for the pregnancy and help the birth mother with her expenses and other needs during the pregnancy?" "Can he emotionally and financially care for a child?" "Would the child's best interests be served by being with him, or the adoptive parents?" Accordingly, if the birth father acted "like a man should" with a baby on the way, he may be tough to defeat in court. If he avoided responsibility, requiring you to step in and fulfill the birth mother's needs, and his lifestyle is not compatible with parenthood, he is more likely to lose.

As a general rule, I think if you are *sure* there will be an objection from the birth father, it is safest to not even start the adoption. Sometimes, however, you may be unsure how a birth father will react, making your decision difficult. For example, the birth father's feelings may vacillate, or he may say things you believe he has no intent to follow through on. In those cases, you may wish to proceed, but you want to be sure the law will be on your side if litigation ends up being required. Many states give alleged/putative fathers a limited time to object, such as 30 days.

Not all states are "notice" states, however. Many are "registry" states. A registry is completely different in that it puts the burden on the birth father, not the adoptive parents. Men in these states typically must voluntarily register themselves as the possible father of (an expected) child in order to later seek to establish any rights. Their failure to do so will normally result in the termination of their rights when a designated period has passed, often 30 days. A court hearing will still be required to terminate his rights, but often all that must be established is his failure to register. Some registry states may still give him the right to object at the hearing, and usually his burden will be the same as described in notice states, where his degree of responsibility and the best interests of the child are considered.

Perhaps soon altering the above information is the pending "Proud Father" legislation. This is a bill pending in Congress which, if passed, will create a national birth father registry. It would likely supplement, not replace, state registries. At this time, the bill is still being amended, so its implications are presently unknown. It is believed, however, that even if it passes that it would not markedly interfere with existing state law, rather be an additional database to check for locating possible birth fathers.

Unknown "John Doe" Birth Fathers. What about if a birth mother has relations with more than one person and is not sure who is the birth father? Do you have to do blood tests? Normally, no. In most cases you give notice to each possible birth father, or see if they listed themselves in the state registry, and see if any of them plans to object. If one or more does, then paternity testing will be required as obviously only that father would have the right to object. If all are agreeable, or apathetic and do nothing, your attorney or agency will simply terminate the rights of every possible father to eliminate any risk.

The state-by-state review provides information about birth father's rights in each state. In some states the laws in this area are either too complex, or too vague, in which case they are not included.

Interstate Compact for the Placement of Children

It is becoming more an more common for adoptions to be interstate, meaning the child is born in one state, and you as adoptive parents live in a different state. Whenever a child is brought across state lines for purposes of adoption, a special law applies called the Interstate Compact for the Placement of Children (the ICPC). Basically, it says that before a child can be brought across state lines, both the "sending state" (where the child was born) and the "receiving state" (where you live) must give their approval in writing. Violating the ICPC can put your adoption at risk. Some states even make violation a criminal offense.

The ICPC applies to both independent and agency adoptions. It normally does not apply to international adoptive placements, however. To obtain Interstate Compact approval, your attorney or agency will initially contact the sending state's Interstate Compact Administrator. Each state has this special office, usually a division of the state's Department of Social Services. Each state has the right to make their own requirements, so for this reason there is no complete uniformity in satisfying the Interstate Compact, adding to its complexity. Generally, however, you will be required to provide your pre-placement home study, the birth mother's health history (and the birth father if it is available), and about half a dozen forms detailing the planned placement and outlining who will have financial and medical responsibility for the child.

Many states will also require the birth mother's consent to adoption and the hospital's discharge summary of the baby before giving their final approval for you to leave the state. If you live in a state where independent adoptions do not require a pre-placement home study, this is the one situation where you will be required to have one. Depending upon your state, you will obtain it through a private adoption agency, a social worker, or a state adoption office.

It commonly takes about one week post-birth for the sending state's Interstate Compact Administrator to have what is needed to give its approval, at which point the documents are forwarded to the sending state for its approval. The receiving state's Interstate Compact Administrator then needs to give its approval for you to transport the child across state lines and come home, and this is usually done within one to two days. In most cases, it is automatic that the required approval will be given, although the bureaucracy to obtain it can be daunting to anyone not an adoption professional.

The state-by-state review provides specifically does not provide each state's Interstate Compact office address and telephone number due to the fact these offices frequently will not take calls from the general public and work only with attorneys or agencies.

The Indian Child Welfare Act

The Indian Child Welfare Act (ICWA), is a federal law taking precedent over state law. Passed into law by Congress in 1978, it was intended to protect Indian culture and keep Indian children from being removed from existing Indian families and placed into non-Indian foster or adoptive homes. The intent of the law is an honorable one, but sadly the language of the law is so vague and far-reaching it has become difficult to apply. Complicating the issue is that some states have enacted their own state ICWA legislation, which may be slightly different than the federal law. We will discuss only the federal ICWA.

The ICWA provides that if a child is a member of an American Indian tribe, or is the biological child of a member and is eligible for membership, that written notice of the planned adoption must be given to the tribe, giving the tribe the right to object and allow Indian adoptive parents to be considered. It also requires a court hearing to find "good cause" to place the child with a non-Indian family (such as the desires of the birth parents, lack of the "Indian" birth parent having a true cultural connection with the tribe, et cetera), and for a judge to witness the birth parent's consent. Under the ICWA a birth parent normally has a longer time in which to withdraw their consent, as the ICWA grants them until the adoption is finalized, which might be six months or more after birth. Obviously, this scenario adds potential risk to you.

On the one hand, very few adoptions are actually affected by the Indian Child Welfare Act. On the other, many adoptions are impacted. How can both those contradictory statements be true? Here's how. Many of the young women placing a child for adoption, when asked about their family background as part of a normal adoption health and social family history, will state they may have a small amount of Indian heritage. In this sense, many adoptions can be affected, as any possible tribe must be contacted to inquire about membership. To find the location of any named tribe, your attorney or agency will usually contact either the Bureau of Indian Affairs, and review the *Tribal Leaders List*. The Bureau of Indian Affairs is a federal government office with its headquarters in Washington, D.C., with regional offices all over the nation. It is then up to any contacted tribe to write back and state if membership exists and the ICWA applies.

Even if it is verified that the child you plan to adopt has some Indian blood does not mean the ICWA applies to your adoption. Every tribe has different rules regarding tribal eligibility. Many require a minimum of twenty-five percent Indian blood, while some use other factors and can accept less. Some tribes have closed membership, perhaps so as to not dilute their existing tribal benefits among a larger group, and will decline membership even for someone who otherwise might be eligible.

If it is determined that the ICWA applies to your adoption, the next inquiry is if the birth parent or child is living or domiciled on the tribal reservation. This increases the tribe's rights as clearly the child has a significant connection to the tribe, and their interest is understandably greater. In these cases, which are very rare, the tribe has the right to block the adoption and have a tribal court hear matters related to the child.

In the few cases where the ICWA does end up applying, normally the birth parent is not living or domiciled on a reservation. In these cases, the tribe has a less significant connection to the birth parent and child, and their rights are weaker as a result.

It should also be known that most tribes are supportive of adoption, even when the adoptive parents are non-Indian. The usual thinking is: "If this is what the birth parent wants, we will respect their decision about whom they've selected as adoptive parents." This is especially true in the many cases where the birth parent has had virtually no connection in her or his life to the tribe, never visiting the reservation or embracing tribal customs, et cetera. For this reason, it is only a small number of tribes that actively seek to disrupt voluntary adoptions. In these cases, however, great caution must be used to do everything correctly. In some cases, such as where a tribe has indicated it will object and the birth parent was living on the tribal reservation, maximizing tribal rights, good judgment may dictate not even starting that adoption.

Birth Mother Financial Assistance

Many adoptions involve almost no financial assistance to the birth mother. Many birth mothers live at home or have a job, and have insurance or Medi-Caid. They don't need, or are too proud to accept, financial help. Often the assistance might be limited to counseling and maternity clothes. However, some adoptions will involve financial assistance. Usually this is due to the birth mother being unemployed, just losing her job and not being employed long enough to qualify for benefits, or perhaps she and the birth father were living together and the pregnancy led to their breakup and now she is homeless. Regardless of the reason, some birth mothers will need your assistance.

Almost every state permits you to assist the birth mother with pregnancy-related assistance. Unlike surrogacy, where some states allow an actual payment for the service of being a surrogate, adoption laws forbids such remuneration. Most states will permit you to help with such basics as medical care, rent, food, utilities maternity clothes, counseling and transportation needs. (See your state's limits in the state-by-state review.) Some states will require a judge's approval prior to the payment, while others do not, perhaps requiring an accounting of all prior expenses to be submitted prior to the granting of the adoption.

Any assistance you provide is basically a gift. That means if she changes her mind and stops the adoption, you can't demand your money back. Neither can you write up a contract that says you will pay her rent in exchange for a baby. That's buying and selling a baby. It is usually wisest to make any pregnancy-related assistance through your agency or attorney. That way, not only does that give them a chance to confirm the payment is legal and appropriate, but it establishes a degree of financial formality with the birth mother.

In most areas of adoption, the closer you are with her, the better. In financial areas, however, it can not only make both you and she feel uncomfortable, it leads to potential conflict. Let's say, for example, she requests assistance with a particular item and you know it falls outside of the permitted pregnancy-related assistance categories. It is much better for the birth mother to be told "no" by your agency or attorney (whom she will view as just doing their job), rather than by you (which she might interpret as being cheap or uncaring).

Some states have specific periods both before and after birth when assistance is allowed. Most, however, use general language like "the pregnancy-related period," which creates some flexibility. In most cases, living assistance starts, if needed at all, several months before the birth, and continues until about six weeks post-birth. As was discussed in Chapter 10, you should be cautious in working with a birth mother if her expenses seem inappropriately high, perhaps seeking to greatly escalate her lifestyle at your expense, even if the assistance is technically legal and falling into permitted pregnancy-related categories.

CHAPTER 13

FINALIZING THE ADOPTION AND POST BIRTH ISSUES

Normally, going to court causes anxiety. It's rare we go there for a "good" reason. In the case of adoptions, however, we go only with joy. This is because most adoptive parents only have to go to court one time, and it's when everything is done and the adoption is ready to be finalized.

The Court Finalization Hearing

When the birth mother's consent has become irrevocable, the birth father has consented (or waived his rights or otherwise had his rights terminated), any other legal obstacles have been satisfied and your home study is complete, your attorney or agency will schedule a court hearing for you to finalize the adoption. (Even in agency adoptions an attorney is normally used for the final hearing.) In almost every state each adoptive parent must be present, as well as the baby and the attorney. The hearing is closed to the general public, although you can invite guests who can be present. Unlike most court hearings, which are quite formal, adoption finalizations tend to be casual and relaxed. In fact, most judges spend more time posing for pictures with the adoptive family and the baby than in conducting legal proceedings.

Usually the hearings start with you being "sworn in." Then you confirm your identity, your desire to adopt the baby, and your willingness to raise the child as your own, with the duties and obligations which accompany that, including the right of inheritance. The judge will then confirm that he or she read the final report from your agency or social worker in which you are recommended as adoptive parents. He or she will then sign and issue what is called a *Decree of Adoption* or *Order of Adoption*, granting the adoption and making you, officially and permanently, parents.

The Amended Birth Certificate

The original birth certificate (naming the biological mother as the child's mother, and with the child's name listed as she elected) will become sealed and technically no longer exist very soon after your adoption is finalized. A new, amended birth certificate will then be issued, listing you as the child's new and only parents. This new birth certificate will not name you as *adoptive* parents, rather just as parents, as if you gave birth yourselves. It will also name the child as you've elected, in the event the birth mother put another first or last name. This new birth certificate will usually take several months to arrive from your state's Birth Registrar or Bureau of Vital Statistics. In the meantime, you can use the *Decree of Adoption* to show your legal status as parents. In the future, when you do the many things parents do, such as registering your child for your local soccer league, little league, and so on, you will only need to show your child's amended birth certificate, as would any parent. The Decree will not be needed, except in a few legal areas, as discussed below.

Obtaining a Social Security Card

When your child's amended birth certificate arrives you can obtain such items as a Social Security card and passport. Some birth mothers will have started the Social Security card process in the hospital, or you might be adopting an older child where one already exists. In those cases, you show the Decree of Adoption and the new birth certificate and have the Social Security information changed.

In most newborn adoptions, however, the hospitals do not have the birth mothers complete Social Security card applications, leaving it to be done by you when the adoption is complete. The Social Security Administration has vacillated regarding how adoptive parents can get a new Social Security card. Previously they could issue one immediately after the finalization hearing, and require only the original birth certificate and the Decree of Adoption. It was not necessary to wait for your amended birth certificate. More recently, however, they have been requiring the Decree of Adoption and the amended birth certificate, although it is uncertain if they will continue this policy.

Even if the birth mother initiated the Social Security card process and a number has been assigned for your child, and only the name change remains to be done in Social Security Administration records, some adoptive parents elect to request a completely new Social Security number for the child, perhaps fearing potential misuse by others in possession of the child's Social Security number prior to the child's completed adoption.

Obtaining a Passport

Once the adoption is finalized, a passport can easily be obtained by awaiting for the child's amended birth certificate, as it names you as the child's mother/father. However, if you need a passport prior to receipt of the amended birth certificate, but subsequent to the granting of the adoption (as the amended birth certificate can take many months to be prepared and available), you can obtain a birth certificate on the child's behalf with the initial birth certificate and the court order granting the adoption.

If you need to travel with the child prior to finalization, you will first need the approval of the supervising agency or government entity overseeing the adoption before removing the child from the country. Additionally, the passport office will require a court order granting permission for the adoptive parents to apply for a passport on the child's behalf.

Taxes, Tax Credits and Dependents

You have the right to name your child as a dependent on your tax forms as soon as you have lawful physically custody. You don't need to wait until the adoption is granted. You will not have a Social Security card number at this early point, however, so the Internal Revenue Service can issue a Temporary Tax Identification Number for your child, to be used in place of a Social Security number on your return.

You are additionally eligible for a federal Adoption Tax Credit as an adoptive parent, and it's substantial. It may even pay for your entire adoption. For adoptions finalized in 2012, if your modified adjusted gross income is $189,710 or less, you are eligible for a $12,650 tax credit per adopted child. (It's per child, so this means a $25,300 tax credit for twins.) Your income can actually go up to $229,710, but the tax credit decreases proportionally when the income exceeds $189,710. Be aware that a *credit* is much better than a mere *deduction*. An example of a deduction would be the interest payment on your home mortgage. The interest is deducted from your gross income, reducing the net income on which you pay taxes. A credit is a dollar for dollar elimination of taxes owed, like giving you back up to $12,650. If you can't use the full credit in the year in which you adopt because you don't have that much tax liability, it can be carried over for several years until fully used.

In both domestic and international adoptions, the credit is only for actual expenses you incurred. So if your adoption only cost $5,500, you could only claim a tax credit of that amount. If you adopted a single child and your expenses were $18,000, you could claim the full $12,650 credit, but would not be able to claim it for the amount in excess. Your adoption expenses are eligible as long as they were lawful expenses, so the traditional expenses we've discussed (medical, living, attorney or agency fees) all qualify. Tax issues are complicated, however, so every adoptive parent should consult a tax professional. You might find that your state even has an additional state tax credit, or other tax benefit.

The tax credit also exists in special-needs adoptions. There is one huge difference, however. The $12,650 amount stays the same, but you don't need to show that you actually incurred any expenses. So if your special-needs adoption cost only $500 (since many services may have been provided to you for free or a discounted fee), you are still eligible for the $12,650 tax credit. You will want to make sure your child qualifies as "special-needs" before you count on receiving the credit, so check with your agency or special-needs exchange. Congress determines each year if the tax credit will continue for the following year, and the amount of the credit, and the eligible income requirements.

Post-Birth Agreements

As discussed in more detail earlier, some adoptions are open. Many states provide that the birth mother or father can put an agreement with the adoptive parents in writing, and file the document with the court. These agreements might call for the annual sending of pictures or letters, phone calls or personal contact. These contracts are generally binding, unless their enforcement would no longer serve the best interests of the child.

Even in states where the agreements are specifically permitted, it is interesting that many birth and adoptive parents elect not to use them. Many seem to feel, upon getting to know and trusting each other, that no such formal contract is required. They seem to view this as some might a pre-marital agreement, feeling it taints their relationship. In adoption, however, a birth parent is very dependent upon adoptive parents keeping their promises, so you should never feel insulted if a birth mother indicates she'd like your promises in writing. After all, she's given you her promise in writing (the consent to adoption) that the child is yours forever. Receiving a promise in return is not asking too much. Even in states that don't have laws specifically permitting post-birth adoption agreements, they may be deemed enforceable, so you want to make sure that any promises you are asked to make are those you feel comfortable with.

Last Will and Testament

Once your child is adopted, he or she is your heir, just as if born to you. Accordingly, completing your adoption is an excellent time to update your will, or to write one if you don't yet have one. Separate from financial issues, however, is the welfare of your child if you and your spouse were to both die. You will want to consider who shall be the child's guardian, and who would manage your estate to best provide for your child's future.

CHAPTER 14

SURROGACY

This is a book on adoption. To adequately discuss the issue of surrogacy would take a book in itself, and indeed, many books exist on the subject. Accordingly, this chapter is to just give you a basic primer of how surrogacy works, the different types available, and some basic pros and cons. This brief overview might help you compare it to adoption if you are considering it as one of your family building options. There are two types of surrogacy: traditional and gestational.

Traditional Surrogacy

In traditional surrogacy, the surrogate is artificially inseminated, and she carries the child to term. It is her own egg that is fertilized, so she is the biological mother of the child. The sperm is that of the intended father (let's think of him as the adoptive father) or a sperm donor. In most states, after she releases the child to the intended parents, a step-parent adoption occurs, as the intended/adoptive father is the biological father, and his wife is the adopting parent. At this point any parental rights of the surrogate would end. Although this method was initially popular, with the advancement of new medical procedures, few surrogacies are now of the traditional variety.

Gestational Surrogacy

In gestational surrogacy, the surrogate is implanted with an embryo via in vitro fertilization. The embryo is composed of the fertilized egg of the intended mother or egg donor. The egg was fertilized by the sperm of the intended/adoptive father or a sperm donor. In a gestational surrogacy, the surrogate is not genetically related to the child she is carrying. In most states, her rights as the birthing mother (and her husband's if applicable) are usually terminated in the fifth to eight month of the pregnancy via a court adjudication of parentage. This gives rights to the intended parents upon the birth of the child, based upon the contract terms and the decisions reached by the parties prior to the pregnancy taking place. The vast majority of surrogacies are gestational.

The Role of the Attorney

Just as attorneys are deemed advisable in adoption, it is the same in surrogacy. You will want someone to screen potential surrogates to confirm she appear emotionally able to fulfill the role as surrogate, and that her health background is appropriate, particularly if you are planning a traditional surrogacy (since it is her egg). Contracts will be required to not only define her (and your) duties and fees, but prescribe what will happen if things don't go as planned, such as a miscarriage. If she is married, her husband will have rights in most states, and that issue must be addressed. Many members of the American Academy of Adoption Attorneys also practice in the field of assisted reproduction. Although their bios in Chapter 15 do not include information on surrogacy experience, the AAAA website (adoptionattorneys.org) provides which members offer services in this field.

Costs

Surrogacy is normally quite a bit more expensive than adoption. There are two reasons for this. One is the medical costs involved in the surrogacy. The other is the fees of the surrogate. Unlike adoption, where a birth mother can't receive any gain (other than her pregnancy-related costs like food and rent), a surrogate can legally be paid a fee in most states. In a traditional surrogacy, the medical fees involved in the insemination, program fees, and the fees of the surrogate herself will usually total from $35,000 to $60,000. A gestational surrogacy will usually cost an additional $6,000 to $22,000 for the medical fees involved in the in vitro fertilization.

Risks and Issues

Just as in adoption, surrogacy involves risks. A surrogate might fail to become pregnant, meaning the medical costs are for naught. Her contracted fee, and that of the program which is overseeing the surrogacy, will be reduced, but some compensation will be required. If the pregnancy is initially successful but there is a miscarriage, she might be owed a larger portion of her fee, or her full fee. The same is true regarding the program overseeing the surrogacy.

There are also legal risks. In a traditional surrogacy, since the surrogate is the biological mother, she may seek to void the contract and seek to maintain her parental rights. Her rights will be particularly strong in states where there is no specific authorization for surrogacy contracts. Even in gestational surrogacy, where she has no biological connection with the child, she might seek to establish custody or visitation. In these cases the courts are most likely to uphold the initial intent of the parties as set down in the contract, usually benefiting the intended/adoptive parents. For this reason, gestational surrogacy is seen as having few legal risks.

There are some very troubling issues which can occur in surrogacy. One term you will see in surrogacy contracts is "selective reduction." This means if the pregnancy is determined to be multiple births (not uncommon with fertility drugs and the in vitro process) the intended/adoptive parents may have the legal right in their contract to terminate the viability of the other births. "Selective termination" is another issue, faced when the expected baby is seen to have a serious medical problem, such as Down's Syndrome, giving them the right to terminate the pregnancy. Conflicts over such issues keep some adoption attorneys and agencies from crossing into the field of surrogacy.

Although the cost is higher, and the risk is more than doubled in surrogacy (the difficulty in achieving the pregnancy to even start the surrogacy/adoption, and risks of the surrogacy changing her mind), many people continue to pursue surrogacy. The typical reason is the intended parents want the child to be fully or half their biological child.

CHAPTER 15

STATE-BY-STATE REVIEW

Each state has different laws and procedures. You will want to review the laws for your home state, and all states in which you are considering working. Provided is information about each state's unique adoption laws and procedures, a listing of American Academy of Adoption Attorney members and their biographies, as well as contact information for the state's adoption office and adoption exchange (waiting children).

State Adoption Office Information

The following is listed for every state:

- The state office overseeing adoption within the state (including the address, phone number, website address and email address for general information requests). The primary source for adoption state office information presented is the U.S. Department of Health.
- The state adoption exchange. (In most cases this will be a website, permitting online viewing of waiting and special-needs children within the state. Please see Appendix A for national and regional exchanges.)

Summary of State Laws and Procedures

Many key legal issues are explored individually for each state. The information was compiled via independent research of state statutes and data provided by attorneys practicing within each state. Be aware that laws can change without notice, be interpreted differently, or applied by individual judges or authorities in different ways. Consultation with an attorney or licensed agency is necessary before initiating an adoption. The following information is provided for each state and the District of Columbia, allowing you to see the pros and cons of each state, and determine which states might be right for you:

- Are both independent and agency adoptions permitted?
- Is a pre-placement home study required for an independent adoption?
- Who does the home study in an independent adoption?
- What are the typical costs of independent and agency adoption home studies?
- Which type of adoption is more popular within that state? Independent or agency?
- Who can file a Petition for Adoption within the state? Is it only residents, or can non-residents do so? (The latter is indicated when the legal summary indicates the Petition can be filed within the state if the baby is born there, the birth mother lives there, or the agency supervising the placement is located there.)
- How open are most newborn adoptions?
- Are the adoptive parents permitted to help with the birth mother's pregnancy-related assistance, and if so, for what specific items?
- Can adoptive parents advertise for a birth mother?
- When does the birth mother sign her consent?
- Who must witness the consent?
- How soon after birth may the birth mother sign the consent?
- Does she have a set period in which to withdraw her consent, and if so, for how long and with what legal burden?
- Is the consent process different within for independent and agency adoptions?

- If the birth mother is a minor does she need the consent of a parent or a guardian ad litem. (This information will only be listed if it is required, so its absence means there is no such requirement.)
- What are the birth father's rights? Is there a putative birth father registry or is separate notice required? Only putative (typically this means non-marital fathers) are discussed as this is the most common type of birth father in adoption and their rights vary tremendously state-by-state. Men who are married to the birth mother (or who have otherwise escalated their rights, such as where they were living with and supporting an existing child) generally have rights equal to the birth mother, meaning their consent is normally required.
- How quickly is the baby released from the hospital to the adoptive parents, and what documents or procedures are required? Is an intermediary needed?
- How long does it take after the baby's placement before the final hearing is set to finalize the adoption?
- Must the adoptive parents and the baby appear in court for the final hearing granting the adoption?

Adoption Attorneys

Only attorneys who are members of the American Academy of Adoption Attorneys (over 300 members nationwide, discussed in Chapter 3) are listed. Each member was sent a detailed questionnaire about their law practice and the information provided is a summary of their replies. To find the most up-to-date contact information for AAAA members, as well as see members' photographs, you may wish to visit the American Academy of Adoption Attorney's website: www.adoptionattorneys.org.

Some attorneys' biographies are shorter than others, perhaps indicating the author did not receive their questionnaire, the attorney did not complete it fully, or completed one for a previous book by the author, in which case previously provided data was used.

Private Adoption Agencies

To view a listing of private adoption agencies for each state (including their address, telephone and fax number, website and email address) please visit adoption101.com and its Agency Adoption page.

*   *   *   *   *

ALABAMA

State Adoption Office: Alabama Department of Human Resources; PO Box 30400; Montgomery, AL 36130-4000; Phone: (334) 242-8112; http://www.dhr.state.al.us/page.asp?pageid=306

State Adoption Exchange: Families 4 Alabama's Kids; Toll-Free: (866) 425-5437; fwilson@dhr.state.al.us; http://www.dhr.state.al.us/Page.asp?pageid=483

State laws and procedures:

General Information. Alabama permits both independent and agency adoption. Approximately 60% of Alabama's infant adoptions are completed via independent adoption; 40% via agencies. Advertising is permitted. To file a Petition for Adoption within Alabama either the adoptive parents or the child to be adopted must be born there (so non-resident adoption is possible). Normally, adoptions are finalized three months after the child is placed with the adoptive parents.

Independent Adoption. A pre-placement home study of the adoptive parents is normally required before a child may be placed in their home, although a court has the authority in some circumstances to allow a child to be placed before the home study is completed. The home study may be conducted by the state adoption office, a licensed adoption agency or an individual licensed by the state as a private independent practitioner (usually a licensed social worker). The fee for the state office is $300. Private agency home studies are typically less than $1,500.

The birth mother and the adoptive parents are not required by law to meet and share identities, although most elect to do so voluntarily. The adoptive parents are permitted to assist the birth mother with pregnancy-related expenses, such as medical, legal and living costs. The child may be placed with the adoptive parents directly upon his or her release from the hospital. Most hospitals have a special form for the birth mother to sign allowing the child's release to the adoptive parents. Normally no court order is required.

The birth mother may sign her consent to the adoption before or after the birth. If signed before the birth it must be signed before a probate judge. If signed after the birth it may be witnessed by a probate judge, a representative of a licensed adoption agency or a notary public. Most birth mothers sign their consents before, or within a few days after, the birth. If the birth mother is under the age of 19 she must be appointed a guardian ad litem before she signs her consent, to be sure she understands her rights. This individual is usually an attorney whose fees, usually paid by the adoptive parents, average $200.

There is a five-day period after the consent is signed, or the birth occurs, whichever is later, in which the birth mother has the automatic right to withdraw her consent. After the five days have elapsed, but within 14 days of the signing or the birth (whichever occurs first), the consent can only be withdrawn by the birth mother proving to a court the child's best interests would be served by being removed from the adoptive parents. After the 14-day period has elapsed, the consent can only be withdrawn upon proof of fraud, duress or legal mistake.

Alabama has a putative birth father registry. Putative birth fathers are required to register no later than 30 days post-birth or their consent is implied. The identity of men listed with the registry can only be released by court order. Many counties additionally require notice to a putative birth father if known by the birth mother, even if he does not file with the registry. If the putative birth father objects, the court will look at his behavior during the pregnancy and see if he abandoned his responsibilities toward the mother/fetus and if the best interests of the child will be served by adoption.

Agency Adoption. There is no difference regarding the process in which a birth mother signs her consent to adoption in an independent or agency adoption. The information provided above regarding

independent adoption (e.g. when it can be signed, before whom, legal burden to seek to withdraw a signed consent, requirement for guardian ad litem) is identical regarding agency adoption.

Some agencies within Alabama agree to do identified adoptions. Some agencies will also agree to make immediate hospital "at risk" placements.

American Academy of Adoption Attorney members:

David Broome; 155 Monroe St., P.O. Box 1944, Mobile, AL 36633 (251) 432-9933 ● d.broome@adoptionattorneys.org
A graduate of the University of Alabama School of Law, he has been practicing law since 1977.

Bryant "Drew" Whitmire, Jr.; 215 Richard Arrington Jr. Blvd. N, #501, Birmingham, AL 35203; Tel: (205) 324-6631 ● dwhitm@bellsouth.net
A graduate of the University of Alabama School of Law, he has been practicing law since 1972. He estimates he has completed 160 adoptions last year (75 independent; 75 agency; 10 intercountry readopts).His clients locate their own birth mother. He accepts contested cases.

ALASKA

State Adoption Office: Alaska Department of Health and Social Services; Office of Children's Services; 350 Main Street, 4th Floor; PO Box 110630; Juneau, AK 99811-0630; Phone: (907) 465-2145; http://www.hss.state.ak.us/ocs/Adoptions/default.htm

State Adoption Exchange: Alaska Adoption Exchange; Phone: (206) 441-6822; http://www.akae.org/

State laws and procedures:

General Information.   Alaska permits both independent and agency adoption. Approximately 50% of Alaska's infant adoptions are completed via independent adoption; 50% via agencies. Advertising is permitted. To file a Petition for Adoption within Alaska either the adopting parents, or the child being adopted, must reside there (typically defined as being born there in a newborn adoption), or the agency having custody must be located there (so non-resident adoption is possible). Normally, adoptions are finalized approximately three to six months after the child is placed in the adoptive parents' custody. The adoptive parents and the child being adopted are required to appear at the final court hearing, but this can often be done telephonically.

Independent Adoption. A pre-placement home study of the adoptive parents is required before a child may be placed in their home, although a judge has discretion to waive this requirement. The pre and post-placement home study is done by a licensed social worker at a usual fee of approximately $750.

The birth mother and adoptive parents are not required by law to meet and share identities, although some do so voluntarily. The adoptive parents are permitted to assist the birth mother with pregnancy-related medical, legal and living expenses. The child may be placed with the adoptive parents directly upon his or her release from the hospital, although each hospital has its own forms and policies.

The birth mother signs a consent to adoption, which can be witnessed by either a judge or a notary public, and can be signed anytime after birth. Once signed, she has ten days thereafter with the automatic right to withdraw it. After the initial ten days have elapsed, she can only withdraw it by proving to a court the child's best interests would be served by being removed from the adoptive parents. Once the adoption is finalized by a judge, the consent becomes irrevocable.

Alaska has no putative birth father registry. Notice must be given to putative fathers unless they can't be found. The notice is a twenty day notice of the final adoption hearing. Mere proof of his paternity is often enough to block an adoption, if that is the birth father's desire.

Agency Adoption.   The information provided above regarding independent adoption is identical regarding agency adoption with the exception of the birth mother's consent. In an agency adoption she signs a *relinquishment*. Once signed, she has ten days with the automatic right to withdraw it. Once the ten days have elapsed, it is irrevocable. The relinquishment must be witnessed by a judge.

Some agencies within Alaska agree to do identified adoptions. Few agencies agree to make immediate hospital "at risk" placements.

American Academy of Adoption Attorney members:

Robert B. Flint; 745 W.4th Avenue, Suite 200, Anchorage, AK 99501 Tel: (907) 771-8300 ● r.flint@adoptionattorneys.org
A graduate of the Georgetown University School of Law, he began practicing law in 1963.

ARIZONA

State Adoption Office: Arizona Department of Economic Security; Administration for Children, Youth and Families; PO Box 6123 - 940A; Phoenix, AZ 85007; Phone: (602) 542-5499; http://www.de.state.az.us/dcyf/adoption/default.asp
State Adoption Exchange: Arizona Department of Economic Security; PO Box 17951; Tucson, AZ 85731; Phone: (520) 327-3324; http://www.de.state.az.us/dcyf/adoption/meet.asp

State laws and procedures:

General Information. Arizona permits both independent and agency adoption. Approximately 65% of Arizona's infant adoptions are completed through independent adoption; 35% via agencies. Advertising is permitted. To file a Petition for Adoption in Arizona the adoptive parents must be residents of the state, generally for at least 90 days. Normally, adoptions are finalized in court within three months if the child was under the age of six months when the Petition for Adoption was filed, otherwise the finalization is usually in six months. The adoptive parents and the child being adopted are required to appear at the final court hearing.

Independent Adoption. A pre-placement home study of the adoptive parents, resulting in "certification" of the adoptive parents, is usually

216

required before a child is placed in the adoptive parents' home. In some cases where there is no certification, a placement with the adoptive parents may be made, provided a petition for temporary custody order is filed with 5 days of the placement (and then a hearing must then be held within 10 days). The home study may be conducted by the state adoption office or a licensed private agency. The cost of the home study varies. Once the home study is completed it must be filed with the juvenile court, allowing the adoptive parents to be certified as adoptive parents, after which time the adoptive placement can occur. If the adoptive parents were unable to complete a pre-placement home study, they may request a court to issue a temporary custody order, allowing them to have immediate custody of the child and complete their home study after the placement.

The birth mother and adoptive parents are not required by law to meet and share identities, although most do so voluntarily. The adoptive parents are permitted to assist the birth mother with pregnancy-related expenses, but the payment of her living expenses requires advance court approval if the total expenses are in excess of $1,000. The child may be placed with the adoptive parents directly upon release from the hospital, but some hospitals require that the release be made directly to the attorney or agency handling the adoption.

The birth mother may sign her consent to the adoption no sooner than 72 hours after the birth. It must be witnessed by a notary public or two witnesses over the age of 18. Most consents to are signed three to four days after the baby's birth. Once the consent to adoption is signed it is irrevocable, unless the birth mother can prove it was signed based upon fraud, duress or undue influence.

Arizona has a putative birth father registry. Putative birth fathers must be given notice if identified by the birth mother, or if they are listed with the birth father registry. To receive a legal notice the birth father must file with the putative father registry within 30 days of the child's birth. Alternatively, notice can be served on a putative father prior to the birth, and in such cases he has 30 days to file a paternity action. Failure to file a paternity action within 30 days results in the putative father having no legal right to bring a court action and his consent is not required.

Agency Adoption. There is no difference regarding the process in which a birth mother signs her consent to adoption in an independent or agency adoption. The information provided above regarding independent adoption (e.g. when it can be signed, before whom, legal burden to withdraw a signed consent) is identical regarding agency adoption.

Some agencies within Arizona agree to do identified adoptions. Some agencies will also agree to make hospital "at risk" placements.

American Academy of Adoption Attorney members:

Michael J. Herrod; 1221 East Osborn, Suite 105, Phoenix, AZ 85014
Tel: (602) 277-7000 ● m.herrod@adoptionattorneys.org

Philip (Jay) McCarthy; 508 N. Humphreys St., Flagstaff, AZ 86001
(928) 779-4252 ● mccarthyweston.com ● Jay@mccarthyweston.com
A graduate of the Creighton Law School, he has been practicing law since 1980. He estimates he has completed more than 600 adoptions in his caree, and completes 80 annually: 75% independent; 25% agency. He does assist in creating adoptive matches.

Rita A. Meiser; 1440 E. Missouri Ave. #201, Phoenix, AZ 85014
Tel: (602) 650-2473 ● www.meiserlaw.com ●
rmeiser@meiserlaw.com
A graduate of the University of Arizona School of Law, she has been practicing law since 1976. She is an adoptive parent.

Scott E. Myers; 3180 E. Grant Rd. Tucson, AZ 85716
Tel: (520) 327-6041 ● scott@smyerslaw.com
A graduate of the Louisiana State University School of Law, he has been practicing law since 1975. He accepts contested adoption cases.

Kathryn Pidgeon; 3131 E. Camelback Rd, #200, Phoenix AZ 85016
Tel: (602) 522-8700 ● k.pidgeon@adoptionattorneys.org
A graduate of the University of Miami, she has been practicing law since 1989..

Daniel I. Ziskin; P.O. Box 7447, Phoenix, AZ 85011
Tel: (602) 234-2280● dan@adoptz.com

A graduate of the Arizona State University School of Law, he has been practicing law since 1975. He estimates he has completed 1,300 adoptions in his career, and completes 40 annually: . 97% independent; 2% agency; 1% international. He does assist in creating adoptive matches. He is an adoptive parent.

ARKANSAS

State Adoption Office: Arkansas Department of Human Services; PO Box 2620; Little Rock, AR 72203; Phone: (501) 682-9273; http://www.state.ar.us

State Adoption Exchange: Arkansas Adoption Resource Exchange; PO Box 1437; Slot S565; Little Rock, AR 72203-1437; Phone: (501) 682-8959; linda.dismuke@arkansas.gov; http://www.accessarkansas.org

State laws and procedures:

General Information. Arkansas permits both independent and agency adoption. Approximately 40% of Arkansas' infant adoptions are completed via independent adoption; 60% via agencies. Advertising is permitted but some newspapers place restrictions on whom may place ads. To file a Petition for Adoption within Arkansas either the adopting parents, or the birth mother or legal father of the child being placed for adoption, must be residents of the state (usually at least 4 months pre-birth for a birth parent). This makes non-resident adoption possible in many instances. If it is an agency adoption the Petition can also be filed there if the adoption agency having custody of the child is located in Arkansas. Normally, adoptions are finalized approximately 11-14 days after the child's placement with the adoptive parents. The adopting parents are required to appear in court for the final hearing.

Independent Adoption. A pre-placement home study of the adoptive parents is not technically required before a child is placed in their home, but most all judges will require one. To do the home study, the state adoption office's maximum fee is $200, but its services are usually limited to finding homes for children who are wards of the state. Fees for home studies by private agencies and social workers average $600. If a pre-placement home study was done, the court will usually waive any post-placement home study requirement (not surprising when considering Arkansas finalizes its adoptions as soon as 11 days after birth).

The birth mother and the adoptive parents are not required by law to meet and share identities, although most do so and share at least first names voluntarily. The adoptive parents are permitted to assist the birth mother with pregnancy-related medical, legal and living expenses. The child may be placed with the adoptive parents directly upon his or her discharge from the hospital. Each hospital has different policies regarding releasing the child, however. Most require either a court order authorizing the release, a copy of the birth mother's consent to the adoption, or a similar formal authorization to release the child.

The birth mother may sign her consent any time after the birth. It is witnessed by a judge or notary public. If the birth mother is under the age of 18 she must be appointed a guardian ad litem prior to her signing of the consent to be sure she understands her rights. Once the consent is signed the birth mother has ten days to revoke the consent via affidavit with the court with no legal burden.

Arkansas has a putative birth father registry. Notice is only given to birth fathers who file with the registry prior to the filing of the Petition for Adoption. Putative birth fathers who register must additionally show they established a significant relationship with the child.

Agency Adoption. There is no difference regarding the process in which a birth mother signs her consent to adoption in an independent or agency adoption. The information provided above regarding independent adoption (e.g. when the consent can be signed, legal burden to withdraw a signed consent) is identical regarding agency adoption, although the consent may be witnessed by a representative of the adoption agency and a notary.

Some agencies agree to do identified adoptions. Some agencies also agree to make immediate hospital "at risk" placements.

American Academy of Adoption Attorney members:

Sandra Bradshaw; 207½ Main St; P.O. Box 249, Crossett, AR 71635
Tel: (870) 364-4300 • s.bradshaw@adoptionattorneys.org
A graduate of the University of Mississippi School of Law, she has been practicing law since 1992.

Eugene T. Kelley; 303 West Walnut Street, Rogers, AR 72757
Tel: (479) 636-1051 • newworldawaits.com
A graduate of the University of Arkansas School of Law, he has been practicing law since 1968.

Kaye H. McLeod; 210 Linwood Court, Little Rock, AR 72205
Tel: (501) 663-6224 • k.mcleod@adoptionattorneys.org
A graduate of the University of Arkansas School of Law, she has been practicing law since 1981. She estimates she has completed more than 1,600 adoptions in her career, and completes 60 annually: 90% independent; 5% agency; 5% intercountry. She received the Congressional Angel in Adoption Award in 2002.

Keith H. Morrison; 1882 North Starr Drive, Fayetteville, AR 72701
Tel: (479) 521-5820 • h.morrison@adoptionattorneys.org

CALIFORNIA

State Adoption Office: California Department of Social Services; Child and Youth Permanency Branch; 744 P Street -- MS 19-69; Sacramento, CA 95814; Phone: (916) 651-7464; http://www.childsworld.ca.gov

State Adoption Exchange: California Kids Connection; Phone: (510) 272-0204; kidsconnection@familybuilders.org; http://www.CAKidsConnection.com

State law and procedures:

General Information. California permits both independent and agency adoption. Approximately 85% of California's infant adoptions are completed via independent adoption; 15% via agencies. Advertising is permitted only by licensed adoption agencies. To file a Petition for Adoption in California the adopting parents must reside there or the baby must be born there (making non-resident adoption available). Normally, adoptions are finalized 7 to 10 months after the placement of the child with the adoptive parents. The adopting parents and child being adopted are required to appear in court for the final hearing, although a court may waive their appearance for good cause.

Independent Adoption. A pre-placement home study of the adoptive parents is not required before a child is placed in their home. It may be done voluntarily, however, and if so is done by a licensed private adoption agency, and it is called an Independent Adoption Pre-Assessment. The post-placement home study may be conducted by the State Department of Social Services or a county adoption agency designated by the Department of Social Services to perform independent adoption services for that county. The state fee for the home study is $4,500. (However, if an Independent Adoption Pre-Assessment was completed prior to the minor's placement, the fee is reduced to $1,550.)

The birth mother is required by law to personally select the adoptive parents with full sharing of identities. Although it is not required by law that they meet in person, this is done in virtually all adoptions. The adoptive parents are permitted to assist the birth mother with pregnancy-related legal, medical, counseling and living expenses. The child may be placed with the adoptive parents directly from the hospital upon the birth mother's signature on a standard hospital form entitled the Health Facility Minor Release.

The birth mother must receive advice and information, called an Advisement of Rights, from a licensed social worker approved by the state as an Adoption Services Provider (often referred to as an ASP), or a licensed adoption agency acting as an ASP, at least ten days before she signs her consent to adoption. The consent form is called the Adoption Placement Agreement, which is also signed by the adoptive parents, and outlines the rights and duties of each party. It may only be signed after the birth mother's medical discharge from the hospital. The Adoption Services Provider then sends the birth mother's consent and related documents to the State Department of

Social Services (or its designated county entity) which will assign an adoption caseworker who will oversee the remainder of the adoption.

The Adoption Placement Agreement is normally signed hours or days after the hospital discharge. However, it is not an effective forfeiture of rights by the birth mother until one of two events occur, whichever occurs first: 1) The birth mother can sign a Waiver of Right to Revoke Consent in the presence of the State Department of Social Services or designated county agency anytime after signing the Adoption Placement Agreement (or a simpler option is to have it witnessed by the ASP, which is permitted if the birth mother was represented by independent counsel - and in either case the Waiver of Right to Revoke Consent becomes irrevocable the next business day); or 2) if the birth mother does not elect to sign a Waiver of Right to Revoke Consent, her consent to adoption becomes permanent and irrevocable automatically on the 31st day after the signing of the Adoption Placement Agreement.

California does not have a putative birth father registry. "Alleged" birth fathers (which generally speaking means non-marital birth fathers and those who are not listed on the birth certificate - usually referred to in other states as "putative" fathers) must be given notice of alleged paternity and adoption, unless they can't be located with due diligence. If an alleged birth father objects in court, he must prove he acted responsibly to meet the birth mother's needs, and also that he objected promptly to the adoption. If he can establish both those things, he must be proven "unfit" to terminate his rights. If he can't prove he did both these things, the adoptive parents must only prove the child's best interests are served by being with them, rather than the birth father. Alleged birth fathers wishing to cooperate may sign either a *Waiver of Notice* or *Denial of Paternity* before the birth, witnessed by a notary public, and either form can be filed with the court post-birth and result in the termination of his parental rights.

Agency Adoption. The birth mother may sign a consent to adoption, called a "relinquishment" in agency adoptions, anytime after her hospital discharge. It must be witnessed by a representative of a licensed adoption agency. Once the relinquishment it signed and satisfactorily filed with and acknowledged by the State Department of Social Services, the relinquishment is irrevocable, except when revoked with the agreement of the adoption agency, or proof of fraud or duress. A birth mother may request the adoption agency to delay the effective date of her signed relinquishment for a period, usually up to 30 days, in which case it can be withdrawn at will within the stated time. Most other laws and procedures are the same as in independent adoption.

Virtually all agencies agree to do identified adoptions. Most will also make "at risk" placements directly to the adoptive parents from the hospital.

American Academy of Adoption Attorney members:

G. Darlene Anderson; 127 E. Third Ave. #202, Escondido, CA 92025
Tel: (760) 743-4700 ● g.anderson@adoptionattorneys.org

David H. Baum; 16255 Ventura Blvd., Suite 704, Encino, CA 91436
Tel: (818) 501-8355 ● adoptlaw.com ● adoptlaw@ix.netcom.com
A graduate of the Loyola School of Law, he has been practicing law since 1978. He estimates he has completed 1,000 adoptions in his career and completes 60 annually: 80% independent; 20% agency. He does assist in creating adoptive matches. He is an adoptive parent and past president of the Academy of California Adoption Lawyers.

Timothy J. Blied; 400 N. Tustin Avenue, #209, Santa Ana, CA 92705
Tel: (949) 863-0200 ● sbsmlaw.com ● admin@sbsmlaw.com
A graduate of the Pepperdine University School of Law, he has been practicing law since 1979. He is an adoptive parent.

D. Durand Cook; 10170 Culver Boulevard, Culver City, CA 90232
Tel: (323) 655-2601 ● adoption-option.com
A graduate of California Western School of Law, he has been practicing law since 1970.

Douglas Donnelly; 1332 Santa Barbara St, Santa Barbara, CA 93101
Tel: (805) 962-0988 ● Adoptionlawfirm.com ●
Doug@adoptionlawfirm.com
A graduate of the Loyola University of Los Angeles, he has been practicing law since 1977. He estimates he has completed more than 2,000 adoptions in his career, and completes 66 annually: 90% independent; 10% agency. He does assist in creating adoptive

matches. He is an adoptive parent and past president of the Academy of California Adoption Lawyers.

Alison Foster Davis; 1120 Tully Rd. Modesto, CA 95350
Tel: (209) 524-8844 ● fcadoptions.org
A graduate of the University of the Pacific, McGeorge School of Law, she has been practicing law since 1992. She is the executive director of an adoption agency. She received the Congressional Angel in Adoption award in 2010.

Jane A. Gorman; 80 Stone Pine Rd., #101 Half Moon Bay, CA 94019; Tel: (650) 560-0123 ● jagorman@aol.com
A graduate of the Western State School of Law, she has been practicing law since 1986. She limits her practice to contested adoption litigation and has been involved in more than 2,000 such cases. She is the past president of both the Academy of California Adoption Lawyers and American Academy of Adoption Attorneys.

Marc Gradstein; 80 Stone Pine Rd., #101, Half Moon Bay, CA 94019; Tel: (650) 560-0123 ● PlaceBaby4Adoption.com
A graduate of the New York University School of Law, he has been practicing law since 1973.

Randall B. Hicks; 7177 Brockton Ave, #218, Riverside, CA 92506
Tel: (951) 787-8300 ● randallhicks.com ● ranhicks@aol.com
A graduate of Pepperdine University School of Law, he has been practicing law since 1986. He estimates he has completed more than 1,000 adoptions in his career, and last year completed approximately 35, most of them newborn placements in domestic adoptions. He reports 90% of his clients find a birth mother through his office; 10% find their own birth mother. He is the author of several "how to" adoption books.

Allen Hultquist; 28581 Old Town Front St. #212, Temecula, CA 92590; Tel: (951) 302-7777 ● AdoptinginCalifornia.com ● achadopt@linkline.com
A graduate of the Western State University College of Law of San Diego, he has been practicing law since 1981. He estimates he has completed 1,500 adoptions in his career and completes 45 annually:

90% independent; 10% agency. He assists in creating adoptive matches.

Joy L. Kolender; 11348 Monticook Court, San Diego, CA 92127
Tel: (858) 485-9823 ● adoptionatty@aol.com
A graduate of the University of San Diego School of Law, she has been practicing law since 1984. She estimates she has completed 700 adoptions in her career and completes 50 annually: 98% independent, 2% agency. She reports 4% of her clients find a birth mother through her office; 96% find their own birth mother. She is an adoptive parent.

Karen R. Lane; 100 Wilshire Bl. #2075, Santa Monica, CA 90401
Tel: (310) 393-9802 ● klane-adopt.com ● karenrlane@sbcglobal.net
She has been practicing law since 1979..

Steven Lazarus; 4640 Admiralty Way #500, Marina Del Ray, CA 90292; Tel: (310) 496-5758 ● swlfamilyformationlaw.com ●
s.lazarus@adoptionattorneys.org

Shannon M. Matteson; 3190 Old Tunnel Road, Lafayette, CA 94549
Tel: (925) 297-4626 ● familyformation.com ●
s.matteson@adoptionattorneys.org

Diane Michelsen; 3190 Old Tunnel Rd., Lafayette, CA 94549
Tel: (925) 945-1880 ● familyformation.com ●
diane@familyformation.com
A graduate of Golden Gate University School of Law, she has been practicing law since 1980. She completes approximately 50 adoptions annually and assists in creating adoptive matches. She is a past president of the American Academy of Adoption Attorneys.

Kristine Pogalies; 3033 Fifth Ave, Suite 430, San Diego, CA 92103
Tel: (619) 231-2085 ● kpogalies@stocksfentin.com
A graduate of Thomas Jefferson School of Law, she has been practicing law since 1993. She estimates she has completed 250 adoptions in her career and completes 20 annually: 98% independent; 2% agency. She does assist in creating adoptive matches.

David Radis; 1801 Century Park East, 24th Fl, Los Angeles, CA 90067
Tel: (310) 552-0536 ● radis-adopt.com ● radis@radis-adopt.com
A graduate of the Southwestern School of Law, he has been practicing law since 1974. He estimates he has completed more than 3,000 adoptions in his career and completes 45 annually: 50% independent, 50% agency. He does assist in creating adoptive matches.

Susan Romer; 829 Sonoma Avenue, Santa Rosa, CA 95404
Tel: (415) 643-4523 ● adamsromer@aol.com
A graduate of the Golden Gate University School of Law, she has been practicing law since 1993.

Jed Somit; 1970 Broadway, Suite 625, Oakland, CA 94612
Tel: (510) 839-3215 ● jedsomit.com ● j.somit@adoptionattorneys.org
A graduate of Boalt Hall School of Law, he has been practicing law since 1976. His practice concentrates on difficult, unusual, and contested adoptions and adoption-related legal issues.

Janis K. Stocks; 3033 Fifth Avenue, Suite 430, San Diego, CA 92101
Tel: (619) 231-2025 ● jstocks@stocksfentin.com

Robert R. Walmsley; 120 El Paseo, Santa Barbara, CA 93101,
Tel: (805) 845-7700 ● jarettewalmsley.com ●
r.walmsley@adoptionattorneys.org
A graduate of Whittier College School of Law, he has been practicing law since 1987.

Felice A. Webster; 4525 Wilshire Bl., #201, Los Angeles, CA 90010
Tel: (323) 664-5600 ● felicewebster.com ●
f.webster@adoptionattorneys.org
A graduate of Loyola Law School, she has been practicing law since 1974. She estimates she completes 70 adoptions annually: 40% independent; 60% agency. She assists in creating adoptive matches.

Marc Widelock; 1801 Oak St., P.O. Box 21270; Bakersfield, CA 93390; Tel: (661) 587-3110 ● thestork.com ● widelock@thestork.com
A graduate of Western State University, he has been practicing law since 1986. He estimates he has completed more than 1,000 adoptions

in his career. Approximately 90% of his practice consists of adoptions and of those 95% are independent and 5% agency. He does assist in creating adoptive matches.

Nanci R. Worcester; 1253 High Street, Auburn, CA 95603
Tel: (530) 888-1311 ● adoption-center.com ●
adopt@adoption-center.com
A graduate of Southwestern School of Law, she has been practicing law since 1981. She estimates she has completed more than 2,000 adoptions in her career and completes 50 annually: 90% independent; 10% agency. She does assist in creating adoptive matches. She is an adoptive parent.

Ted Youmans; 505 S. Villa Real Dr. #112, Anaheim Hills, CA 92807
Tel: (714) 408-2900 ● center4familybuilding.com ●
t.youmans@adoptionattorneys.org
A graduate of Whittier School of Law, hehas been practicing since 1987. He estimates he completes 40 adoptions annually; 80% independent; 20% agency. He does assist in creating adoptive matches.

COLORADO

State Adoption Office: Colorado Department of Human Services (CDHS); 1575 Sherman Street, 2nd Floor; Denver, CO 80203-1714; Phone: (303) 866-3197; www.changealifeforever.org

State Adoption Exchante: The Adoption Exchange; Phone: (303) 755-4756; kids@adoptex.org ; http://www.adoptex.org

State laws and procedures:

General Information. Colorado permits only agency adoption, although "direct" adoption is permitted where the child is placed with a close family relative (known as "kinship adoption") or when the child has been in the adoptive parents' care for one year or longer, in limited circumstances. Advertising laws regarding adoption are ambiguous but it is generally permitted. To file a Petition for Adoption within Colorado the adopting parents are not required to reside there, as long as the child-placing agency is located there (allowing non-resident adoption). In interstate adoptions, Colorado ICPC charges a $175.00 fee. Normally, adoptions are finalized six months after the placement of the child with the adoptive parents.

A pre-placement home study of the adopting parents is required before a child can be placed in their home. The home study may be performed by the county Department of Human Services (usually where the child is a ward of the state) or a licensed adoption agency. The cost for pre and post-birth home study services is usually about $2,500 when done by private agencies.

Although birth mothers and adoptive parents are not required by law to meet in person, many elect to do so voluntarily. Adopting parents are permitted to assist with pregnancy-related expenses. The child is typically released directly from the hospital to the custody of the adoption agency, which will usually elect to immediately place the child with the adoptive parents. Identified adoptions are common.

There are two methods to terminate a birth mother's parental rights. The traditional method is, rather than sign a consent to adoption, she files a Petition for Relinquishment with the court anytime after the birth. It need only be witnessed by a notary public. A court hearing is then scheduled, usually within several weeks. At the hearing the birth mother confirms to the court that she has received agency relinquishment counseling and it is determined the relinquishment will serve the child's best interests. Once the court has entered the Order of Relinquishment, it can only be revoked within 90 days if proven it was obtained by fraud or duress.

The other method is where a birth mother files an Expedited Petition for Relinquishment, which allows the court to order her parental rights relinquished without the necessity of a court hearing. This cannot be filed until at least four days have elapsed after birth, and the child must be under one year of age. Upon filing, the court is permitted to terminate the birth mother's rights in no more than seven business days. Not all Colorado courts accept Expedited Petitions, however.

Colorado does not have a putative birth father registry. Notice must be given to all putative fathers, unless their identity is unknown, then notice must be by publication. Once notice is given, the birth father has 30 days after birth in which to object. If he elects to object, his rights can be terminated only if proven he failed to establish a substantial and positive relationship with the child, has not promptly taken substantial responsibility, is unfit, or cannot personally assume legal and physical custody. If the birth mother has filed an Expedited Petition for Relinquishment, the birth father's time in which to object is shorted to 20 days from the date of the notice, or the date the relinquishment proceeding is filed, whichever occurs later.

Most agencies within Colorado agree to do identified adoptions. Most agencies also agree to make immediate hospital "at risk" placements directly from the hospital before an Order of Relinquishment is entered by the court.

American Academy of Adoption Attorney members:

W. Thomas Beltz; 729 S. Cascade Ave. Colorado Springs, CO 80903
Tel: (719) 473-4444 ● bestlawllp.com ● wtbeltz@bestlawllp.com
A graduate of the Washington University School of Law, he has been practicing law since 1973.

Virginia Frank; 35715 US Hwy 40, #105(a), Building D, Evergreen, CO 80439; Tel: (303) 756-4673 ●: v.frank@adoptionattorneys.org

Seth A. Grob; 31425 Forestland Drive, Evergreen, CO 80439
Tel: (303) 679-8266 ● sethgrob.com ● s.grob@adoptionattorneys.org
A graduate of the University of California at Los Angeles School of Law, he has been practicing law since 1991. He estimates he has completed 600 adoptions in his career and completes 60 adoptions annually: 40% independent; 50% agency; 10% international. He does not assist in creating adoptive matches. He is a member of the National Association of Counsel for Children.

Daniel A. West; 729 S. Cascade Avenue, Colorado Springs, CO 80903
Tel: (719) 473-4444 ● beltzandwest.com ●
d.west@adoptionattorneys.org

CONNECTICUT

State Adoption Office: Connecticut Department of Children and Families; Bureau of Adoption and Interstate Compact Services; 505 Hudson Street; Hartford, CT 06106; Phone: (860) 550-6467; http://www.state.ct.us

State Adoption Exchange: Connecticut Department of Children and Families
Phone: (860) 550-6578; vera.esdaile@po.state.ct.us; http://www.adoptuskids.org/states/ct/index.aspx

State laws and procedures:

General Information. Connecticut only permits agency adoption. However, identified adoptions are permitted, where the birth mother was located outside the agency, as long as the attorney or intermediary did not receive a fee for locating the birth mother. Accordingly, all adoptions within Connecticut are agency adoptions. Advertising is permitted. To file a Petition for Adoption within Connecticut the adopting parents must reside there. Normally, adoptions are finalized 6 to 12 months after the placement of the child with the adoptive parents. The adoptive parents are required to appear in court for the final hearing, although many courts waive this requirement.

A pre-placement home study of the adopting parents is required before a child can be placed in their home. The home study may be performed by the Department of Children and Youth Services or a licensed adoption agency. The Department of Children Services charges no fee for their home study services, but their services are usually limited to children being adopted who are wards of the state. The fees of private agencies are usually on a sliding scale and for most adoptive parents will be about $10,000.

Birth mothers and adoptive parents are not required by law to meet in person, although some elect to do so voluntarily. Normally, full identities are not disclosed. Adopting parents are permitted to assist with pregnancy-related expenses, such as medical, legal and living costs, although any assistance must be paid through the agency and not directly to the birth mother. Assistance living expenses cannot exceed $1,500 without special court approval. The child may not be released directly to the adoptive parents from the hospital. Instead, the child is released to the custody of the adoption agency. In some cases the agency will elect to immediately place the child with the adoptive parents as an "at risk" placement before the child is permanently free for adoption.

The consent to adoption process is made by the birth mother or the agency filing a voluntary Petition to Terminate Parental Rights with the court. This petition to voluntarily terminate parental rights may not be signed by the birth mother until at least 48 hours have elapsed after the birth and must be witnessed by a notary public. The birth mother later signs a Consent to Termination of Parental Rights, also witnessed by a notary, which is presented in a court hearing approximately four weeks later. The birth mother need not appear at that hearing.

If the birth mother is under the age of 18 a guardian ad litem, usually an attorney, shall be appointed prior to her signing of the consent to termination of parental rights to be sure she understands her legal rights. The consent may also not be signed until the birth mother has received mandatory counseling. The consent cannot be withdrawn once the court has approved the consent and resulting termination of parental rights, except upon proof of fraud or coercion.

Connecticut does not have a putative birth father registry. Notice must be given to any putative father, and if he can't be located, then notice by publication is required. If he elects to object the adoption can't proceed without his consent absent a finding of grounds, such as abandonment.

American Academy of Adoption Attorney members:

Pamela Nolan Dale; 140 Fair Oak Drive, Fairfield, CT 06824
Tel: (203) 319-1440 ● p.dale@adoptionattorneys.org

Donald B. Sherer; 1010 Summer Street, #101, Stamford, CT 06905
Tel: (203) 327-2084 ● d.sherer@adoptionattorneys.org

Janet S. Stulting; One Constitution Plaza, Hartford, CT 06103
Tel: (860) 251-5000 ● jstulting@goodwin.com
A graduate of the University of Connecticut, she has been practicing law since 1980.

DELAWARE

State Adoption Office: Delaware Department of Services for Children, Youth and Their Families (DSCYF); Division of Family Services; 1825 Faulkland Road; Wilmington, DE 19805-1195; Phone: (302) 633-2655; http://www.state.de.us

State Adoption Exchange: Adoption Center of Delaware Valley; Phone: (215) 735-9988; acdv@adopt.org; http://www.acdv.org/waiting_children.html

State laws and procedures:

General Information. Delaware permits only agency adoption, although independent adoption (with no pre-placement home study requirement) is permitted if the child being adopted is a close relative. Identified agency adoption is also permitted. Advertising is only permitted by adoption agencies. To file a Petition for Adoption within Delaware either the adopting parents must reside there or the child must be born there (making non-resident adoption possible). Adoptions are normally finalized six months to one year after the birth or the placement of the child with the adoptive parents. The adopting parents and the child are generally not required to appear in court for the final hearing.

A pre-placement home study of the adopting parents is required before a child may be placed in their home. The home study must be conducted by a licensed adoption agency. The fee varies but may range from $2,000 to $15,000. The birth mother and adoptive parents are not required by law to meet in person and share identities, although some do so voluntarily. Adopting parents are permitted to assist with pregnancy-related expenses, such as medical, legal and living costs, although they must be paid through the agency and not directly to the birth mother. Any direct payments are not permitted.

The child may not be released directly to the adoptive parents from the hospital. Instead, the child is released to the custody of the adoption agency. In some cases the agency will elect to immediately place the child with the adoptive parents as an "at risk" placement where the child is not yet permanently free for adoption. About half of Delaware's infant adoptions are identified adoptions.

The birth mother may sign her consent to adoption anytime after the birth. (A birth father may sign before the birth.) The consent to adoption must be witnessed by a notary public and executed before individuals designated by statute, including a judge or court-approved individual or an attorney not representing the adoptive parents or adoption agency. The consent is signed and filed with the court, in conjunction with a voluntary Petition for Termination of Parental Rights. A birth mother has the right to revoke her consent to adoption within 60 days of the filing of the adoption petition containing her consent, at which time the appropriate state or private agency shall write a report to the court, and the court shall rule as it deems best.

Delaware has a putative birth father registry. A birth father must register either before the birth, or within 30 days after the birth, to be entitled to notice of an action to terminate his rights. Many judges, however, will additionally require notice by publication.

Identified adoptions are common and most agencies will agree to make them. Many agencies will also agree to make immediate hospital "at risk" placements.

American Academy of Adoption Attorney members:

Deborah E. Spivack; 800 King St, 1st Floor, Wilmington, DE, 19801 Tel: (215) 763-5550 ● familybuildinglaw.net ● d.spivack@adoptionattorneys.org

DISTRICT OF COLUMBIA

State Adoption Office: District of Columbia Child and Family Services Agency; 400 6th Street SW; Washington, DC 20024; Phone: (202) 727-4733; www.dhs.dc.gov

State Adoption Exchange: District of Columbia Child and Family Services Agency; Phone: (202) 442-6188; SJackson@cfsa-dc.org

State laws and procedures:

General Information. The District of Columbia permits both independent and agency adoption. Approximately 75% of the District of Columbia's infant adoptions are completed via independent adoption; 25% via agencies. Advertising is permitted. To file a Petition for Adoption in the District of Columbia the adoptive parents must have resided there for one year, or in some circumstances less if they intend to make it their permanent residence. If it is an agency adoption the Petition may also be filed there if the adoption agency having custody of the child is located there (making non-resident adoption possible). Usually, adoptions are finalized approximately six to eight months after the child's placement with the adoptive parents. The adoptive parents and the child are normally required to appear in court for the final hearing.

Independent Adoption. A pre-placement home study is not required of the adoptive parents before a child may be placed in their home. The post-placement home study may be conducted by the state adoption office or a licensed adoption agency. The cost varies. Attorneys are not permitted to "match" birth mothers and adoptive parents.

The adoptive parents and the birth mother are not required by law to meet in person and share identities, although many do so voluntarily. The adoptive parents are permitted to assist the birth mother with pregnancy-related medical and legal expenses. Living expense assistance is not permitted. The child may be released from the hospital upon his or her discharge directly to the adoptive parents, although each hospital has different policies. Some hospitals will accept a release form while others require a court order.

The birth mother may sign her consent anytime after the birth. It may be witnessed by a person authorized to take acknowledgments, such as a notary public, or in some cases an adoption agency representative or representative of the Mayor of the District of Columbia. Absent proof of fraud or undue influence, the consent is generally considered irrevocable upon filing it with the court, assuming the child has been placed in the custody of the adoptive parents.

The District of Columbia does not have a putative birth father registry. Notice must be given, unless the birth father can't be located.

Agency Adoption. All aspects of agency adoption are the same with the following exceptions. A pre-placement home study is required in an agency adoption. Also, a birth mother may sign her consent to the adoption, called a relinquishment in an agency adoption, anytime following the birth. She must also have received counseling prior to the signing of the relinquishment. Once the relinquishment is signed, there is a 14 day period in which the birth mother may automatically withdraw her consent by written request. After the 14 days have elapsed, the relinquishment can only be withdrawn upon proving to a court that fraud or undue influence was used. Once the adoption is finalized the relinquishment is basically irrevocable.

Many adoption agencies within the District of Columbia do identified adoptions. Many will also agree to make "at risk" placements of the child with the adoptive parents directly from the hospital before relinquishments are irrevocable.

American Academy of Adoption Attorney members:

Jody Marten; 3360 Tennyson St., NW, Washington, DC 20015
Tel: (202) 537-0496 ● jodymarten.com ● jmartennis@aol.com
A graduate of the University of Baltimore, she has been practicing law since 1985.

Mark McDermott; 910 17th Street NW, #800, Washington, DC 20006
Tel: (202) 331-1440 ● mtm-law.com ● mcdermott@mtm-law.com
A graduate of the Indiana University School of Law, he has been practicing law since 1974. He estimates he has completed 1,400 adoptions in his career an completes 60 annually: 65% independent; 10% agency; 25% international. He does not assist in creating adoptive matches. He is an adoptive parent and a past-president of the American Academy of Adoption Attorneys. He is also licensed in Maryland and Virginia.

Please be aware that many attorneys located in neighboring states, particularly Virginia and Maryland, also practice in the District of Columbia. You may wish to see more information about them in their state listings.

FLORIDA

State Adoption Office: Florida Department of Children and Families; Office of Family Safety; 1317 Winewood Boulevard, Building 6; Tallahassee, FL 32399-0700; Phone: (850) 922-5055; http://www.dcf.state.fl.us/adoption/

State Adoption Exchange: Florida Department of Children and Families; (same address as above); Phone: (850) 921-8357; Kathleen_Waters@dcf.state.fl.us; http://www.dcf.state.fl.us/adoption/

State laws and procedures:

General Information. Florida permits both independent and agency adoption. Approximately 60% of Florida's infant adoptions are completed via independent adoption; 40% via agencies. Advertising is permitted but only by a Florida-licensed attorney or agency. To file a Petition for Adoption within Florida the adoptive parents or the child must reside there. Normally, adoptions are finalized three to four months after the child's placement with the adoptive parents. The adoptive parents are required to appear in court for the final hearing in some regions, but in others the courts are willing to excuse their appearance in person.

Independent Adoption. A pre-placement home study of the adoptive parents is required before a child may be placed in their home. The home study may be conducted by a licensed private adoption agency, licensed social worker or the state adoption office if no agency is available in that region. The cost varies.

The adoptive parents and birth mother are not required by law to meet in person and share identities, although some do so voluntarily. The adoptive parents are permitted to assist the birth mother with pregnancy-related expenses, although they may not continue beyond six weeks after the birth. Court approval is required for all expenses, but this is often done at the conclusion of the adoption. Expenses totaling over $5,000 require advance court approval, however. The child may be released from the hospital directly to the adoptive parents, usually by means of a release form to the attorney who in turns places the child with the adoptive parents.

When the child being adopted is under the age of six months, the birth mother may sign her consent 48 hours after the birth or the day she is medically discharged from the hospital, whichever is sooner. It must be witnessed by two witnesses and a notary public. Most birth mothers sign their consents two days after birth. Once signed, the consent is irrevocable unless fraud or duress is proven. However, if the child being adopted was over the age of six months when adopted, there is a three-day revocation period.

Florida has a putative birth father registry. Putative birth fathers must register prior to the birth, or prior to the date a petition is filed to terminate parental rights, and confirm their willingness and intent to support the child.

Agency Adoption. There is no difference regarding the process in which a birth mother signs her consent to adoption in an independent or agency adoption. The information provided above regarding independent adoption (e.g. when it can be signed, before whom, legal burden to seek to withdraw a signed consent) is identical regarding agency adoption.

Some agencies within Florida agree to do identified adoptions, as well as agree to make immediate hospital "at risk" placements.

American Academy of Adoption Attorney members:

Ginger S. Allen; 16831 N.E. 6th Ave. N. Miami Beach, FL 33162
Tel: (305) 653-2474 ● adoptionflorida.org ●
g.allen@adoptionattorneys.org
A graduate of St. Thomas University School of Law, she has been practicing law since 1995.

Danelle Dykes Barksdale; 418 W. Platt Street, Tampa, FL 33606
Tel: (813) 258-3355 ● floridaadoptionattorney.com ●
d.barksdale@adoptionattorneys.org

Cheryl Eisen-Yeary; 370 Camino Gardens Bl. #107, Boca Raton, FL 33432; Tel: (561) 330-9901 ● eisenlawoffice.com ●
c.yeary@adoptionattorneys.org

Madonna M. Finney; 1535 Killearn Center Blvd., Suite A-1, Tallahassee, FL 32309; Tel: (850) 577-3077 ● madonnafinney.com ● m.finney@adoptionattorneys.org
A graduate of the University of Florida School of Law, she has been practicing law since 1988. She estimates she has completed 400 adoptions in her career and completes 40 annually: 95% independent; 5% agency. She does assist in creating adoptive matches.

Robison R. Harrell; 3 Clifford Drive Shaliman, FL 32579
Tel: (850) 651-5225 ● adoptioncenter.org ● adoptioncenter@aol.com
A graduate of the Florida State University School of Law, he has been practicing law since 1970.

Michelle Hausmann; 2423 Quantum Blvd, Boynton Beach, FL 33426; Tel: (561) 732-7030 ● hausmann&hickman.com ● 2adopt@bellsouth.net
A graduate of the Nova University School of Law, she has been practicing law since 1990.

Amy U. Hickman; 2423 Quantum Blvd., Boynton Beach, FL 33426
Tel: (561) 732-7030 ● hausmann&hickman.com ● 2adopt@bellsouth.net
A graduate of the University of Florida School of Law, she has been practicing law since 1989.

Brian Kelly; 3821 Atlantic Bl, P.O. Box 10007, Jacksonville, FL 32247; Tel: (904) 348-6400 ● adoption-USA.com ● b.kelly@adoptionattorneys.org
A graduate of the University of Florida School of Law, he has been practicing law since 1983.

Anthony Marchese; 4010 Boy Scout Blvd., #590, Tampa, FL 33607
Tel: (813) 877-6643 ● anthonymarchese.com

Linda McIntyre; 2 NE 5th Avenue, Delray Beach, FL 33483
Tel: (561) 272-1422 ● lindamcintyre.net ● l.mcintyre@adoptionattorneys.org
A graduate of the Nova Southeastern University School of Law, she has been practicing law since 1984.

Nicole Ward Moore; 1604 S. Bumby Avenue, Orlando, FL 32806
Tel: (407) 898-8015 • floridaadoptionattorney.com •
n.moore@adoptionattorneys.org
A graduate of the University of Florida, she has been practicing law
since 2005. Her agency completes 170 adoptions annually: 50%
independent; 50% agency. (Offices also in St. Cloud, Tampa, Naples.)

Mary Ann Scherer; 2001 E. Commercial Bl, Ft. Lauderdale, FL
33308; Tel: (954) 564-6900 • adoptionflorida.com •
m.scherer@adoptionattorneys.org

Michael A. Shorstein; 3821 Atlantic Blvd, P.O. Box 10007,
Jacksonville, FL 32247; Tel: (904) 348-6400 • adoption-usa.com •
adoption@shorsteinkelly.com
A graduate of Florida State University School of Law, he has been
practicing law since 1986.

Susan L. Stockham; 4017 Swift Road, Sarasota, FL 34231
Tel: (941) 924-4949 • stockhamlaw.com • susan@stockhamlaw.com
A graduate of the University of Florida School of Law, she has been
practicing law since 1981.

Patricia Strowbridge; 1516 E. Colonial Dr., Suite 202, Orlando, FL
Tel: (407) 894-1525 • strowbridge.com • patricia@strowbridge.com
A graduate of Georgetown University Law Center, she has been
practicing law since 1988. She estimates she completes 100 adoptions
annually. She does assist in creating adoptive matches.

Cynthia Stump Swanson; 2830 NW 41st Street, Suite M,
Gainesville, FL 32606; Tel: (352) 375-5602 • swansonlawcenter.com
• c.swanson@adoptionattorneys.org
A graduate of University of Florida School of Law, she has been
practicing since 1982. She estimates she completes 20 adoptions
annually: 100% independent. She assists in creating adoptive matches.

Jeanne Trudeau Tate; 418 W. Platt St. Tampa, FL 33606
Tel: (813) 258-3355 • floridaadoptionattorney.com •
j.tate@adoptionattorneys.org.   A graduate of the University of
Florida School of Law, she has been practicing law since 1982.

Christine Welch; 3800 W. Bay to Bay Blvd, #13, Tampa, FL 33629
Tel: (813) 835- 6000 ● christinewelch.com ●
cwelch@adoptionattorneys.org

Brian J. Welke; 531 North Bay Street, Eustis, FL 32726
Tel: (352) 357-0400 ● floridaadoptionattorney.net ●
bwelke@adoptionattorneys.org
A graduate of University of Tulsa School of Law, he has been
practicing law since 1997. He estimates he completes 50 adoptions
annually: 75% independent; 25% agency. He does assist in creating
adoptive matches.

Jeffrey Wood; One Financial Plaza, #2602, Fort Lauderdale, FL
33394
Tel: (954) 764-6006 ● mmdpa.com ● j.wood@adoptionattorneys.org

GEORGIA

State Adoption Office: Georgia Department of Human Resources;
Division of Family and Children Services; 2 Peachtree Street NW --
85th Floor, Suite 460; Atlanta, GA 30311; Phone: (404) 657-3619
http://dfcs.dhr.georgia.gov

State Adoption Exchange: My Turn Now Photolisting; Phone: (404)
657-3479; http://167.193.144.179/mtnmenu2.asp

State laws and procedures:

General Information. Georgia permits both independent and agency
adoption. Approximately 75% of Georgia's infant adoptions are
completed via independent adoptions; 25% via agencies. Attorneys
are not permitted to locate birth mothers for adoptive parents to start
adoption planning for a fee. Advertising is not permitted, except by
licensed adoption agencies. To file a Petition for Adoption in Georgia
the adoptive parents must reside there for six months. Normally,
adoptions are finalized within four months of the placement of the
child and filing of the Petition for Adoption. The adoptive parents and
the child are required to appear at the final court hearing.

Independent Adoption. A pre-placement home study of the adoptive parents is not required of the adoptive parents before a child is placed in their home. The post-placement home study may be conducted by a licensed private adoption agency or other court appointed individual. The fee varies.

The adoptive parents and birth mother are not required by law to meet in person and share identities, although many do so voluntarily. The adoptive parents are permitted to assist the birth mother with medical expenses only. The child may be placed with the adoptive parents immediately upon discharge from the hospital, usually through the attorney by means of a "Third Party Discharge" form.

The birth mother may sign her consent (called a surrender) anytime after the birth. It must be witnessed by a notary public and an additional witness. Most consents are signed within several days of the birth. There is a ten-day period after the signing of the consent in which the birth mother has the automatic right to withdraw her consent. After the ten-day period has expired the consent is irrevocable, except upon proof of fraud or duress.

Georgia has a putative birth father registry. A putative father must be given notice if his identity is known, or if he has filed with the registry. Upon notice, he has 30 days to file his objection or his rights will be terminated.

Agency Adoption. There is no difference regarding the process in which a birth mother signs her surrender in an independent or agency adoption, although agencies must wait until at least 24 hours after birth and an agency representative acts as an additional witness. Also, a pre-placement home study is required in agency adoptions.

Many agencies within Georgia agree to do identified adoptions. Many agencies agree to make immediate hospital "at risk" placements.

American Academy of Adoption Attorney members:

Ruth F. Claiborne; 60 Lenox Pointe, NE, Atlanta, GA 30324
Tel: (800) 407-0931, ext. 223 ● gababylaw.com ●
ruth@gababylaw.com.   A graduate of the University of California
Hastings College of Law, she has been practicing law since 1976.

Rhonda L. Fishbein; Overlook 1, 2849 Paces Ferry Rd., Suite 215, Atlanta, GA 30339; Tel: (770) 437-8582 • rfishbeinadoption-law.com • rlfishbein@bellsouth.net
A graduate of Benjamin N. Cardozo School of Law, she has been practicing law since 1982. She estimates she has completed 1,300 adoption in her career and completes 300 adoptions annually: 45% independent; 45% agency; 10% international. She does not assist in creating adoptive matches. She is an adoptive parent and the founder and director of a licensed adoption agency.

Karlise Y. Grierz; 811 Duffield Drive NW, Atlanta, GA 30318
Tel: (404) 658-9999 • grierlawoffice.com •
k.grier@adoptionattorneys.org

Jerrold W. Hester; 235 Scientific Drive, #2000, Norcross, GA 30092
Tel: (770)446-3645 • hesterlawfirm.net •
j.hester@adoptionattorneys.org
A graduate of the University of Georgia School of Law, he has been practicing law since 1975. He has completed more than 2,000 adoptions in his career and completes about 60 annually. He was the recipient of the Congressional Angel in Adoption Award in 2002.

Sherriann H. Hicks; 368 South Perry Street, Lawrenceville, GA 30045; Tel: (678) 985-3011 • thehickslawgroup.com •
shhicks@bellsouth.net
A graduate of the University of Memphis School of Law, she has been practicing law since 1993.

Richard Horder; 3490 Piedmont Road NE, #350, Atlanta, GA 30305
Tel: (404) 812-0843 • kilpatrickstockton.com •
r.hoarder@adoptionattorneys.org
A graduate of the University of Florida School of Law, he has been practicing law since 1971. He is an adoptive parent.

Michael S. Jennings; 130 Jordan Drive, Chattanooga, TN 37421
Tel: (423) 892-2006 • m.jennings@adoptionattorneys.org

James B. Outman; P.O.Box 942075, Atlanta, GA 31141
Tel: (404) 317-3044 ● gababylaw.com ● jim@gababylaw.com
A graduate of the Georgetown University School of Law, he has been practicing law since 1971.

Josie Redwine; 2440 Sandy Plains Rd., Suite 7, Marietta, GA 30066
Tel: (770) 579-6070 ● redwineattorney.com ● redwinepc@aol.com
A graduate of the Georgia State University School of Law, she has been practicing law since 1996.

Irene Steffas; 4343 Shallowford Road, Bldg. H, Suite 1, Marietta, GA; Tel: (770) 642-6075 ● i.steffas@adoptionattorneys.org

Lori M. Surmay; 60 Lenox Pointe, NE, Atlanta, GA 30324
Tel: (404) 442-6933 ● gababylaw.com ●
l.surmay@adoptionattorneys.org

Lynn McNeese Swank; 118 North Ave., #6, Jonesboro, GA 30236
Tel: (770) 477-5318 ● swanklaw.com ● swanklaw@mindspring.com
She has been practicing law since 1975.

Diane Woods; 707 Whitlock Avenue, G-5, Marietta, GA 30064
Tel: (770) 429-1001 ● d.woods@adoptionattorneys.org

HAWAII

State Adoption Office: Hawaii Department of Human Services; 810 Richards Street, Suite 400; Honolulu, HI 96813; Phone: (808) 586-5698; http://www.hawaii.gov

State Adoption Exchange: Central Adoption Exchange of Hawaii: Phone: (808) 586-5698; Fax: (808) 586-4806

State laws and procedures:

General Information. Hawaii permits both independent and agency adoption. Approximately 90% of Hawaii's newborn adoptions are via independent adoption; 10% via private agencies. Advertising is permitted by law, but most Hawaii newspapers refuse to accept advertising by adoptive parents. To file a Petition for Adoption in Hawaii either the adopting parents must reside there, or the child to be adopted must have been born there or reside there (making non-resident adoption possible). If it is an agency adoption the Petition for Adoption can additionally be filed in Hawaii if the agency having custody of the child is located there. Normally, adoptions are finalized two to six months after the placement of the child with the adoptive parents. At least one of the adopting parents and the child are required to appear at the final hearing.

Independent Adoption. A pre-placement home study of the adoptive parents is not required before a child may be placed in their home. In fact, there is no requirement for even a post-placement home study, although the court has discretion to require one. If a home study is required, it may be conducted by any person or organization approved by the court, usually a licensed social worker. The fee for the home study is typically $1,500.

The birth mother and adoptive parents are not required by law to meet in person and share identities, although most elect to do so voluntarily. The adopting parents are permitted by law to assist with the birth mother's pregnancy-related medical, legal and living expenses. The child may be released from the hospital directly to the adoptive parents, usually by the birth mother signing a hospital form authorizing the release.

The birth mother may sign her consent to the adoption anytime after the birth. It may be witnessed by a notary or a judge. Once the consent is signed and the child has been placed with the adoptive parents, the consent can only be withdrawn if the best interests of the child would be served by being removed from the adoptive parents. Once the adoption is finalized by the court, there is a one-year period where the adoption can be "set aside" and the consent revoked if fraud or duress is proved.

Hawaii requires notice to birth fathers. This notice to putative birth fathers is usually by personal notice or publication. If he has not objected at, or prior to, the noticed hearing to terminate his rights, his rights are terminated. If he elects to object, the court will consider the best interests of the child and rule accordingly.

Agency Adoption. There is no difference regarding the process in which a birth mother signs her consent to adoption in an independent or agency adoption, other than the fact a home study is required in agency adoptions. The information provided above regarding independent adoption (e.g. when it can be signed, before whom, legal burden to seek to withdraw a signed consent) is identical regarding agency adoption.

Many agencies in Hawaii agree to do identified adoptions, as well as make immediate "at risk" placements before consents are irrevocable.

American Academy of Adoption Attorney members:

Laurie A. Loomis; 1001 Bishop Street, #2850, Honolulu, HI 96813
Tel: (808) 524-5066 • l.loomis@adoptionattorneys.org
A graduate of the Catholic University School of Law, she has been practicing law since 1985.

IDAHO

State Adoption Office: Idaho Department of Health and Welfare; Division of Family and Community Services: 450 West State Street, 5th Floor, PO Box 83702; Boise, ID 83702; Phone: (208) 334-5697; http://www.healthandwelfare.idaho.gov

State Adoption Exchange: Idaho's Wednesday's Child: Phone: (208) 345-6646; http://www.idahowednesdayschild.org/

State laws and procedures:

General Information. Idaho permits both independent and agency adoption. Approximately 60% of Idaho's infant adoptions are completed via independent adoption; 40% via agencies. Advertising is not permitted. To file a Petition for Adoption in Idaho the adoptive parents must reside there, usually for a minimum of six months prior to filing the Petition for Adoption. Normally, independent adoptions are finalized approximately three months after the placement of the child with the adoptive parents, while agency adoptions take seven months. The adopting parents and the child are required to appear in court for the final hearing.

Independent Adoption. A pre-placement home study of the adopting parents is required before a child can be placed in their home. The home study is usually performed by a licensed private adoption agency or licensed social worker approved to perform home studies. The fee averages $600 to $1,200.

The adoptive parents and birth mother are not required by law to meet in person and share identities, although it is often done voluntarily. The adopting parents are permitted to assist the birth mother with medical and legal expenses related to the pregnancy. Living expense assistance is permitted up to $500 without court approval, and up to $2,000 with court approval. The child may be released to the adoptive parents directly from the hospital upon discharge, although the forms and procedures among hospitals varies. Some hospitals require the attorney to be present at the discharge.

The birth mother may sign her consent to the adoption anytime after the birth, and it must be witnessed by a judge. Most judges will require at least 48 hours to pass after birth before the signing of the consent. The consent is irrevocable upon signing. Most consents are signed several days after the birth.

Idaho has a putative birth father registry. A putative birth father must file a paternity action and register that he has done so before termination proceedings are commenced, or before the child is placed for adoption, whichever occurs first.

Agency Adoption. There is no difference regarding the process in which a birth mother signs her consent to adoption in an independent or agency adoption. The information provided above regarding independent adoption (e.g. when it can be signed, before whom, legal burden to seek to withdraw a signed consent) is identical regarding agency adoption.

Most agencies within Idaho agree to do identified adoptions. Most agencies will also agree to make immediate hospital "at risk" placements.

American Academy of Adoption Attorney members:

Alfred E. Barrus; P.O. Box 487, Burley, ID 83318
Tel: (208) 678-1155 • a.barrus@adoptionattorneys.org
A graduate of the University of Idaho School of Law, he has been practicing law since 1974. He is an adoptive parent.

Bart D. Browning; P.O. Box 1846, 516 Hansen Street East, Twin Falls, ID 83303; Tel: (208) 733-7180 •
b.browning@adoptionattorneys.org

Mark R. Iverson; 921 W. Broadway, Suite 301, Spokane, WA 99201
Tel: (509) 462-3678 • adoptionwa.com •
m.iverson@adoptionattorneys.org

Jeffrey T. Sheehan; 702 W. Idaho Street, Suite 1100, Boise, ID 83702
Tel: (208) 287-4429 • idahofamilylaw.com •
jsheenan@adoptionattorneys.org

ILLINOIS

State Adoption Office: Illinois Department of Children and Family Services: Service Intervention; 405 E. Monroe, Springfield, IL 62701; Phone: (217) 785-2509; http://www.state.il.us/dcfs

State Adoption Exchange: Adoption Information Center of Illinois (AICI): Phone: (312) 346-1516; aici@adoptinfo-il.org; http://www.adoptinfo-il.org

State laws and procedures:

General Information. Illinois permits both independent and agency adoption. It is difficult to distinguish the percentage of independent and agency adoptions in Illinois as the vast majority of newborn adoptions are "identified" adoptions, where both attorneys and agencies have a united role. Advertising is permitted, but only by individuals (adoptive parents) from any state, and only by agencies and attorneys located in Illinois. Out-of-state agencies/attorneys/

facilitators cannot advertise. To file a Petition for Adoption within Illinois the adopting parents must reside there, usually for a minimum of six months prior to the filing of the Petition for Adoption. If it is an agency adoption, the Petition for Adoption can additionally be filed within Illinois if the adoption agency having custody of the child is located there (making non-resident adoption possible). Illinois residents adopting from another state are required to have not only a pre-placement home study, but also a foster license. Normally, adoptions are finalized six months after the placement of the child with the adoptive parents. The adoptive parents and the child are required to appear in court for one hearing, but counties differ on whether that appearance must be at an initial, or a final hearing.

Independent Adoption. A pre-placement home study of the adoptive parents is normally not required before a child may be placed in their home. A few counties, however, may require a pre-placement interview (e.g. Cook County). The post-placement home study may be conducted by the state adoption office, county social services agency, a licensed private adoption agency or other court approved individual. The fee varies.

Attorneys cannot be paid for creating adoptive matches, meaning they can assist in birth mother matching, but not for compensation. The adoptive parents and the birth mother are not required by law to meet in person, although it is done voluntarily in most cases. The adopting parents are permitted to assist the birth mother with her pregnancy-related expenses, including living costs incurred 120 days before the due date and up to 60 days after the child's birth. Advance court approval is required if the total amount exceeds $1,000. The child may be placed directly with the adopting parents immediately upon hospital discharge, although a court order giving temporary legal custody to the adopting parents is sometimes required. Other hospitals may require a short-term guardianship appointment.

The birth mother may sign a traditional consent to the adoption no sooner than 72 hours after the birth. It must be witnessed by a judge, licensed adoption agency, or other individual authorized by the court to act as a witness. Once signed, the consent is irrevocable.

Illinois has a putative birth father registry. Any putative birth father, either identified by the birth mother, or who has registered within 30 days after the birth, must be given notice. A putative father may sign his consent pre-birth, but it is revocable for 72 hours after birth. A putative father may also sign a notarized waiver before or after birth if he denies paternity, and that waiver may be irrevocable.

Agency Adoption. There are few differences regarding the process in which a birth mother signs her consent to adoption in an independent or agency adoption. The information provided above regarding independent adoption is similar regarding agency adoption, except for the following. A pre-placement home study is required. An agency may pay for the birth mother's living expenses without advance court approval. Also, the birth mother may sign her consent to adoption, called a surrender, after 72 hours have elapsed after the birth. It may be witnessed by a representative of the adoption agency and a notary public. Once signed, the surrender is irrevocable, except upon proof of fraud or duress.

Some agencies within Illinois agree to handle identified adoptions. Many agencies also agree to make "at risk" placements.

American Academy of Adoption Attorney members:

Shelley B. Ballard; 221 N. LaSalle St., Suite 1136, Chicago, IL 60601; Tel: (312) 673-5312 ● familybuildinglaw.com ●
sballard@familybuildinglaw.com
A graduate of Northwestern University School of Law, she has been practicing law since 1987. She estimates she has completed approximately 3,000 adoptions in her career and completes 100-150 annually: 60% independent; 10% agency; 30% international. She does assist in creating adoptive matches. She is an adoptive parent.

Kirsten Crouse Bays; 1513 University Dr., Charleston, IL 61920
Tel: (217) 345-6099 ● iladoptlaw.com ● kbays@charter.net
A graduate of the Washington University School of Law in St. Louis, she has been practicing law since 1994.

Deborah Crouse Cobb; 515 West Main St., Colinsville, IL 62234
Tel: (618) 344-6300 ● iladoptlaw.com ● debcobb@sbcglobal.net
A graduate of the Washington University School of Law in St. Louis, she has been practicing law since 1984.

Nidhi Desai; 221 N. LaSalle Street, Suite 1136, Chicago, IL 60601
Tel: (312) 673-5312 ● n.desai@adoptionattorneys.org

Joseph H. Gitlin; 111 Dean Street, Woodstock, IL 60098
Tel: (815) 338-0021 ● gitlin.com

Theresa Rahe Hardesty; 7513 N. Regent Place, Peoria, IL 61614
Tel: (309) 692-1087 ● TRHAdopt@comcast.net
A graduate of the DePaul University School of Law, she has been
practicing law since 1977. She estimates she has completed 3,500
adoptions in her career, and completes 150 annually: 10%
independent; 75% agency; 15% international.

Michelle M. Hughes; 221 N. LaSalle St., #2020, Chicago, IL 60601
Tel: (312) 857-7287 ● m.hughes@adoptionattorney.org
A graduate of the University of Chicago School of Law, she has been
practicing law since 1989. She estimates she has completed more than
2,000 adoptions in her career and completes 220 annually: 2%
independent; 85% agency; 13% international. She does assist in
creating adoptive matches.

Kimberly Kuhlengel-Jones; 255 E. St. Louis Street; P.O. Box 186,
Nashville, IL 62263; Tel: (618) 327-3093 ● kuhlengel@earthlink.net
A graduate of the Southern Illinois University School of Law at
Carbondale, she has been practicing law since 1995.

Richard Lifshitz; 211 W. Wacker Drive, #1100, Chicago, IL 60606
Tel: (312) 236-7089 ● lifshitzlaw.com ●
rlifshitz@adoptionattorneys.org
A graduate of the Washington University School of Law, he has been
practicing law since 1976. He estimates he has completed 3,000
adoptions in his career and completes 50 adoptions annually: 60%
independent; 10% agency; 30% international. He does not assist in
creating adoptive matches.

Sheila Maloney; 633 Rogers Street, #102, Downers Grove, IL 60515
Tel: (630) 570-5050 ● iladoptionlawyer.com ● stmesq@msn.com
A graduate of the John Marshall School of Law, she has been
practicing law since 1986. She estimates she has completed more than

1,000 adoptions in her career and completes 75 annually: 15% independent; 75% agency; 10% international. She is an adoptive parent.

Kathleen Morrison; 70 W. Madison St. #2100, Chicago, IL 60602
Tel: (312) 977-4477 ● chicagoadoptionattorney.com
● k.morrison@adoptionattorneys.org
A graduate of the John Marshall School of Law, she has been practicing law since 1976. She estimates she has completed 7,500 adoptions in her career and completes 250 annually: 25% independent; 45% agency; 30% international. She does not assist in creating adoptive matches. She is a past president of the American Academy of Adoption Attorneys.

Denise J. Patton; 4760 Fairfax Avenue, Palatine, IL 60067
Tel: (847) 925-9072 ● d.patton@adoptionattorneys.org

Sally Wildman; 200 N. LaSalle St., Suite 2750, Chicago, IL 60601
Tel: (312) 726-9214 ● swildmanlaw.com ●
s.wildman@adoptionattorneys.org
A graduate of DePaul University School of Law, she has been practicing law since 1985. She estimates she has completed over 400 adoptions in her career and completes 15 annually: 20% independent; 50% agency; 30% international. She does not assist in creating adoptive matches. She is a past-chairperson of the American Bar Association Adoption Committee.

INDIANA

State Adoption Office: Indiana Department of Child Services: 402 West Washington Street, Room W364; Indianapolis, IN 46204; Phone: (317) 234-4211; http://www.in.gov/fssa/adoption/

State Adoption Exchange: Indiana's Adoption Program: Toll-Free: (888) 252-3678; adoption@iquest.net; http://www.adoptachild.in.gov

State laws and procedures:

General Information. Indiana permits both independent and agency adoption. Approximately 65% of Indiana's infant adoptions are completed via independent adoption; 35% via agencies. Advertising is permitted. To file a Petition for Adoption within Indiana the adopting parents must reside within the state, except if the child is designated as hard-to-place, then out-of-state residents may adopt in-state. Normally, adoptions are finalized three months to one year after the placement of the child with the adoptive parents. The adoptive parents are required to appear in court for the final hearing.

Independent Adoption. A pre-placement home study of the adoptive parents is required before a child can be placed in their home. The post-placement home study may be done by the state adoption office or a licensed private adoption agency. The fee varies.

Adoptive parents and birth mothers are not required to meet in person and share identifying information, although it is sometimes done voluntarily. The adoptive parents are permitted to assist the birth mother with pregnancy-related expenses, but the maximum total which can be paid is $3,000 whether the adoption will occur in, or out of, Indiana. The child may be placed directly with the adoptive parents from the hospital, although generally a court order is required.

The birth mother may sign her consent to the adoption anytime after the birth. It must be witnessed by a judge or a notary public. Most consents are signed within several days of the birth. Once the consent is signed it may be withdrawn with 30 days only by proving the child's best interests would be served by being removed from the adoptive parents, or that fraud or duress existed. However, if the birth mother elects to appear in court to confirm her consent, the consent becomes irrevocable immediately at the time of the court appearance. This appearance may usually be made by telephone.

Indiana has a putative birth father registry. Failure of a putative father to register during the pregnancy, or the latter of the filing of the Petition for Adoption or 30 days following the birth, constitutes an irrevocable implied consent to adoption, relieving any requirement to notice.

Agency Adoption. There is no difference regarding the process in which a birth mother signs her consent to adoption in an independent or agency adoption. The information provided above regarding independent adoption is identical regarding agency adoption.

Some agencies in Indiana agree to do identified adoptions. Some agencies will also agree to make immediate hospital "at risk" placements.

American Academy of Adoption Attorney members:

Michael Bishop; 8888 Keystone Crossing, #1200, Indianapolis, IN 46240; Tel: (317) 573-8888 ● m.bishop@adoptionattorneys.org

Lisa M. Bowen-Slaven; 832 N. Detroit Street, LaGrange, IN 46761
Tel: (260) 463-4949 ● slavenlaw.com ●
l.slaven@adoptionattorneys.org
A graduate of the Valpariaso University School of Law, she has been practicing law since 1993.

Rebecca S. Bruce; 108 N. Liberty Street, Suite A, Muncie, IN 47305
Tel: (765) 286-1776 ● adoptindiana.org ●
r.bruce@adoptionattorneys.org
A graduate of the Indiana University School of Law - Indianapolis, she has been practicing law since 1998. She completes 100 adoptions annually: 35% independent; 60% agency; 5% international. She does assist in creating adoptive matches.

John Q. Herrin; Capital Center South Tower, 201 N. Illinois Street, Suite 1700, Indianapolis, IN 46204
Tel: (317) 580-4848 ● j.herrin@adoptionattorneys.org

Timothy J. Hubert; 20 NW First St., 9th floor; P.O. Box 916, Evansville, IN 47706
Tel: (812) 424-7575 ● zsws.com ● t.hubert@adoptionattorneys.org

Joel D. Kirsh; 2930 E. 96th Street, Indianapolis, IN 46240
Tel: (317) 575-5555 ● kirsh.com ● joel@kirsh.com
A graduate of the Indiana University School of Law at Indianapolis, he has been practicing law since 1984. He estimates he has completed

more than 3,000 adoptions in his career, and last year completed approximately 100. His practice is limited to adoptions, all newborn placements. He reports 50% of his clients find a birth mother through his office; 50% find their own birth mother. He also assists with step-parent, grandparent, adult, foster care and foreign adoptions.

Steven M. Kirsh; 2930 E. 96th Street, Indianapolis, IN 46240
Tel: (800) 333-5736; (317) 575-5555 ● kirsh.com ●
s.kirsh@adoptionattorneys.org
A graduate of the Indiana University School of Law, he has been practicing law since 1979. He estimates he has completed more than 3,000 adoptions in his career and completes 100 annually: 95% independent; 5% agency. He is a past president of the American Academy of Adoption Attorneys and the 2005 recipient of the Congressional Angels in Adoption Award.

Michael G. Naville; 506 State Street; New Albany, IN 47151
Tel: (812) 949-1000 ● m.naville@adoptionattorneys.org

Sally A. Thomas; 506 State Street, New Albany, IN 47151
Tel: (812) 949-1000 ● lorchnaville.com ● sthomas@lorchnaville.com
A graduate of the Northeastern University School of Law, she has been practicing law since 1984.

Keith M. Wallace; 401 SE 6th Street, Suite 202, Evansville, IN 47713; Tel: (812) 479-9900 ● ftia.org ● kwallace@ftia.org
A graduate of the Valparaiso University School of Law, he has been practicing law since 1983.

IOWA

State Adoption Office: Iowa Department of Human Services (DHS): Hoover State Office Building, 5th Floor; 1305 East Walnut Avenue; Des Moines, IA 50319-0114; Phone: (515) 281-5358; http://www.dhs.state.ia.us

State Adoption Exchange: KidSake Foster/Adopt Iowa: Phone: (515) 289-4649; kidsake@iakids.org; http://www.iakids.org

State laws and procedures:

General Information. Iowa permits both independent and agency adoption. Approximately 60% of Iowa's infant adoptions are completed via independent adoption; 40% via agencies. Advertising is permitted. To file a Petition for Adoption within Iowa either the adoptive parents must reside there or the child is born and resides there (making non-resident adoption possible). Normally, adoptions are finalized seven months after the placement of the child with the adoptive parents. The adopting parents and the child are required to appear in court for the final hearing, although some courts may waive the requirement for out-of-state residents and allow them to appear with their attorney by telephone.

Independent Adoption. A pre-placement home study of the adoptive parents is required before a child can be placed in their home. The home study is performed by a certified adoption investigator (a person certified by the state to perform home studies) or a licensed adoption agency. The fee varies from approximately $600 to $2,000. The post-placement evaluation is $500-$1,500.

The adoptive parents and birth mother are not required by law to meet in person and share identities, although in some cases it is done voluntarily. The adoptive parents are permitted to assist the birth mother with pregnancy-related medical, legal and living expenses, although if she is receiving welfare, she may be required to reimburse the welfare office the amount she received from the adoptive parents. The birth mother must also be offered three hours of counseling, although she may waive it. Children may be placed directly with the adoptive parents from the hospital, although many hospitals require a court order. Occasionally a short-term foster home placement is made until the birth mother's consent is irrevocable.

Normally, the juvenile court will appoint a custodian for the child, who will witness the birth mother signing her consent to adoption, called a Release of Custody. The birth mother cannot sign the Release of Custody until at least 72 hours after the birth. Once signed, there is a 96-hour period in which the birth mother has the automatic right to withdraw it. A termination of parental rights hearing is then scheduled after the expiration of the 96-hour period. After the 96-hour period, but before the termination of parental rights hearing, the birth mother can withdraw her consent if she can show good cause to do so, usually proof of fraud or duress. After the court order terminating parental rights, the consent is irrevocable.

Iowa has a putative birth father registry. A putative father may file a Declaration of Paternity with the Department of Vital Statistics. Those who do, or who can be identified by the birth mother as a possible birth father, are entitled to notice. The notice will be of a termination of parental rights hearing.

Agency Adoption. There is no difference regarding the process in which a birth mother signs her consent to adoption in an independent or agency adoption. The information provided above regarding independent adoption (e.g. when it can be signed, before whom, legal burden to seek to withdraw a signed relinquishment) is identical regarding agency adoption.

Some agencies within Iowa agree to do identified adoptions. Few agencies agree to make immediate hospital "at risk" placements.

American Academy of Adoption Attorney members:

Maxine M. Buckmeier; 600 Fourth Street, Suite 304: P.O. Box 634, Sioux City, IA 51102
Tel: (712) 233-3660 ● m.buckmeier@adoptionattorneys.org

Lori L. Klockau; 402 S. Linn Street, Iowa City, IA 52240
Tel: (319) 338-7968 ● brayklockau@bkfamilylaw.com
A graduate of the Iowa University School of Law, she has been practicing law since 1991..

Kenneth Nelson; 3112 Brockway Road, Waterloo, IA 50704
Tel: (319) 291-6161 ● kenneth-nelson.com ●
k.nelson@adoptionattorneys.org

Susan Kubert Sapp; 233 S. 13th Street, Suite 1900, Lincoln, NE 68508; Tel: (402) 474-6900 ● clinewilliams.com ●
s.sapp@adoptionattorneys.org

KANSAS

State Adoption Office: Kansas Department of Social and Rehabilitation Services, Children and Family Policy Division: Docking State Office Building - 5th Floor South; 915 SW Harrison, Room 551-S; Topeka, KS 66612-1870; Phone: (785) 296-0918; http://www.srskansas.org

State Adoption Exchange: Coming Home Kansas: Phone: (785) 274-3100; Fax: (785) 274-3188; https://www.cominghomekansas.org

State laws and procedures:

General Information. Kansas permits both independent and agency adoption. Approximately 85% of Kansas' infant adoptions are completed via independent adoption; 15% via agencies. Advertising is permitted if done by a licensed adoption agency, although many newspapers will accept an advertisement if accompanied by a letter from an attorney. To file a Petition for Adoption within Kansas either the adoptive parents must reside there or the child is born there and the birth mother resides there (making non-resident adoption possible). If it is an agency adoption the Petition for Adoption can also be filed there if the adoption agency having custody of the child is located there. Normally, independent adoptions are finalized one to two months after the child's placement with the adoptive parents; one to six months for agency adoptions. The adopting parents are required to appear in court for the final hearing, but some judges will waive this requirement.

Independent Adoption. A pre-placement home study of the adoptive parents is required before a child can be placed in their home, although the court has discretion to waive this requirement. The home study may be conducted by a licensed clinical social worker or licensed private adoption agency. Most home study fees total approximately $850.

Adoptive parents and birth mothers are not required by law to meet in person and share identities, although it is sometimes done voluntarily. The adoptive parents are permitted to assist with pregnancy-related expenses, such as medical, legal and living costs.

The child may be released from the hospital directly to the adoptive parents, but a court order granting the adoptive parents temporary custody is required.

The consent to adoption may be signed no sooner than 12 hours after the birth. It may be witnessed by a judge or a notary public. Most consents are signed from 12 hours to only several days after the birth. If the birth mother is under the age of 18 she must have her own attorney prior to signing the consent to adoption. Usually the attorney's fees, typically only several hundred dollars, are paid by the adoptive parents. Once signed, the consent is irrevocable, except by clear and convincing evidence it was not freely and voluntarily given.

Kansas does not have a putative birth father registry. Notice must be given to putative fathers, unless due diligence shows they can't be found. Once notice is given, he has 30 days to object after birth. If he objects, it must be shown he is unfit, abandoned the child, rape of the birth mother, or failed to support the birth mother during the last six months of the pregnancy.

Agency Adoption. There is no difference regarding the process in which a birth mother signs her consent to adoption in an independent or agency adoption, although agencies call the consent a *relinquishment.* The information provided above regarding independent adoption (e.g. when it can be signed, before whom, legal burden to seek to withdraw a signed consent) is identical regarding agency adoption.

Some agencies within Kansas agree to do identified adoptions. Some agencies will agree to make immediate hospital "at risk" placements.

American Academy of Adoption Attorney members:

Martin W. Bauer; 100 N. Broadway, Suite 500, Wichita, KS 67202 Tel: (316) 265-9311 ● m.bauer@adoptionattorneys.org

Michael J. Belfonte; 1125 Grand Blvd. #1301, Kansas City, MO 64106; Tel: (816) 842-3580 ● m.belfonte@adoptionattorneys.org

Jill Bremyer; P.O. Box 443, McPherson, KS 67460
Tel: (620) 241-0554 ● bwisecounsel.com ●
jbarcher@bwisecounsel.com
A graduate of the Washburn University School of Law, she has been practicing law since 1980. Approximately 25% of her practice consists of adoptions (typically 75% independent; 25% agency). She does not assist in creating adoptive matches.

Allan A. Hazlett; 1622 Washburn,Topeka, KS 66604
Tel: (785) 232-2011 ● a.hazlett@adoptionattorneys.org
A graduate of the University of Kansas School of Law, he has been practicing law since 1967. He is a past president of the American Academy of Adoption Attorneys.

Douglas J. Keeling; 200 East First St., Suite 202, Wichita, KS 67202
Tel: (316) 265-2210 ● d.keeling@adoptionattorneys.org
A graduate of the Washburn University School of Law, he has been practicing law since 1984. He is an adoptive parent.

Kevin Kenney; 7301 Mission Road, #243, Prairie Village, KS 66208
Tel: (913) 671- 8008 ● kevinwkenney.com ●
k.kenney@adoptionattorneys.org

Richard A. Macias; 901 North Broadway, Witchita, KS 67214-3531
Tel: (316) 265-5245 ● r.macias@adoptionattorneys.org

Joseph N. Vader; 104 E. Poplar, Olathe, KS 66061
Tel: (913) 764-5010 ● jvader@sbcglobal.net
A graduate of the Washburn University School of Law, he has been practicing law since 1964.

KENTUCKY

State Adoption Office: Kentucky Cabinet for Families and Children: 275 East Main Street - 3CE; Frankfort, KY 40621; Phone: (502) 564-2147; http://chfs.ky.gov

State Adoption Exchange: Special Needs Adoption Program (SNAP): Phone: (502) 564-2147; deborah.green@ky.gov; https://apps.chfs.ky.gov

State laws and procedures:

General Information. Kentucky permits both independent and agency adoption. Approximately 80% of Kentucky's infant adoptions are completed via independent adoption; 20% via agencies. Advertising is not permitted. To file a Petition for Adoption within Kentucky the adopting parents must reside there. Normally, adoptions are finalized three to four months after the placement of the child. The adoptive parents are required to appear in court for the final hearing.

Independent Adoption. A pre-placement home study of the adoptive parents is required before a child can be placed in their home. The home study is conducted by either the state adoption office or a licensed agency. The fee, in the form of a "filing fee," is $200 if done by the state adoption office. There is no fee when the adoptive parents reside out of state and will not be completing their adoption in Kentucky. The state will not start the pre-placement home study until a specific child has been identified, and will only conduct the home study if the adoptive parents' income does not exceed 200% of the poverty level. Those in excess of that amount, which will be most adoptive parents, have their home study done by a private agency. Typical fees range from $1,700 - $2,500.

The adopting parents and the birth mother are not required to meet in person and share identities, although some do so voluntarily. The adoptive parents are permitted to assist the birth mother with pregnancy-related expenses, such as medical, legal and living costs. The child may be released directly from the hospital to the adoptive parents if they have a pre-approved home study from a Kentucky licensed adoption agency and/or if they have a temporary custody order from the court. Each hospital has different forms and procedures regarding the child's release.

The birth mother may assent to the adoption in one of two ways, either by signing a *Voluntary and Informed Consent,* or by filing a voluntary *Petition to Terminate Parental Rights* with the court. The former is less complicated, although it does not become irrevocable until 20 days after signing and approval of the adoption placement. The latter option is more secure, as it is irrevocable upon the judge signing the order terminating the birth mother's rights. If the birth mother is a minor, a guardian ad litem is appointed for her. Neither the *Voluntary and Informed Consent* nor the voluntary *Petition to Terminate Parental Rights* can be signed and filed until at least 72 hours after birth.

Depending upon the county, the hearing on the *Petition to Terminate Parental Rights* may be scheduled immediately after this 72 hour period or within 30 days, and if the birth mother appears with her attorney, and a guardian ad litem is appointed for the child, the court can often issue its order terminating her rights, if the adoption placement has been approved by the Cabinet for Health and Family Services.

Kentucky does not have a putative birth father registry. Notice is only given to a man married to the birth mother, who lived with her during the pregnancy or was identified by her affidavit (although she is not required to name non-marital relationships). Men in these categories will be given 20 days notice in which to file their objection. Some counties will not enter an order terminating birth father's rights for 60 days, when abandonment is presumed.

Agency Adoption.   There is no difference regarding the process in which a birth mother indicates her consent to adoption in an independent or agency adoption, except that the simpler *Voluntary and Informed Consent* method is unavailable in agency adoptions. Otherwise, the information provided above regarding independent adoption (e.g. when it can be signed, before whom, legal burden to seek to withdraw a signed consent, etc.) is identical regarding agency adoption.

Although adoption agencies in Kentucky sometimes arrange "open" adoptions, identified adoptions (where the adoptive parents and birth parents initially became acquainted outside the agency) are not permitted. Some agencies agree to make hospital "at risk" placements.

American Academy of Adoption Attorney members:

Carolyn S. Arnett; 2518 Frankfort Avenue, Louisville KY 40206
Tel: (502) 585-4368 ● c.arnett@adoptionattorneys.org
A graduate of the University of Louisville School of Law, she has been practicing law since 1984. She completes 50 adoptions annually, 100% of them independent. She does assist in creating adoptive matches.

Mitchell A. Charney; 9301 Dayflower Street, Prospect, KY 40059
Tel: (502) 589-4440 ● m.charney@adoptionattorneys.org
A graduate of the University of Louisville School of Law, he has been practicing law since 1970. He estimates he has completed more than 500 adoptions in his career and completes 11 annually: 60% independent; 35% agency; 5% international. He does assist in creating adoptive matches.

Ellie Goldman; 333 W. Vine St., Suite 1201, Lexington, KY 40507
Tel: (859) 381-1145 ● e.goldman@adoptionattorneys.org
Ellie Goldman, a graduate of the University of Kentucky School of Law, has been practicing law since 1976. She estimates she has completed 400 adoptions in her career and completes 17 annually: 75% independent; 25% agency. She does assist in creating adoptive matches.

Gregory K. Northcutt; P.O. Box 996, Calvert City, KY 42029
Tel: (270) 5714 ● g.northcutt@adoptionattorneys.org

Waverley Townes; 401 W. Main Street, #1900, Louisville, KY 40202
Tel: (502) 589-4404 ● w.townes@adoptionattorneys.org

Michael R. Voorhees; 11159 Kenwood Road, Cincinnati, OH 45242
Tel: (513) 489-2555 ● mike@ohioadoptionlawyer.com
Michael Voorhees has been practicing law since 1987 and estimates he completes 150 annually: 60% independent; 30% agency; 10% international. He rarely assists in creating adoptive matches.

LOUISIANA

State Adoption Office: Louisiana Department of Social Services: Office of Community Services; 333 Laurel Street -- PO Box 3318; Baton Rouge, LA 70821; Phone: (225) 342-4086; http://www.dss.state.la.us

State Adoption Exchange: Louisiana Adoption Resource Exchange (LARE): Toll-Free: (800) 259-3428; cbilliod@dss.state.la.us; http://www.adoptuskids.org

State laws and procedures:

General Information. Louisiana permits both independent and agency adoption. Approximately 50% of Louisiana's infant adoptions are completed via independent adoption; 50% via agencies. Advertising is not permitted, except by licensed adoption agencies. To file a Petition for Adoption within Louisiana the adoptive parents must reside there, or the birth parent relinquishing custody must be domiciled for at least eight months in Louisiana and surrender the child there (making non-resident adoption possible). Normally, independent adoptions are finalized 14 months after the placement of the child; agency adoptions are usually finalized in eight months. The adoptive parents are required to appear in court for the final hearing.

Independent Adoption. A pre-placement home study of the adoptive parents is required before the child can be placed in their home, unless a court specifically approves a direct placement without a home study. Upon completion of a pre-placement home study the adoptive parents receive a *Certification for Adoption.* The home study may be conducted by a licensed private adoption agency, licensed social worker, psychologist or psychiatrist. The individual or agency which conducts the home study also issues the *Certification for Adoption.* The cost of the pre and post-placement home study services typically varies from $1,000 to $1,500.

The birth mother and adoptive parents are not required to meet in person, but the name of the adoptive parents or their attorney must be provided on the consent form signed by the birth mother. The adoptive parents are permitted to assist the birth mother with pregnancy-related medical, legal and living expenses. The child may be released directly from the hospital to the adoptive parents, but some will require releasing the child to the attorney handling the adoption. Hospitals vary widely on this policy.

The birth mother may sign her consent to adoption, called a *surrender*, no sooner than five days after the birth. She must have her own attorney to advise her. The surrender must be witnessed by a notary and two witnesses, as well as her attorney. If the birth mother is under the age of eighteen, she must also have her parent, or a guardian (called a tutor) sign the surrender as well. Once signed, the surrender is irrevocable, but for proof of fraud or duress.

Louisiana has a putative birth father registry. Notice must be given to any putative fathers who either list themselves with the registry, or who can be identified by the birth mother. If the birth mother signs a pre-birth *Notice of Intent to Surrender*, notice can be given to the putative father pre-birth, and if he does nore object within 15 days from the date of notice (even if pre-birth) his consent to the adoption will not be required. Alternately, he can be given notice after birth, when the birth mother has signed her surrender, and he is given 15 days from the date of that notice to object.

Agency Adoption. There is no difference regarding the process in which a birth mother signs her consent to adoption in an independent or agency adoption, except that a birth mother need not have her own attorney, and instead the witnessing attorney can be the agency's attorney. The information provided above regarding independent adoption (e.g. when the surrender can be signed, before whom, legal burden to seek to withdraw a signed surrender) is identical regarding agency adoption.

Some agencies agree to do identified adoptions. Some agencies will also agree to make immediate hospital "at risk" placements.

American Academy of Adoption Attorney members:

Terri Hoover-Odom; 500 N. 7th Street, West Monroe, LA 71294; Tel: (318) 387-8811 ● centerforadoption.com ● terridebnam@jam.rr.com
A graduate of the Loyola University School of Law at New Orleans, she has been practicing law since 1986.

Edith H. Morris; 1515 Poydras Street, #1870, New Orleans, LA 70112; Tel: (504) 524-3781 ● e.morris@adoptionattorneys.org
A graduate of Loyola University School of Law, she has been practicing law since 1985.

Noel E. Vargas II; 146 N. Telemachus Street, New Orleans, LA 70119; Tel: (504) 488-0200 ● n.vargas@adoptionattorneys.org

MAINE

State Adoption Office: Maine Department of Health and Human Services (DHHS - BCFS); Bureau of Child and Family Services: 221 State Street; Augusta, ME 04333-0011; Phone: (207) 287-2976; http://www.afamilyforme.org

State Adoption Exchange: A Family For ME; Toll-Free: (877) 505-0545; info@afamilyforme.org; http://www.afamilyforme.org

State laws and procedures:

General Information. Maine permits both independent and agency adoption. Advertising is permitted by adoption agencies licensed in Maine. To file a Petition for Adoption within Maine the adoptive parents, or the child to be adopted, must reside there (making non-resident adoption possible). If it is an agency adoption, the Petition for Adoption may also be filed in Maine if the adoption agency having custody of the child is located there. Normally, independent adoptions are finalized one to two months after the placement of the child with the adoptive parents. Agency adoptions are typically finalized six months after placement. The adoptive parents are required to appear in court for the final hearing, although the court may waive this requirement.

Independent Adoption. A pre-placement home study of the adoptive parents is not required before a child can be placed in their home. The post-placement home study is performed by a licensed private adoption agency. The fee varies but is typically $1,600.

The birth parents and adoptive parents are not required to meet and share identities, although it is sometimes done voluntarily. Adoptive parents may assist the birth mother by paying pregnancy-related medical, legal and living expenses. The child may be released to the adoptive parents directly from the hospital, usually upon the birth mother's signature on a Power of Attorney and/or hospital release forms.

The consent to adoption may be signed any time after the birth. It must be witnessed by a probate judge and cannot be taken before the Petition for Adoption has been filed. The consent may be withdrawn only within three days of signing the consent. After the three-day period has elapsed, the consent can only be withdrawn upon proof of fraud or duress.

Maine does not have a putative birth father registry. Putative fathers must be given notice post-birth, then they have 20 days in which to file their objection/paternity action. If they can't be located, notice by publication is required, which then allows a 35 day period from the first day of publication.

Agency Adoption. There is little difference regarding the process in which a birth mother signs her consent to adoption in an independent or agency adoption, although the consent form employed by adoption agencies is called a *Surrender and Release.* Also, a pre-placement home study is required. The remaining information provided above regarding independent adoption (e.g. when the consent can be signed, before whom, legal burden to seek to withdraw a signed consent) is identical regarding agency adoption.

Some agencies within Maine do identified adoptions. Few agree to do immediate hospital "at risk" adoptions.

American Academy of Adoption Attorney members:

Judith M. Berry; 28 State Street, Gorham, ME 04038
Tel: (207) 839-7004 ● judithberryme@aol.com
A graduate of the University of Maine School of Law, she has been practicing law since 1991. She estimates she has completed more than 500 adoptions in her career and completes 100 annually: 20% independent; 70% agency; 10% international. She is an adoptive parent.

Abigail King Diggins; P.O. Box 7950, Portland, ME 04112
Tel: (207) 772-2800

MARYLAND

State Adoption Office: Maryland Department of Human Resources: 311 West Saratoga Street; Baltimore, MD 21201; Phone: (410) 767-7506; http://www.dhr.state.md.us

State Adoption Exchange: Maryland Adoption Resource Exchange (MARE): (same as above); Phone: (410) 767-7359; Phone: (410) 767-7737; mare@dhr.state.md.us; http://www.adoptuskids.org

State laws and procedures:

General Information. Maryland allows both independent and agency adoption. Approximately 60% of Maryland's infant adoptions are completed through independent adoption; 40% via agency. Advertising is permitted. Intermediaries, other than licensed adoption agencies, are not permitted to receive compensation for locating a birth mother to create an adoptive match for adoptive parents. Adoptive parents can file their Petition for Adoption in Maryland if they reside there or if the baby was born there (making non-resident adoption possible). Adoptions are usually finalized 3 to 6 months after the filing of the Petition for Adoption. The adoptive parents and the child to be adopted are required to appear at the final court hearing, although a court may waive the requirement.

Independent Adoption. Adoptive parents are not technically required to have a pre-placement home study completed before a child is placed in their home, although the adoptive parents must be granted a temporary custody order by a judge to take custody (and most courts require a pre-placement home study). The home study may be performed by a licensed adoption agency, court investigator, social worker or county social services department. The fee for the home study varies from free to approximately $2,300 based upon who performs the home study, and the county in which the adoptive parents live.

The birth parents and adoptive parents are not required to meet and share identities. However, many voluntarily agree to meet in person. Identities are shared in many cases. Adoptive parents may assist the birth mother by paying her pregnancy-related medical and legal expenses. Assistance with living costs is not permitted. The child may be placed with the adoptive parents directly from the hospital, but a court order granting the adoptive parents temporary legal custody is required.

The birth mother may sign her consent to the adoption anytime after the birth. A witness is required, but the statutes do not appear to specify if it must be a judge, social worker, or similar person. Most consents are signed one to four days after the birth. The birth mother has the automatic right to withdraw the consent for a period of 30 days after signing. Once the 30-day period has passed her consent is irrevocable.

Maryland does not have a putative birth father registry. Notice must be given and if he can't be found notice by publication is required. Putative father's rights are normally severed if they do not object within 30 days of notice.

Agency Adoption. There is no difference regarding the process in which a birth mother signs her consent to adoption in an independent or agency adoption except that a pre-placement home study is required, and that the child must be in the adoptive parents' care for six months prior to finalization. The information provided above regarding independent adoption (e.g. when the consent can be signed, before whom, legal burden to seek to withdraw a signed consent) is identical regarding agency adoption. Some agencies agree to do identified adoptions. Some agencies also agree to do immediate hospital "at risk" placements.

American Academy of Adoption Attorney members:

Jeffrey E. Badger; P.O. Box 259, Salisbury, MD 21803
Tel: (410) 749-2356 ● longbadger.com ● jbadger@longbadger.com
A graduate of the Washington & Lee University School of Law, he has been practicing law since 1980. He is an adoptive parent.

Ellen Ann Callahan; 12600 War Admiral Way, Gaithersburg, MD 20878; Tel: (301) 258-2664 ● adoptinmaryland.com ● e.callahan@adoptionattorneys.org

Jennifer Fairfax; 827 Woodside Parkway, Silver Spring, MD 20910 Tel: (301) 221-9651 ● jenniferfairfax.com ● j.fairfax@adoptionattorneys.org

John R. Greene; 156 South St., Annapolis, MD 21401 Tel: (410) 268-4500 ● familiesthruadoption.com ● jrgreenelaw@comcast.net
A graduate of the New York Law School, he has been practicing law since 1976. He estimates he has completed 1,000 adoptions in his career and completes 75 annually: 50% independent; 30% agency; 20% international. He does assist in creating adoptive matches.

Sherry L. Leichman; 51 Monroe Street, #1605, Rockville, MD 20850; Tel: (301) 545-1840 leichmansnyderlaw.com ● s.leichman@adoptionlawyer.org

Harvey Schweitzer; 4520 East-West Hwy, #700, Bethesda, MD 20814; Tel: (301) 469-3382 ● schweitzerlaw.com ● h.schweitzer@adoptionattorneys.org

Margaret E. Swain; P.O. Box 219, Riderwood, MD 21139; 301 W. Pennsylvania Ave., Towson, MD 21204
Tel: (410) 583-0688 ● m.swain@adoptionattorneys.org
A graduate of the University of Baltimore School of Law, she has been practicing law since 1987. She estimates she has completed 300 adoptions in her career and completes 70 annually: 85% independent; 10% agency; 5% international. She does not assist in creating adoptive matches.

Carolyn Thaler; 29 W. Susquehanna Ave., #205, Towson, MD 21204 Tel: (410) 828-6627 ● c.thaler@adoptionattorneys.org
A graduate of University of Baltimore School of Law.

Peter J. Wiernicki; 11140 Rockville Pike, #620, Rockville, MD 20852; Tel: (301) 230-2446 • p.wiernicki@adoptionattorneys.org
A graduate of the University of Baltimore School of Law, he has been practicing law since 1986. He is also licensed to practice law in Virginia and the District of Columbia.

Michele Zavos; 1400 Spring Street, #460, Silver Spring, MD 20910
Tel: (301) 562-8220 • zavosjunckerlawgroup.com •
m.zavos@adoptionattorneys.org

Please be aware that some attorneys located in neighboring states, particularly Virginia and the District of Columbia, also practice in Maryland. You may wish to see more information about them in those state listings.

MASSACHUSETTS

State Adoption Office: Massachusetts Department of Social Services: 24 Farnsworth Street; Boston, MA 02210; Phone: (617) 748-2267; http://www.mass.gov;

State Adoption Exchange: Massachusetts Adoption Resource Exchange, Inc. (MARE): Phone: (617) 542-3678; http://www.mareinc.org

State laws and procedures:

General Information. Massachusetts permits only agency adoption, unless the child is a blood relative. Accordingly, most all of Massachusetts' infant adoptions are completed via agency adoption. Advertising is permitted only by licensed adoption agencies. To file a Petition for Adoption within Massachusetts either the adoptive parents, or the child, must reside there (making non-resident adoption possible). Massachusetts law enforces open adoption agreements. Normally, adoptions are finalized seven to twelve months after the placement of the child with the adoptive parents. The adoptive parents and the child are required to appear in court for the final hearing.

A pre-placement home study of the adoptive parents is required before a child can be placed in their home. The home study must be performed by a licensed adoption agency. The fee varies among private agencies for pre and post-placement home study services from $2,500 to over $12,000, depending upon the services rendered.

It is not required that the birth mother and adoptive parents meet in person and share identities, although it is done voluntarily in many cases. Many agencies do identified adoptions, where meetings between the parties occur and identities are usually shared. The adoptive parents are permitted to assist with pregnancy-related medical, legal and living expenses. The child may be released directly from the hospital to the adoptive placement as an "at risk" placement if the agency authorizes the release.

The consent to adoption, called a *surrender*, may be signed no sooner than the fourth day after birth. It must be witnessed by a notary and two witnesses. The surrender is irrevocable upon signing, but for proof of fraud and duress.

Massachusetts has a putative birth father registry, but it seems to be deemed ineffective by the courts, at least in its present form. Accordingly, all putative fathers are given notice, or if they can't be found then give notice by publication, of an action to terminate their rights. The birth father must file an objection in court prior to a specified date in the notice, usually approximately two months later. At that hearing the child's best interests and the birth father's fitness will be considered.

American Academy of Adoption Attorney members:

Susan L. Crockin; 29 Crafts Street, Suite 500, Neweton, MA 02460
Tel: (617) 332-7070 ● s.crockin@adoptionattorneys.org

Herbert D. Friedman; 92 State Street, 7th floor, Boston, MA 02109
Tel: (617) 723-7700 ● massadopt.com ●
h.friedman@adoptionattorneys.org

Karen K. Greenberg; 220 Cedar St., Wellesley Hills, MA 02481
Tel: (781) 237-0033 ● kongreen.com ● kkg@kongreen.com
A graduate of the Suffolk University School of Law, she has been practicing law since 1983. She currently concentrates on contested/

problematic adoptions and appeals, while still completing many adoptions annually. She does not assist in creating adoptive matches. She is an adoptive parent and past president of the American Academy of Adoption Attorneys.

Jeffrey M. Kaye; 302 Broadway, Methuen, MA 01844
Tel: (617) 720-0028 ● j.kaye@adoptionattorneys.org

MICHIGAN

State Adoption Office: Michigan Department of Human Services; Child and Family Services Administration: PO Box 30037 -- Suite 413; Lansing, MI 48909; Phone: (517) 373-3513; http:// www.michigan.gov

State Adoption Exchange: Michigan Adoption Resource Exchange (MARE): Phone: (517) 783-6273; http://www.mare.org

State laws and procedures:

General Information. Michigan permits both independent and agency adoptions. Independent adoptions were illegal in Michigan until 1995. It is now estimated approximately 25% of Michigan's newborn adoptions were completed via independent adoption; 75% via agency. Advertising is permitted. To file a Petition for Adoption in Michigan, either the adoptive parents or one of the birth parents must reside there, or the child to be adopted must be physically present there (making non-resident adoptions possible). Normally, adoptions are finalized about six months after placement with the adoptive parents.

Independent Adoption. A pre-placement home study of the adoptive parents is required before a child can be placed in their home. The home study must be performed by a licensed adoption agency. The fee usually ranges from $1,000 to $3,500.

It is not required by law for the birth mother and adoptive parents to meet in person and share identities, but it is usually done. The adoptive parents are permitted to assist the birth mother with pregnancy-related medical and living expenses if of a reasonable amount and supported by receipts. The child may be released directly to the adoptive parents directly from the hospital with the birth mother's signature on a *Temporary Placement Agreement.*

The consent to adoptions can be signed anytime after the birth. It must be taken in court at a hearing, which is usually scheduled by the court anywhere from two days to two months later, depending upon the county. Once signed, the consent is irrevocable and can only be withdrawn upon proof of fraud or duress.

Michigan has a putative birth father registry, where putative fathers can file a *Notice of Intent to Claim Paternity.* If a putative father is personally served with the birth mother's *Notice of Intent to Release or Consent,* he must fie a *Notice of Intent to Claim Paternity* to be entitled to notice of a hearing. Notice must also be given to any putative fathers if known to the birth mother, who were not served with the birth mother's Notice of Intent. Their failure to appear at the scheduled hearing will terminate their rights. If a putative birth father elects to object in court, the court will consider the best interests of the child in determining whether to terminate parental rights.

Agency Adoption. There is no difference regarding the process in which a birth mother signs her consent to adoption in an independent or agency adoption, with the exception that in most cases a birth mother relinquishes her child directly to the agency, rather than making a direct placement to the adoptive parents. Either form of consent is irrevocable upon signing in court.

Most agencies in Michigan agree to do identified adoptions. Many will do immediate "at risk" placements with the adoptive parents before the irrevocable consents are taken if the adoptive parents are properly licensed.

American Academy of Adoption Attorney members:

Herbert A. Brail; 930 Mason St., Dearborn, MI 48124
Tel: (313) 278-8779 ● brail-law.com ● h.brail@adoptionattorneys.org
A graduate of the Wayne State University School of Law, he has been practicing law since 1982.

Lauran F. Howard; 1200 N. Telegraph Road, #452, Pontiac, MI 48341; Tel: (248) 858-0038 ● l.howard@adoptionattorneys.org

Monica Farris Linkner; 6204 Celeste Rd, West Boomfield, MI 48322

Tel: (248) 432-1902 ● linknerlaw.com ● m.linkner@adoptionattorneys.org

A graduate of Wayne State University School of Law, she has been practicing since 1977. She estimates she has completed over 500 adoptions in her career (about 80% are infant adoptions).

Kenneth A. Rathert; 137 N. Park St., Kalamazoo, MI 49007

Tel: (269) 349-6808 ● rathertlaw.com ● kenrathert@rathertlaw.com

A graduate of the Valparaiso University School of Law, he has been practicing law since 1976. He estimates he has completed 400 adoptions in his career and completes 100 annually, 100% of them independent. He does assist in creating adoptive matches.

MINNESOTA

State Adoption Office: Minnesota Department of Human Services; Human Services Building: 444 Lafayette Road; St. Paul, MN 55155-3831; Phone: (651) 282-3793; http://www.dhs.state.mn.us

State Adoption Exchange: Minnesota Adoption Resource Network, Inc.: Phone: (612) 861-7115; info@mnadopt.org; http://www.mnadopt.org

State laws and procedures:

General Information. Minnesota permits both independent (technically called "direct placement: in Minnesota) and agency adoption. Approximately 80% of Minnesota's infant adoptions are completed via independent adoption; 20% via agencies. Advertising is permitted. Attorneys are not permitted to locate birth mothers for adoptive parents. To file a Petition for Adoption within Minnesota the adoptive parents must reside there for a minimum of one year, although a court may waive this requirement. Normally, adoptions are completed no sooner than three months after the child's placement with the adoptive parents. The adoptive parents and the child are required to appear in court for the final hearing.

Independent ("direct placement") Adoption. A pre-placement home study of the adoptive parents is required before a child can be placed in their home, although in emergency situations exceptions may be permitted. The home study must be conducted by a licensed private adoption agency. The fee varies but is usually $2,200 to $6,000.

It is not required for the adoptive parents and birth mother to meet in person and share identities, although some elect to do so voluntarily. The adoptive parents are permitted to assist with the birth mother's pregnancy-related expenses. The child may be released directly from the hospital to the adoptive parents. Normally, however, the child's release must by court order, through an adoption agency, or the birth mother must be discharged with the child then personally give the child to the adoptive parents outside the hospital.

The consent may be signed no sooner than 72 hours after the birth. It may be witnessed by a judge or a licensed adoption agency if that agency provided counseling services to her. If the birth mother did not receive counseling, her consent must be witnessed by a judge. Birth mothers must be offered an independent attorney at the adoptive parents' expense. If the birth mother is a minor, her custodial parent must also sign a consent, and if that parent refuses, a guardian ad litem can be appointed to do so. Most consents are signed within one to two weeks after the birth. Once the consent is signed, the birth mother has the automatic right to withdraw the consent for a period of ten working days. Once the ten days have elapsed, the consent may only be withdrawn upon proof of fraud.

Minnesota has a putative birth father registry. A putative birth father can file anytime up to 30 days after birth. If he fails to register, he is not entitled to notice. If he does register, he must be given notice of his right to initiate a paternity action within 30 days of receiving the notice. If he does not do so, he has waived his right to object, unless he can show good cause for his failure to do so.

Agency Adoption. There is no difference regarding the process in which a birth mother signs her consent to adoption in an independent or agency adoption (e.g. when the consent can be signed, before whom, legal burden to seek to withdraw a signed consent) is identical regarding agency adoption, except there is no right to her own attorney at the adoptive parents' expense.

Some agencies in Minnesota agree to do identified adoptions, as well as make "at risk" placements before consents are irrevocable.

American Academy of Adoption Attorney members:

Gary A. Debele; 121 S. Eighth St., #1100, Minneapolis, MN 55402
Tel: (612) 335-4288 ● wbdlaw.com ● gary.debele@wbdlaw.com
A graduate of the University of Minnesota School of Law, he has been practicing law since 1987. He estimates he has completed 250 adoptions in his career and completes 35 annually: 85% independent; 10% agency; 5% international. He does not assist in creating adoptive matches. He is an adoptive parent.

Jody Ollyver DeSmidt; 121 S. Eighth St, #1100, Minneapolis, MN 55402
Tel: (612) 335-4284 ● wbdlaw.com ● jody.desmidt@wbdlaw.com
A graduate of the William Mitchell College of Law, she has been practicing law since 1982. She estimates she has completed over 800 adoptions in her career and completes 40 annually: 65% independent; 30% agency; 5% international. She does not assist in creating adoptive matches.

Stacia W. Driver; 121 S. 8th Street, #1100, Minneapolis, MN 55402
Tel: (612) 335-4295 ● wbdlaw.com ● s.driver@adoptionattorneys.org

Jessica J. W. Maher; 121 S. 8th St, #1100, Minneapolis, MN 55402
Tel: (612) 335-4291 ● wbdlaw.com ● Jessica.maher@wbdlaw.com

Brittany Shively; 111 Third Avenue South #360, Minneapolis, MN 55401; Tel: (612) 332-7772 ● b.shively@adoptionattorneys.org

Judith Vincent; 111 Third Avenue S., #360, Minneapolis, MN 55401
Tel: (612) 332-7772 ● adoptionlaw-mn.com ●
jvincent@adoptionlaw.mn.com
A graduate of the University of Minnesota School of Law, she has been practicing law since 1978. She estimates she has completed more than 2,500 adoptions in her career and completes 100 annually: 60% independent; 38% agency; 2% international. She does not assist in creating adoptive matches. She is an adoptive parent.

Wright S. Walling; 121 S. Eighth St., #1100, Minneapolis, MN 55402; Tel: (612) 340-1150 • wbdlaw.com • w.walling@adoptionattorneys.org

MISSISSIPPI

State Adoption Office: Mississippi Department of Human Services; Division of Family and Child Services: 750 North State Street; Jackson, MS 39202; Phone: (601) 359-4981; http://www.mdhs.state.ms.us

State Adoption Exchange: Mississippi Adoption Resource Exchange: Phone: (601) 359-4407; http://www.mdhs.state.ms.us

State laws and procedures:

General Information. Mississippi permits both independent and agency adoption. Advertising is permitted. To file a Petition for Adoption in Mississippi either the adoptive parents must be residents, the child must be born there, or the adoption agency having custody of the child must be located there. Normally, adoptions are finalized approximately six months after the placement of the child with the adoptive parents, but the court can waive this period and dramatically shorten it. The adoptive parents and the child to be adopted are often not required to appear in court for the final hearing.

Independent Adoption. A home study of the adoptive parents is required, but need not be completed before a child is placed in their home. The home study must be done by a licensed social worker working for an adoption agency. The court may waive any post-placement agency visits to the adoptive home.

It is not required by law that the adoptive parents and birth mother meet in person and share identities, although many do so voluntarily. The adoptive parents are permitted by law to assist the birth mother with pregnancy-related medical, legal and living expenses. The child may be released directly to the adoptive parents from the hospital, usually through an attorney.

The consent to adoption cannot be signed sooner than 72 hours after the birth. There are no state statutory laws governing the possible withdrawal of a consent to adoption, but case law indicates that once the consent is signed it is irrevocable, except for proof of fraud or duress. The state statute also does not mention who, if anyone, must act as a witness to the signing of the consent. As a practical matter, however, all consents are normally witnessed by a notary public.

Mississippi does not have a putative birth father registry. Putative birth fathers are given personal notice, or by publication if they can't be located, of the action to terminate their parental rights. The the putative father's identity is unknown, the court determines what, if any, notice is required.

Agency Adoption. There is no difference regarding the process in which a birth mother signs her consent to adoption in an independent or agency adoption, except that a pre and post-placement home study is routinely done, usually at a cost of about $1,300. The other information provided above regarding independent adoption (e.g. when the consent can be signed, before whom, legal burden to seek to withdraw a signed consent) is identical regarding agency adoption.

Some agencies in the state agree to do identified adoptions, as well as make immediate "at risk" placements before consents are signed.

American Academy of Adoption Attorney members:

Wes Daughdrill; 210 East Capitol St., Suite 2000; P.O. Box 23059, Jackson, MS 39225; Tel: (601) 360-9030 ● 279youngwilliams.com ● wes.daughdrill@youngwilliams.com
A graduate of the University of Missisippi School of Law, he has been practicing law since 1993.

Dan J. Davis; 352 N. Spring Street: P.O. Box 7262, Tupelo, MS 38802
Tel: (662) 841-1090 ● d.davis@adoptionattorneys.org
A graduate of University of Iowa, he has been practicing law since 1989. He estimates he completes 50 adoptions annually: 60% independent; 30% agency; 10% international. He does not assist in creating adoptive matches.

MISSOURI

State Adoption Office: Missouri Department of Social Services: 615 Howerton Court; PO Box 88; Jefferson City, MO 65103-0088; Phone: (573) 751-3171; http://www.dss.mo.gov

State Adoption Exchange: Missouri Adoption Photolisting: http://www.adoptuskids.org;

State laws and procedures:

General Information. Missouri permits both independent and agency adoption. Approximately 60% of Missouri's infant adoptions are completed via independent adoption; 40% via agencies. Advertising is permitted. To file a Petition for Adoption within Missouri either the adoptive parents, the birth mother, or the child to be adopted, must reside there (making non-resident adoption possible). Normally, adoptions are finalized approximately six months after the placement of the child with the adoptive parents. The adoptive parents and the child are usually required to appear in court for the final hearing.

Independent Adoption. A pre-placement home study of the adoptive parents is required before a child is placed in the adoptive home. It may be conducted by a licensed adoption agency or licensed social worker. The fees vary but typical pre and post-placement home study fees total $1,000 to $5,000.

Adoptive parents and birth mothers are not required by law to meet in person or share identities, although it is done voluntarily in a some cases. The adoptive parents are permitted to assist with pregnancy-related medical, living, counseling and legal expenses. The child may be released directly from the hospital to the adoptive parents, although hospital policies vary. Some hospitals accept a Power of Attorney form while others require a court order called an *Order of Transfer of Custody*.

The consent to adoption of the birth mother can be signed no sooner than 48 hours after the birth. It must be witnessed by a notary or two witnesses. Most consents are signed within several days of the birth. After signing, the consent must then be filed with the court so a judge may approve the consent and issue an order approving the consent. Before the court enters this order the birth mother has the automatic right to withdraw her consent. After the court's order, the consent may only be withdrawn upon proof of fraud or duress.

Missouri has a putative birth father registry. Putative birth fathers must register no later than 15 days after the birth. There is no independent requirement that birth mothers identify putative fathers. A birth father who fails to either register within 15 days, be acknowledged on the birth certificate, or file a paternity action, waives his rights.

Agency Adoption. There is no difference regarding the process in which a birth mother signs her consent to adoption in an independent or agency adoption. The information provided above regarding independent adoption (e.g. when the consent can be signed, before whom, legal burden to seek to withdraw a signed consent) is identical regarding agency adoption.

Some agencies in Missouri agree to do identified adoptions. Some agencies also agree to make immediate hospital "at risk" placements with the adoptive parents before the consents are irrevocable.

American Academy of Adoption Attorney members:

Mary Beck; 2775 Shag Bark, Columbia, MO 65203
Tel: (573) 446-7554 ● law.missouri.edu/beck/ ● beckm@missouri.edu
A graduate of the Missouri University School of Law, she has been practicing law since 1988.

Michael Belfonte; 1125 Grand Blvd., #1301, Kansas City, MO 64106
Tel: (816) 842-3580 ● m.belfonte@adoptionattorneys.org

Timothy B. Brassil; 4390 Lindell Boulevard, St. Louis, MO 63108
Tel: (314) 534-5110 ● t.brassil@adoptionattorneys.org

Daniel M. Buescher; 214 Elm Street, #102, Washington, MO 63090
Tel: (636) 390-2202 ● d.buescher@adoptionattorneys.org
A graduate of Washington University, he has been practicing law since 1964. He estimates he completes 40 adoptions annually: 60% independent; 39% agency; 1% international. He does assist in creating adoptive matches.

Catherine W. Keefe; 222 S. Central Ave., #708, Clayton, MO 63105
Tel: (314) 726-6242 ● ckeefe@keefebrodie.com
A graduate of the St. Louis University School of Law, she has been practicing law since 1986. She estimates she has completed more than 500 adoptions in her career, and last year completed approximately 37 (15 independent; 12 agency; 10 intercountry). Approximately 30% of her practice consists of adoptions (typically 50% independent; 30% agency; 20% intercountry), and of these 75% are newborn placements, 25% are toddlers or above. She reports all of her clients locate their own birth mother.

Sanford P. Krigel; 4550 Belleview, Kansas City, MO 64111
Tel: (816) 756-5800 ● krigelandkrigel.com ● s.krigel@adoptionattorneys.org
A graduate of the St. Louis University School of Law, he has been practicing law since 1976.

Allan F. Stewart; 222 S. Central St., Suite 501, St. Louis, MO 63105
Tel: (314) 863-8484 ● vdrm22825@sbclgobal.net
A graduate of the St. Louis University School of Law, he has been practicing law since 1973.

F. Richard Van Pelt; 1524 E. Primrose, Suite A , Springfield, MO 65804; Tel: (417) 886-9080 ● www.vanpeltlaw.com ● r.vanpelt@adoptionattorneys.org
A graduate of the University of Missouri at Columbia School of Law, he has been practicing law since 1983.

Kay A. Van Pelt; 1524 E. Primrose Suite A , Springfield, MO 65804
Tel: (417) 886-9080 ● www.vanpeltlaw.com ● k.vanpelt@adoptionattorneys.org
A graduate of the University of Missouri at Columbia School of Law, she has been practicing law since 1983.

Betty Wilson; 401 Locust St., #406, Columbia, MO 65205
Tel: (573) 443-3134 ● www.owwlaw.com ● bwilson@owwlaw.com
A graduate of the University of Missouri School of Law at Columbia, she has been practicing law since 1975.

MONTANA

State Adoption Office: Montana Department of Public Health and Human Services (DPHHS): PO Box 8005; Helena, MT 59604-8005; Phone: (406) 841-2400; hlutz@mt.gov; http://www.dphhs.mt.gov

State Adoption Exchange: Montana Waiting Children Photolistings: (same as above); Phone: (866-936-7837); askaboutadoption@mt.gov; http://www.adoptuskids.org

State laws and procedures:

General Information. Montana permits both independent (called "direct placement") and agency adoption. Approximately 50% of Montana's infant adoptions are completed via independent adoption; 50% via agencies. Advertising is not permitted. To file a Petition for Adoption within Montana the adoptive parents must be residents of the state. Normally, adoptions are finalized approximately six months after the child's placement with the adoptive parents. The adoptive parents and the child are required to appear in court for the final hearing.

Independent Adoption. A pre-placement home study of the adoptive parents is required. The home study may be conducted by a licensed adoption agency or licensed social worker. The fee for the pre-and post placement home study ranges from $1,000 - $2,000.

It is required by law that the adoptive parents and birth mother share identities, and virtually all meet each other in person. The adoptive parents are allowed by law to assist the birth mother with pregnancy-related expenses, including living expenses. The child can be released to the adoptive parents directly from the hospital.

The consent, called a *relinquishment of parental rights and consent to adoption*, may be signed no sooner than 72 hours after the birth. It may be witnessed by a notary or representative of the court or a licensed adoption agency. It is later filed with the court and a request to a judge is made to enter an *Order Terminating Parental Rights*. Prior to the order being issued, the birth mother may seek to withdraw her consent only if she can prove fraud or duress in the signing of the consent. Once the order is issued the consent is irrevocable.

Montana has a putative birth father registry.

Agency Adoption. There is no difference regarding the process in which a birth mother signs her consent to adoption in an independent or agency adoption. The information provided above regarding independent adoption (e.g. when the consent can be signed and before whom) is identical regarding agency adoption.

Some agencies in Montana agree to do identified adoptions. Some agencies also agree to make immediate hospital "at risk" placements with the adoptive parents before the consents are irrevocable.

American Academy of Adoption Attorney members:

Dennis E. Lind; 201 W. Main Street, Suite 201, Missoula, MT 59802
Tel: (406) 728-0810 • d.lind@adoptionattorneys.org

NEBRASKA

State Adoption Office: Nebraska Department of Health and Human Services: PO Box 95044; 301 Centennial Mall South -- Child and Family Services Division; Lincoln, NE 68509-5044; Phone: (402) 471-9331; http://www.hhs.state.ne.us

State Adoption Exchange: Nebraska Adoption Exchange: Phone: (402) 471-9331; mary.dyer@hhss.state.ne.us; http://www.hhs.state.ne.us

State laws and procedures:

General Information. Nebraska permits both independent and agency adoption. Advertising is permitted. To file a Petition for Adoption within Nebraska the adoptive parents must reside there. Normally, adoptions are finalized approximately seven months after the child's placement with the adoptive parents. The adoptive parents and the child are required to appear in court for the final hearing.

Independent Adoption. A pre-placement home study of the adoptive parents is required before a child can be placed in their home. The home study may be performed by a licensed adoption agency or the Nebraska Department of Social Services (which serves only certain counties in an independent adoption). The fees for pre and post-placement home study services usually range from $1,500 to 2,500.

It is not required by law for the birth mother and adoptive parents to meet in person or share identities, although some elect to do so voluntarily. There are no statutes governing permitted expenses, just case law. The normal practice is to allow adoptive parents to assist the birth mother with pregnancy-related medical and legal expenses. Living expenses are normally not permitted unless there is a significant safety issue for the birth mother and fetus (such as homelessness, or the inability to pay a heating bill in winter, et cetera), to eliminate any possible appearance of improper influence by the adoptive parents. The child may be released to the adoptive parents directly from the hospital, although many hospitals will only arrange the release through an attorney.

The consent can be signed no sooner than 48 hours after the birth. It must be witnessed by a notary and one witness. There are no state statutes governing the withdrawal of a consent to adoption, but case law indicates they are irrevocable, and can only be withdrawn by proof to the court fraud or duress was used, or the child's best interests would be served by being removed from the adoptive parents. Once the adoption is finalized the consent becomes irrevocable.

Nebraska has a putative birth father registry. The birth mother must sign an affidavit identifying all possible putative fathers, who must then be given notice by certified mail or personal service. If he can't be located, notice by publication can be used. He then has 5 days from his receipt of notice, or the birth, whichever is later, to file an objection to adoption with the registry. If he does, he has an additional 30 days to file a paternity action. If he fails to do so his rights will no longer be recognized.

Agency Adoption. There is no difference regarding the process in which a birth mother signs her consent to adoption in an independent or agency adoption, with the exception that the consent is considered irrevocable once: it is signed and the agency has accepted the consent. The information provided above regarding independent adoption (e.g. when the consent can be signed and before whom) is identical regarding agency adoption.

Some agencies in Nebraska agree to do identified adoptions. Some agencies also agree to make immediate hospital "at risk" placements with the adoptive parents before the consents are irrevocable.

American Academy of Adoption Attorney members:

Susan Kubert Sapp; 233 South 13th Street, #1900, Lincoln, NE 68508; and 1125 South 103rd, Omaha, NE 68124
Tel: (402) 474-6900 ● clinewilliams.com ● ssapp@clinewilliams.com
Susan Sapp has completed hundreds of adoptions since 1989. She is a trial attorney and adoptions make up about 25% of her practice.

Kelly N. Tollefsen; 134 South 13th Street, #800, Lincoln, NE 68508
Tel: (402) 438-2500 ● demarsgordon.com ●
k.tollefsen@adoptionattorneys.org
A graduate of the University of Nebraska College of Law, she has been practicing law since 2000.

Please be aware that some attorneys located in neighboring states, particularly Iowa and South Dakota, also practice in Nebraska.

NEVADA

State Adoption Office: Nevada Department of Human Resources; Division of Child and Family Services: 4220 South Maryland Parkway -- Building B, Suite 300; Las Vegas, NV 89119; Phone: (702) 486-7633; http://www.dcfs.state.nv.us

State Adoption Exchange: Nevada Photolisting Service: Toll-Free: (888) 423-2659; http://dcfs.state.nv.us;

State laws and procedures:

General Information. Nevada permits both independent and agency adoption. Advertising is not permitted. To file a Petition for Adoption within Nevada the adopting parents must reside there, and can be filed only after the child has been in the home for 30 days. Normally, adoptions are finalized approximately seven months after the child's placement with the adoptive parents. The adopting parents and the child are required to appear in court at the final hearing, except for non-residents completing an agency adoption, in which case the final appearance can usually be made telephonically.

Independent Adoption. A pre-placement home study of the adoptive parents is required before a child can be placed in their home. The home study may be conducted by the state adoption office (which usually limits its services to foster homes and special needs adoptions) or a licensed adoption agency. The fee varies but can be as inexpensive as $2,000.

It is not required by law that adoptive parents and birth mothers meet in person, although it is usually done voluntarily. It is required that full identities be shared. The adoptive parents are permitted to assist the birth mother with pregnancy-related expenses. The child may be released directly from the hospital to the adoptive parents.

The consent to adoption can be signed no sooner than 72 hours after the birth. It must be witnessed by two witnesses, one of whom must be a social worker, and it must be notarized. The consent is irrevocable once signed.

Nevada does not have a putative birth father registry. Putative fathers must be given notice of an action to terminate their parental rights. If he can't be found, notice by publication will be required, and twenty days thereafter the hearing can occur. The dominant issue of interest to the court is the best interests of the child in determining to terminate a putative father's rights. If a putative father wishes to assent to the adoption, he may sign a consent even prior to the birth.

Agency Adoption. There is no difference regarding the process in which a birth mother signs her consent to adoption in an independent or agency adoption. The information provided above regarding independent adoption (e.g. when it can be signed, before whom, legal burden to seek to withdraw a signed consent) is identical regarding agency adoption.

American Academy of Adoption Attorney members:

Ginny L. Frank; 200 Ridge Street, Suite 75, Reno, NV 89501
Tel: (303) 918-6707 ●adoptionchoices.org

Heather E. Kemp; 7435 W. Azure Road, #110, Las Vegas, NV 89110
Tel: (702) 258-1183 ● kemp-attorneys.com ●
h.kemp@adoptionattorneys.org

Israel "Ishi" Kunin; 3551 E. Bonanza Rd., #110, Las Vegas, NV
89110; Tel: (702) 438-8060 ● kunincarman.com ●
i.kunin@adoptionattorneys.org
A graduate of the Cal-Western School of Law, she has been practicing
law since 1980. She estimates she has completed 500 adoptions in her
career and completes 50 annually: 80% independent; 20% agency.
She does not assist in creating adoptive matches.

Todd L. Moody; 10080 W. Alta Drive, #200, Las Vegas, NV 89145
Tel: (702) 385-2500 ● hutchlegal.com ●
t.moody@adoptionattorneys.org

Eric A. Stovall; 200 Ridge St., Suite 222, Reno, NV 89501
Tel: (775) 337-1444 ● nevadaadoptionlawyer.com ●
e.stovall@adoptionattorneys.org
A graduate of the Nevada School of Law, hehas been practicing law
since 1987. He estimates he has completed more than 250 adoptions
in his career and completes 95 annually: 30% independent; 70%
agency. He does not assist in creating adoptive matches.

NEW HAMPSHIRE

State Adoption Office: New Hampshire Department of Health and
Human Services; Division for Children, Youth and Families: 129
Pleasant Street -- Brown Building; Concord, NH 03301; Phone: (603)
271-4707; http://www.dhhs.state.nh.us

State Adoption Exchange: New Hampshire Department of Health
and Human Services: (same as above); Phone: (603) 271-4707; http://
www.dhhs.state.nh.us

State laws and procedures:

General Information. New Hampshire permits both independent and agency adoption. Approximately 60% of New Hampshire's infant adoptions are completed via independent adoption; 40% via agencies. Advertising is permitted. To file a Petition for Adoption in New Hampshire either the adoptive parents, or the child to be adopted, must be residents of the state (making non-resident adoption possible). If it is an agency adoption the Petition for Adoption may also be filed there if the agency having custody of the child is located in New Hampshire. Normally, adoptions are finalized approximately six months after the child's placement with the adoptive parents.

Independent Adoption. A pre-placement home study of the adoptive parents is required before a child can be placed in their home. The home study may be conducted by a licensed adoption agency. The fee varies.

It is not required by law that the adoptive parents and the birth mother meet in person and share identities, although some elect to do so voluntarily. The adoptive parents are permitted to assist the birth mother with pregnancy-related expenses, including living expenses. The child can be released directly to the adoptive parents from the hospital, although each hospital may employ different release forms.

The consent to adoption, called a *Surrender of Parental Rights*, can be signed no sooner than 72 hours after the birth. It must be witnessed by a judge. The birth parents must be represented by counsel, unless a judge waives that requirement. If the birth parent is under the age of 18 the court may require the consent of a parent as well. Once signed, the surrender can only be withdrawn upon proof of fraud or duress and that the child's bests interests would be served by removal from the adoptive parents.

New Hampshire has a putative birth father registry. Putative birth fathers must register prior to the time the birth mother surrenders her parental rights. If he fails to do so, he has lost his right to claim paternal rights.

Agency Adoption. There is no difference regarding the process in which a birth mother signs her surrender in an independent or agency adoption. The information provided above regarding independent adoption (e.g. when the surrender can be signed and before whom) is identical regarding agency adoption.

Some agencies in New Hampshire agree to do identified adoptions. Some agencies also agree to make immediate hospital "at risk" placements with the adoptive parents before the consents are irrevocable.

American Academy of Adoption Attorney members:

Margaret Cunnane Hall; 37 High Street, Milford, NH 03055
Tel: (603) 673-8323 ● www.margaretchall.com ●
m.hall@adoptionattorneys.org
A graduate of the New England Law School, she has been practicing law since 1979. She estimates she has completed 1,000 adoptions in her career and completes 30 annually: 99% independent; 1% agency. She is an adoptive parent.

Ann McLane Kuster; One Capital Plaza; Concord, NH 03302
Tel: (603) 226-2600 ● www.rathlaw.com ● amk@rathlaw.com
A graduate of the Georgetown Law School, she has been practicing law since 1984.

NEW JERSEY

State Adoption Office: New Jersey Department of Children and Families; Office of Resource Families and Adoption Support:
50 East State Street -- PO Box 717; Trenton, NJ 08625; Phone: (609) 984-6080; http://www.state.nj.us

State Adoption Exchange: New Jersey Division of Youth and Family Services Adoption Exchange: Phone: (609) 984-5453; http://www.state.nj.us

State laws and procedures:

General Information. New Jersey permits both independent and agency adoption. Advertising is permitted. To file a Petition for Adoption within New Jersey the adoptive parents must reside there, or the child must be born there (making non-resident adoption possible). A Petition for Adoption can also be filed there if the child was surrendered to a New Jersey adoption agency. Normally, independent adoptions are finalized ten months after the placement of the child with the adoptive parents. Agency adoptions are usually finalized seven months after placement. The adoptive parents are required to appear in court for the final hearing, but out-of-state residents are often permitted to appear by video conferencing.

Independent Adoption. Birth mothers can be introduced to adoptive parents by intermediaries only if the adoptive parents have a completed home study. The intermediary (which includes attorneys) cannot charge a fee for this service. This home study must be conducted by a licensed non-profit adoption agency. The fee varies.

It is not required by law that the adoptive parents and birth mother meet and share identities, although it is often done voluntarily. The adoptive parents are permitted by law to assist the birth mother with pregnancy-related living, medical, counseling and legal expenses. The child can be placed with the adoptive parents directly from the hospital, but some hospitals require that the birth mother must be discharged with the baby, then personally place the child with the adopting parents outside the hospital.

The consent to adoption can be signed anytime after birth. The consent is not irrevocable until one of two situations occur. The birth parent can appear before a judge and agree to the termination of parental rights. If this is done, usually it is approximately 10-14 days after the birth. If this is not done, the consent cannot be made permanent until a preliminary hearing, which normally occurs several months after the birth and filing of the Complaint for Adoption.

New Jersey does not have a putative birth father registry. Notice is given to any putative birth father of the pending adoption. He has 120 days after birth, or the date of the preliminary hearing, whichever is first, to either amend the birth certificate to be named as the biological father, or file a paternity action. If he does one of these actions he has the right to object and the court will examine his fitness and the best interests of the child. Although there are other procedures to give notice and terminate parental rights, this is the traditional one.

Agency Adoption. The information provided above regarding independent adoption is identical regarding agency adoption, except a birth mother's consent to adoption, called a *surrender*, can be taken no sooner than 72 hours after birth. Once executed, it is irrevocable, except for fraud or duress. A birth parent must also be offered, but is not required to accept, three counseling sessions.

Many agencies in New Jersey agree to do identified adoptions. Many agencies will agree to do immediate hospital "at risk" placements.

American Academy of Adoption Attorney members:

Donald C. Cofsky; 209 Haddon Avenue, Haddonfield, NJ 08033
Tel: (856) 429-5005 ● 209law.com ● dcc@209law.com
A graduate of the Temple University School of Law, he has been practicing law since 1973. He estimates he has completed more than 1,500 adoptions in his career and completes 100 annually: 30% independent; 55% agency; 15% international. He does not assist in creating adoptive matches. He was a recipient of 2005 Congressional Angel in Adoption Award.

Robin Fleischner; 374 Millburn Ave., #303E Millburn, NJ 07041
Tel: (973) 376-6623 ● adoptlawyer.com ● robin@adoptlawyer.com
A graduate of the Yeshiva University, Benjamin N. Cardozo School of Law, she has been practicing law since 1980. She is also licensed to practice in New York. She estimates she has completed more than 1,000 adoptions in her career.

Debra E. Guston; 55 Harristown Road, #202, Glen Rock, NJ 07452
Tel: (201) 447-6660

Elizabeth A. Hopkins; 766 Shrewsbury Ave., Tinton Falls, NJ 07724
Tel: (732) 933-7777 ● peterliska.com ● liz@peterliska.com
A graduate of the Seton Hall School of Law, she has been practicing law since 1984.

Steven B. Sacharow; 1810 Chapel Ave. West, Cherry Hill, NJ 08002
Tel: (856) 661-1919 ● flastergreenberg.com ●
s.sacharow@adoptionattorneys.org

Toby Solomon; 5 Becker Farm Road, Roseland, NJ 07068
Tel: (973) 533-0078 ● tobysolomon.com ●
tsolomon@tobysolomon.com
A graduate of the Seton Hall School of Law, She has been practicing
law since 1983.n

Deborah E. Spivack; P.O. Box 3433, Cherry Hill, NJ 08034
Tel: (856) 857-1155 ● familybuildinglaw.net ●
d.spivack@adoptionattorneys.org

Deborah Steincolor; 80 Park Street, Montclair, NJ 07042
Tel: (973) 743-7500 ● adoptattorney.net ● dsteincolor@aol.com
A graduate of the Delaware Law School of Widener University, she
has been practicing law since 1987. She is also licensed to practice in
New York. She estimates she has completed more than 1,800
adoptions in her career, and last year completed approximately 73 (41
independent; 22 agency; 20 intercountry readopts). Her domestic
adoptions are typically 65% independent; 35% agency, and of these
100% are newborn placements.

NEW MEXICO

State Adoption Office: New Mexico Department of Children, Youth
and Families: PERA Building, Room 254; PO Drawer 5160; Santa Fe,
NM 87502-5160; Phone: (505) 827-8455; http://www.cyfd.org

State Adoption Exchange: New Mexico Department of Children,
Youth and Families: 2920 Carlisle Blvd, Suite G, Albuquerque, NM
87110; www.cyfd.org

State laws and procedures:

General Information. New Mexico permits both independent and
agency adoption. Approximately 75% of New Mexico's infant
adoptions are completed via independent adoption; 25% via agencies.
Advertising is permitted. To file a Petition for Adoption within New
Mexico the adoptive parents must be residents, or the child must be
born there (making non-resident adoption possible). If it is an agency

adoption the Petition for Adoption can also be filed there if the agency having custody of the child is located in New Mexico. Normally, adoptions are finalized four months after the child's placement with the adoptive parents. The adoptive parents are required to appear in court for the final hearing unless good cause (travel distance) can be shown to waive it.

Independent Adoption. A pre-placement home study of the adoptive parents is required before the child is placed in their home. The home study may be conducted by a licensed adoption agency or an independent social worker certified by the Children, Youth and Families Department. The fee varies but typical pre and post-placement services range from $1,500 to $2,500.

It is not required by law that the adoptive parents and birth mother meet in person and share identities, although it is done in most cases voluntarily. The adoptive parents are permitted to assist the birth mother with pregnancy-related expenses, including living expenses, although these expenses must be paid directly to the party supplying the related services and not a third party like the birth mother. The child may be released directly from the hospital to the adoptive parents, although hospitals use various forms for the release.

The consent to adoption, called the Voluntary Relinquishment, can be signed no sooner than 48 hours after the birth. It must be signed before a judge. It is irrevocable upon signing, but for proof of fraud or duress. New Mexico allows for enforceable open adoption agreements.

New Mexico has a putative birth father registry. Putative birth fathers who have registered within ten days of the birth must be served notice. No notice is required to those not registering and their rights are normally terminated at the adoption finalization. must be served if known by the birth mother, or if listed with the registry within 10 days after the birth. Putative fathers are divided into two categories, "acknowledged" fathers (who filed with the registry, or filed a paternity action within 10 days of the birth) and "alleged" fathers (who failed to file). Consent to adoption is required of acknowledged fathers. Alleged fathers' rights can be terminated upon a showing of the best interests of the child.

Agency Adoption. There is no difference regarding the process in which a birth mother signs her consent to adoption in an independent or agency adoption. The information provided above regarding independent adoption (e.g. when it can be signed, before whom and the legal burden to seek to withdraw a signed consent) is identical regarding agency adoption.

Some agencies in New Mexico agree to do identified adoptions. Some agencies also agree to make immediate hospital "at risk" placements.

American Academy of Adoption Attorney members:

Harold O. Atencio; 3809 Atrisco NW, Suite B, P.O. Box 66468, Albuquerque, NM 87193
Tel: (505) 839-9111 ● atenciolawpc.com ● adopt@atenciolawpc.com
A graduate of the University of New Mexico School of Law, he has been practicing law since 1988. He estimates he has completed more than 500 adoptions in his career.

Lisa H. Olewine; 4801 Lang, Suite 110: P.O. Box 93216, Albuquerque, NM 87199
Tel: (505) 858-3316 ● adoptionlaw.com ● nmadoptionlaw.com
A graduate of the University of New Mexico School of Law, she has been practicing law since 2001. Her practice is limited to adoptions (typically 75% independent; 15% agency; 10% intercountry). She is a past president of the Adoption and Foster Care Alliance of New Mexico and is an adoptive parent.

NEW YORK

State Adoption Office: New York State Office of Children and Family Services; New York State Adoption Service: 52 Washington Street, Room 323; Rensselaer, NY 12144; Phone: (518) 473-5754; http://www.ocfs.state.ny.us

State Adoption Exchange: New York State Office of Children and Family Services: (same as above); Phone: (518) 473-5754; carol.mccarthy@dfa.state.ny.us; www.ocfs.state.ny.us

State laws and procedures:

General Information. New York permits both independent and agency adoption. Approximately 70% of New York's infant adoptions are completed via independent adoption; 30% via agencies. Advertising is permitted. It is illegal for an intermediary, other than a licensed agency, to receive compensation for locating a birth mother for adoptive parents to create an adoptive match. To file a Petition for Adoption within New York either the adoptive parents, or the child being adopted, must reside there (making non-resident adoption possible). If it is an agency adoption the Petition for Adoption may be filed in New York if the agency having custody of the child is located there. Normally, adoptions are finalized from three to twelve months after the child's placement with the adoptive parents. The adoptive parents and the child are required to appear in court for the final hearing, although some court will allow an appearance by video conferencing.

Independent Adoption. A pre-placement home study of the adoptive parents is required before a child can be placed in their home. The home study is used to allow the adoptive parents to be "certified" as qualified adoptive parents. If the adoptive parents have not been certified by the time the placement is to occur, a court may permit the adoptive parents to have physical custody of the child if they file a request for temporary guardianship within five days of having obtained custody. The home study may be conducted by a licensed agency, licensed social worker, state adoption office, or other person approved by the court. The fee varies.

It is not required by law that the adoptive parents and birth mother meet in person and share identities, although some elect to do so voluntarily. The adoptive parents are permitted to assist the birth mother with pregnancy-related medical, legal and living expenses. Living assistance is limited to two months pre-birth and one month post-birth. Assistance in excess of these periods requires court approval. The child can be released from the hospital directly to the adoptive parents, although hospitals use different forms and have different policies.

The consent to adoption can be signed anytime after the birth. The consent must be witnessed by a judge or a notary public. Most consents are signed within several days of the birth. If the consent is signed before a judge, it is irrevocable upon signing, but for proof of fraud or duress. If the consent was witnessed by a notary public, the consent may be revoked for a period of 45 days from the time it is signed, but only if a court determines the child's best interests would be served by the child being removed from the adoptive parents.

New York has a putative birth father registry. A putative birth father who registers, or who is identified by the birth mother, must be given notice, giving him the right to offer evidence that he believes adoption is not in the best interests of the child.

Agency Adoption. The information provided above regarding independent adoption is identical regarding agency adoption, with the following exception. The consent to adoption, called a *surrender* in an agency adoption, may be signed anytime after birth. If it is witnessed by a judge the surrender is irrevocable upon signing. The surrender may also be witnessed by a representative of the adoption agency, and one additional witness. If this non-judicial witnessing option is selected, the surrender may be withdrawn by proving the child's best interests would be served, but only until 30 days have elapsed from the time the surrender is signed, and the child must have been placed with the adoptive parents. Once 30 days have elapsed and the child is placed with the adoptive parents, the surrender is irrevocable and can only be withdrawn upon proof of fraud or duress.

Some agencies agree to do identified adoptions. Some agencies also agree to do immediate hospital "at risk" placements.

American Academy of Adoption Attorney members:

Jeanine Castagna; 1225 Franklin Ave., #325, Garden City, NY 11530 Tel: (516) 495-7906 ● jcadoptionlaw.com ● j.castagna@adoptionattorneys.org
A graduate of Hofstra Law School, she has been practicing law since 1997. She estimates she completes 25 annually: 95% independent; 2.5% agency; 2.5% international. She does not assist in creating adoptive matches.

Anne Reynolds Copps; 126 State St., 6th Floor, Albany, NY 12207
Tel: (518) 436-4170 • arcopps.net • a.copps@adoptionattorneys.org
A graduate of the Albany Law School of Union University, she has
been practicing law since 1982. She estimates she has completed more
than 1,000 adoptions in her career.

Robin Fleischner; 11 Riverside Dr. #14 NW. New York, NY 10023
Tel: (212) 362-6945 • adoptsurrogatelaw.com •
robin@adoptlawyer.com
A graduate of the Yeshiva University, Benjamin N. Cardozo School of
Law, she has been practicing law since 1980. She is also licensed to
practice in New Jersey. She estimates she has completed more than
1,000 adoptions in her career, and last year completed approximately
50 (37 independent; 13 agency). Her practice is limited to adoptions
(typically 75% independent; 25% agency), and of these all are
newborn placements.

Gregory A. Franklin; 150 Allens Creek Road, Rochester, NY 14618
Tel: (585) 442-0540 • afylaw.com • gfranklin@afylaw.com
A graduate of the Fordham University School of Law, he has been
practicing law since 1984. He estimates he has completed more than
1,200 adoptions in his career.

Laurie B. Goldheim; 20 Old Nyack Turnpike, #300, Nanuet, NY
10954; Tel: (845) 624-2727 • adoptionrights.com •
lgoldheim@adoptionrights.com
A graduate of the Boston University School of Law, she has been
practicing law since 1990. She estimates she has completed more than
1,200 adoptions in her career and completes 80 annually: 90%
independent; 10% agency. She is an adoptee.

Michael S. Goldstein; 62 Bowman Avenue, Rye Brook, NY 10573
Tel: (914) 939-1111 • adoptgold.com • info@adoptgold.com
201 West 70th Street, Suite 17L, New York, NY 10023
A graduate of the Fordham Law School, he has been practicing law
since 1982. He estimates he has completed 2,200 adoptions in his
career and completes 40 annually: 10% independent; 30% agency;
60% international. He is an adoptive parent and the recipient of the
Congressional Angel in Adoption Award in 2006.

Lisa M. Gibbons; 64 North Park Ave., #203, Rockville Center, NY 11570; Tel: (516) 442-2176 • l.gibbons@adoptionattorneys.org

Kevin P. Harrigan; 2 Clinton Square, Suite 215, Syracuse, NY 13202 Tel: (314) 478-3138 • kevharr@twcny.rr.com
A graduate of the Syracuse University College of Law, he has been practicing law since 1978.

Stephen Lewin; 845 Third Avenue, Suite 1400, New York, NY 10022 Tel: (212) 759-2600 • s.lewin@adoptionattorneys.org

Frederick J. Magovern; 111 John Street, New York, NY 10038 Tel: (212) 962-1450 • f.magovern@adoptionattorneys.org
A graduate of the Fordham University School of Law, he has been practicing law since 1972. He estimates he has completed more than 500 adoptions in his career.

Cynthia Perla Meckler; 8081 Floss Lane, East Amherst, NY 14051 Tel: (716) 741-4164 • c.meckler@adoptionattorneys.org
A graduate of the SUNY Law School at Buffalo, she has been practicing law since 1980. She estimates she has completed more than 1,000 adoptions in her career.

Rebecca L. Mendel; 801 2nd Ave., 10th Floor, New York, NY 10017 Tel: (212) 972-5430 • r.mendel@adoptionattorneys.org
A graduate of Benjamin N. Cardozo School of Law, she has been practicing law since 1998.

Suzanne B. Nichols; 800 Westchester Ave. #641 North, Rye Brook, NY 10573; Tel: (914) 697-4870 • rlnlaw.com • adoptnpro@aol.com
A graduate of the New York Law School, she has been practicing law since 1985. She is also licensed to practice law in New Jersey. She estimates she has completed more than 1,000 adoptions in her career.

Brendan C. O'Shea; 40 Beaver Street, Albany, NY 12207 Tel: (518) 432-7511 • gdwo.net • boshea@gdwo.net
A graduate of the Albany Law School, he has been practicing law since 1980. He estimates he has completed more than 1,000 adoptions

in his career and completes 85 annually: 20% independent; 75% agency; 5% international.

Douglas H. Reiniger; 801 2nd Avenue, New York, NY 10017
Tel: (212) 972-5430 ● d.reiniger@adoptionattorneys.org
A graduate of the Fordham Law School, he has been practicing law since 1981.

Benjamin J. Rosin; 801 2nd Avenue, New York, NY 10017
Tel: (212) 972-5430 ● brosin@lawrsm.com
A graduate of the Columbia University School of Law, he has been practicing law since 1966. He estimates he has completed more than 1,000 adoptions in his career, and last year completed approximately 30 (10 independent; 20 agency). He is an adoptive parent.

Nina E. Rumbold; 116 Kraft Avenue, Suite 3, Bronxville, NY 10708
Tel: (914) 779-1050 ● adoptionlawny.com ●
n.rumbold@adoptionattorneys.org
A graduate of the New York University School of Law, she has been practicing law since 1978. She estimates she completes 60 adoptions annually: 55% independent; 29% agency; 16% international.

Denise Seidelman; 116 Kraft Avenue, Suite 3, Bronxville, NY 10708
Tel: (914) 779-1050 ●_adoptionlawny.com ●
d.seidelman@adoptionlawny.com
A graduate of the Washington College of Law, she has been practicing law since 1980. She estimates she has completed more than 500 adoptions in her career and completes 60 annually: 55% independent; 29% agency; 16% international.

Mary Walsh Schneider; 653 Plank Rd. #111, Clifton Park, NY 12065
Tel: (518) 371-9910 ● friendsinadoption.org ●
m.walshsnyder@adoptionattorneys.org

Laurie Slavin; 275 Fair Street, Suite 22, Kingston, NY 12401
Tel: (845) 338-0700 ● hudsonvalleyadoptionservices.org ●
l.slavin@adoptionattorneys.org

Deborah Steincolor; 845 Third Ave. #1400, New York, NY 10022
Tel: (212) 421-7807 ● adoptattorney.net ● dsteincolor@aol.com
A graduate of the Delaware Law School of Widener University, she
has been practicing law since 1987. She estimates she has completed
more than 1,800 adoptions in her career and completes 93 annually:
65% independent; 35% agency.

NORTH CAROLINA

State Adoption Office: North Carolina Division of Social Services;
Division of Social Services: 325 North Salisbury; Street, Suite 715 --
2409 Mail Service Center; Raleigh, NC 27699-2409; Phone: (919)
733-9464; http://www.dhhs.state.nc.us/dss/adopt

State Adoption Exchange: North Carolina Kids Adoption and Foster
Care Network: 330 South Greene Street, Suite 200; Greensboro, NC
27401; Phone: (336) 217-9770; nckids@uncg.edu; http://
www.adoptuskids.org

State laws and procedures:

General Information. North Carolina permits both independent and
agency adoption. Approximately 80% of North Carolina's infant
adoptions are completed via independent adoption; 20% via agencies.
Advertising is permitted only by licensed adoption agencies or
adoptive parents with completed home studies. To file a Petition for
Adoption the adoptive parents must reside there, usually for at least
six months, or the minor must be born there or resided there for at
least six months. Normally, adoptions are finalized approximately six
months after the child's placement with the adoptive parents. The
adoptive parents and child to be adopted are usually not required to
appear in court for the final hearing.

Independent Adoption. A pre-placement home study ("pre-placement
assessment") is required of the adoptive parents before a child is
placed in their home. The home study may be conducted by a licensed
adoption agency, or in some areas, the county department of social
services. The fee varies.

It is required that the adoptive parents and birth mother share identities. Virtually all will also voluntarily meet in person. A copy of the adoptive parents' home study must be offered to the birth mother. The adoptive parents are allowed to assist the birth mother with pregnancy-related medical and legal expenses. Assistance with living expenses is normally permitted, but usually for not more than six weeks after birth. The child may be released from the hospital directly to the adoptive parents.

The consent to adoption may be signed anytime after the birth by the birth mother. (The birth father can usually sign before birth.) It must be witnessed by a notary or the clerk of the Superior Court. The birth mother has the automatic right to withdraw her consent for a period of 7 days after signing. If the placement occurs before the home study is delivered to the birth mother, she has an additional five business days. Once these time periods have elapsed the consent is irrevocable, but upon proof of fraud or duress.

North Carolina does not have a putative birth father registry. Notice must be given to putative fathers (although North Carolina uses the terms "wed" and "unwed") and they have 30 days in which to object after notice, if the notice was received post-birth. If he elects to object, he must prove he did all of the following things before the Petition for Adoption was filed: acknowledge paternity; communicate with the birth mother; and provide support.

Agency Adoption. There is no difference regarding the process in which a birth mother signs her consent to adoption in an independent or agency adoption with one exception. The information provided above regarding independent adoption (e.g. when it can be signed, before whom, and the legal burden to seek to withdraw a signed consent) is identical regarding agency adoption. However, it is not required that the adoptive parents' home study be offered to the birth mother (although it may still voluntarily be offered).

Few agencies within North Carolina agree to do identified adoptions. Some will agree to make immediate hospital "at risk" placements.

American Academy of Adoption Attorney members:

Bobby D. Mills; P.O. Box 1677, Raleigh, NC 27602
Tel: (919) 821-1860 ● bmills@adoptionattorneys.org
A graduate of the Wake Forest School of Law, he has been practicing law since 1985. He estimates he completes 50 adoptions annually: 50% independent; 50% agency. He does not assist in creating adoptive matches.

Sharon A. Thompson; 400 W. Main St., Suite 502, Durham, NC 27701; Tel: (919) 688-9646 ● stlawgroup.com ● s.thompson@adoptionattorneys.org

W. David Thurman; 301 S. McDowell St., #608, Charlotte, NC 28204; Tel: (704) 377-4164 ● thurmanwilsonboutwell.com ● w.thurman@adoptionattorneys.org
A graduate of the North Carolina School of Law, he has been practicing law since 1983. He estimates he has completed 2,500 in his career and completes 150 annually: 50% independent; 40% agency; 10% international. He does not assist in creating adoptive matches.

Brinton D. Wright; 324 W. Wendover Ave. #107, Greensboro, NC 27408; Tel: (336) 373-1500 ● wendoverlaw.com ● b.wright@adoptionattorneys.com
A graduate of Wake Forest University School of Law, he has been practicing law since 1976. He estimates he has completed more than 1,000 adoptions in his career and completes 60 annually: 90% independent; 5% agency; 5% international. He does not assist in creating adoptive matches. He is an adoptive parent.

NORTH DAKOTA

State Adoption Office: North Dakota Department of Human Services (NDDHS); Children and Family Services Division: State Capitol, Department 325; Bismarck, ND 58505; Phone: (701) 328-4805; http://www.state.nd.us

State Adoption Exchange: North Dakota Department of Human Services: (NDDHS) (same as above); Phone: (701) 328-2316; dhseo@state.nd.us; http://www.state.nd.us

State laws and procedures:

General Information. North Dakota permits only agency adoption, although identified agency adoptions as done within the state are very similar to independent adoption. Advertising is not expressly permitted or barred by law, so most interpret that as it being permitted. To file a Petition for Adoption within North Dakota the adoptive parents must reside there, or the agency having custody of the child must be located there (permitting non-resident adoption). Normally, adoptions are finalized approximately seven months from the child's placement with the adoptive parents. The adoptive parents and the child are required to appear in court for the final hearing.

      A pre-placement home study of the adoptive parents is required before a child can be placed in their home. The home study may be conducted by a licensed adoption agency. The fee typically varies from $7,000 to $8,000 for pre and post-placement services.

      It is not required by law that the adoptive parents and birth mother meet in person and share identities, although some elect to do. However, if the adoption is designated an "identified adoption" full identities are shared. The adoptive parents are permitted to assist the birth mother with pregnancy-related medical, legal and living expenses. The child may be released directly to the adoptive parents from the hospital if they are licensed as foster parents. Otherwise, a court order is required if the placement occurs prior to the birth mother's termination of parental rights. The latter option is more common in identified adoptions.

      The birth mother shows her assent to the adoption by filing a *Petition for Relinquishment* with the court. If she is under the age of

18, a guardian at litem must be appointed to be sure she understands the proceedings. Her signature must be witnessed by a notary or a representative of a licensed adoption agency. Although the Petition for Relinquishment can be signed and filed before the child's birth, the Petition will not be heard until at least 48 hours after the birth, or the signing of the Petition, whichever occurs later. Once the court has granted the birth mother's Petition for Relinquishment, the child cannot be reclaimed by the birth mother, unless proved to the court within 30 days that fraud or duress was used to obtain her consent.

North Dakota does not have a putative birth father registry. A putative birth father is entitled to notice and if he can't be found notice is given by publication. He is given notice of an action to terminate his parental rights. If he elects to object, the adoptive parents must normally prove he is unfit.

American Academy of Adoption Attorney members:

William P. Harrie; 201 N. 5th Street, Suite 1800; P.O. Box 2626, Fargo, ND 58102
Tel: (701) 237-5544 ● w.harrie@adoptionattorneys.org

OHIO

State Adoption Office: Ohio Department of Job and Family Services; Office of Children and Families: 255 E. Main Street; Columbus, OH 43215; Phone: (614) 466-9274; http://jfs.ohio.gov/oapl/index.htm

State Adoption Exchange: AdoptOHIO: (same as above); Phone: (614) 466-9274; ; http://www.odjfs.state.oh.us

State laws and procedures:

General Information. Ohio permits both independent and agency adoption. Approximately 70% of Ohio's infant adoptions are completed via independent adoptions; 30% via agencies. Advertising is not permitted. To file a Petition for Adoption within Ohio either the adoptive parents must reside there, the child must be born there, or a birth parent must reside there (making non-resident adoption possible). If it is an agency adoption, the Petition for Adoption may also be filed in Ohio if the agency having custody of the child is located there. Normally, independent adoptions are finalized approximately six months after the child's placement with the adoptive parents; agency adoptions normally 6 months to one year. The adoptive parents are required to appear in court for either the final or interlocutory hearing.

Independent Adoption. A pre-placement home study is required before a child can be placed in the adoptive parents' home. Depending upon the policy of the county in which the Petition for Adoption is filed, the home study may be conducted by the state adoption office, a private licensed agency or a person approved by the court. The fee varies.

It is not required by law that the adoptive parents and birth mother meet in person and share identities, although some elect to do so voluntarily. The adoptive parents are permitted to assist the birth mother with pregnancy-related medical and legal expenses, and living expenses not to exceed $3,000 if incurred during the pregnancy and up to 60 days post-birth. The child may be released directly from the hospital to the adoptive parents, although a court order is sometimes required.

The consent to adoption can be signed no sooner than 72 hours after the birth, or the completion of the social work assessment, whichever occurs later. The birth mother must personally appear in court and request placement of the child with the adoptive parents. Once the placement is approved by the court, the child is placed in the custody of the adoptive parents and they may file their Petition for Adoption. Courts in different counties in Ohio differ. Some enter an *Interlocutory Order of Adoption* after the child has been with the adoptive parents for 30 days. This Interlocutory Order then becomes final about six months after the placement. Other counties do not enter an Interlocutory Order and wait about six months after the placement and enter a *Final Decree of Adoption*. The consent of the birth mother becomes irrevocable upon the entry of either the Interlocutory Order, or Final Decree, whichever occurs first. Prior to the granting of either order, the birth mother can withdraw her consent based only upon proving the child's best interests would be served.

Ohio has a putative birth father registry. Putative birth fathers must register no later than 30 days after the birth. If he registers and elects to object a key issue the court will examine is if he supported the birth mother during the pregnancy.

Agency Adoption. The information provided above regarding independent adoption is similar regarding agency adoption, except the birth mother executes a *surrender*, giving custody of the child to the adoption agency. The surrender can be signed no sooner than 72 hours after birth or the completion of the social work assessment, whichever occurs later. It is irrevocable upon signing. If the child is under the age of six months, the birth mother is not required to appear in court.

Some agencies in Ohio agree to do identified adoptions. Some agencies also agree to do immediate hospital "at risk" placements.

American Academy of Adoption Attorney members:

James S. Albers; 88 North Fifth Street, Columbus, OH 43215
Tel: (614) 464-4414 • j.albers@adoptionattorneys.org

Margaret L. Blackmore; 536 S. High Street, Columbus, OH 43215
Tel: (614) 221-1341 • tblattorneys.com •
p.blackmore@adoptionattorneys.org

Julia A. Cain; 34 South Main Street, Rittman, OH 44270
Tel: (330) 927-3120 • j.cain@adoptionattorneys.org
A graduate of the Ohio State University College of Law, she has been practicing law since 1989. She estimates she completes 30 adoptions annually: 25% independent; 70% agency; 5% international. She does assist in creating adoptive matches.

Susan G. Eisenman; 3363 Tremont Rd. #304, Columbus, OH 43221
Tel: (614) 326-1200 • s.eisenman@adoptionattorneys.org
A graduate of the Ohio State University School of Law, she has been practicing law since 1974. She estimates she has completed more than 2,000 adoptions in her career and completes 85 annually: 30% independent; 52% agency; 18% international. She does assist in creating adoptive matches. She is an adoptive parent.

Ellen Essig; 105 East Fourth St., Suite 400, Cincinnati, OH 45202
Tel: (513) 721-5151 • surrogatesearch.com •
e.essig@adoptionattorneys.org
A graduate of the Chase College of Law, she has been practicing law
since 1986.

Patrick A. Hamilton; 400 S. Fifth St., #103, Columbus, OH 43215
Tel: (614) 464-4532 • aphamiltonlaw.com •
p.hamilton@adoptionattorneys.org

John C. Huffman; 540 Market Street, Lima, OH 45801
Tel: (419) 227-3423 • j.huffman@adoptionattorneys.org

Jerry M. Johnson; 400 West North Street, Lima, OH 45801
Tel: 419) 222-1040 • hjlaw.biz • j.johnson@adoptionattorneys.org
A graduate of the Ohio Northern University School of Law, he has
been practicing law since 1975. He estimates he has completed more
than 600 adoptions in his career. He accepts contested adoption cases.

Carolyn Mussio; 3411 Michigan Avenue, Cincinnati, OH 45208
Tel: (513) 871-8855 • c.mussio@adoptionattorneys.org

Lori S. Nehrer; 111 Stow Ave., Suite 100, Cuyahoga Falls, OH
44221
Tel: (330) 928-3373 • l.nehrer@adoptionattorneys.org
A graduate of the Georgetown University Law Center, she has been
practicing law since 1985. She estimates she has completed 700
adoptions in her career and completes 80 annually: 40% independent;
59% agency; 1% international. She does assist in creating adoptive
matches. She is an adoptive parent.

Rosemary E. Pomeroy; 3 Crosswoods Building, 200 E. Campus
View Blvd.#200, Columbus OH 43235 • Tel: (614) 985-3650 •
ebnerpomlaw.com • r.pomeroy@adoptionattorneys.org
A graduate of the Detroit College of Law, she has been practicing law
since 1988. She has completed over 500 in her career and complete
about 60 annually.

Mary E. Smith; 1200 Edison Plaza, 300 Madison Ave, Toledo, OH 43604; Tel: (419) 243-6281 ● m.smith@adoptionattorneys.org

James Swaim; 15 West Fourth Street, Dayton, OH 45402
Tel: (937) 223-5200 ● j.swaim@adoptionattorneys.org

Micheal R. Voorhees; 11159 Kenwood Road, Cincinnati, OH 45242
Tel: (513) 489-2555 ● m.voorhees@adoptionattorneys.org
He has been practicing law since 1987. He estimates he has completed 800 adoptions in his career and completes 150 annually: 60% independent; 30% agency; 10% international.

OKLAHOMA

State Adoption Office: Oklahoma Department of Human Services: 907 South Detroit, Suite 750; Tulsa, OK 74120; Phone: (918) 588-1735; http://www.okdhs.org/adopt

State Adoption Exchange: Oklahoma Adoption Exchange: Phone: (405) 521-2475; linda.foster@okdhs.org; http://www.okdhs.org

State laws and procedures:

General Information. Oklahoma permits both independent and agency adoption. Approximately 60% of Oklahoma's infant adoptions are completed via independent adoption; 40% via agencies. Advertising is permitted by adoptive parents having a completed home study. To file a Petition for Adoption in Oklahoma either the adoptive parents must reside there, or the child to be adopted must show significant contacts with the state, usually by being born there or having resided there at least six months. In interstate adoptions, Oklahoma ICPC charges a $300 fee. Normally, adoptions are finalized approximately 7-12 months after the placement of the child with the adoptive parents. The adoptive parents and the child are required to appear in court for the final hearing.

Independent Adoption. A pre-placement home study of the adoptive parents is required before a child can be placed in their home. It may be conducted by a licensed adoption agency, Department of Human Services, or a person approved by the court. The fee for pre and post-placement home study services is $750 to $2,000 in some regions and is higher in others.

It is not required by law that the adoptive parents and birth mother meet in person and share identities, although in some cases it is done voluntarily. The adoptive parents are permitted to assist the birth mother with pregnancy-related expenses, although living assistance may not be provided directly to the birth mother, except that adoptive parents are permitted to give a one-time gift to the birth mother of no greater value than $100. Prior court approval is required for any living assistance exceeding $1,000. The child may be released directly from the hospital to the adoptive parents, although hospital policies differ. Some hospitals accept special release forms, while others require a court order.

The consent to adoption can be signed anytime after the birth by the birth mother. (A non-marital father may sign his consent before the birth witnessed by a notary public, which becomes irrevocable 15 days after signing.) The birth mother's consent must be witnessed by a judge. If the birth mother is under the age of 16 the consent of one of the birth mother's parents, or her guardian, is also required. Most consents are signed within 4-5 days of the birth. The consent to adoption is irrevocable immediately upon signing. It may only be withdrawn upon proof of fraud or duress, or the adoptive parents' failure to file their Petition for Adoption within nine months.

Oklahoma has a putative birth father registry. Notice must be given to birth fathers who are identified by the birth mother, have filed with the birth father registry or who cohabited with the birth mother within the 10 months preceding the birth. The notice will be of an action to terminate his parental rights. If he appears at the hearing and elects to object, he will first have to prove paternity. Then the key issue will usually be if the putative father financially supported the birth mother during the pregnancy to the extent his financial ability permitted. If he claims he had no opportunity to do so, he will have to show he made sufficient efforts to determine if he fathered a child and offer support.

Agency Adoption. There is no difference regarding the process in which a birth mother signs her consent to adoption in an independent or agency adoption. The information provided above regarding independent adoption (e.g. when the consent can be signed, before whom, legal burden to seek to withdraw a signed consent) is identical regarding agency adoption.

Some agencies in Oklahoma agree to do identified adoptions.

American Academy of Adoption Attorney members:

Barbara K. Bado; 1800 Canyon Park Circle, #301, Edmond, OK 73013
Tel: (405) 340-1500 ● badoandbadoattorneys.com ●
b.bado@adoptionattorneys.org
A graduate of the American University, Washington College of Law, she has been practicing law since 1978.

John T. Bado; 1800 Canyon Park Circle, #301, Edmond, OK 73013
Tel: (405) 340-1500 ● badoandbadoattorneys.com ●
j.bado@adoptionattorneys.org
A graduate of the Baylor University, he has been practicing law since 1971. He is also licensed to practice in Texas.

Virginia Frank; 201 North Broadway, Suite 107A, Moore, OK 73160
Tel: (888) 749-0169 ● adoptionchoices.org ●
v.frank@adoptionattorneys.org
A graduate of Oklahoma City University School of Law, she has been practicing since 1992. She estimates she completes 200 annually: 10% independent; 89% agency; 1% international. She does not assist in creating adoptive matches.

Jennifer K. Kern; 2700 Bank of America Center; 15 W. 6th Street, Tulsa, OK 74119; Tel: (918) 587-0101 ● newtonoconnor.com ●
jkern@newtonoconnor.com
A graduate of the University of Tulsa College of Law, she has been practicing law since 2003. She estimates she completes 18 adoptions annually: 65% independent; 35% agency. She does assist in creating adoptive matches.

Mark Morrison; 524 W. Evergreen St.; P.O. Box 1623, Durant, OK 74702; Tel: (580) 924-1661 ● m.morrison@adoptionattorneys.org

John M. O'Connor; 15 W. Sixth St., Suite 2700, Tulsa, OK 74119 Tel: (918) 587-0101 ● newtonoconnor.com ● joconnor@newtonoconnor.com
A graduate of the University of Tulsa College of Law, he has been practicing law since 1981. He estimates he has completed 350 adoptions in his career and completes 18 annually: 65% independent; 35% agency. He does assist in creating adoptive matches.

Peter K. Schaffer; 204 N. Robinson Ave., #2305, Oklahoma City, OK 73102; Tel: (405) 239-7707 ● p.schaffer@adoptionattorneys.org
A graduate of the Oklahoma City University, he has been practicing law since 1974. He estimates he has completed more than 350 adoptions in his career.; 75% of which are independent and 25% agency adoptions.

Paul E. Swain III; 406 South Boulder Ave. #423, Tulsa, OK 74103 Tel: (918) 599-0100 ● swainlaw.com ● p.swain@adoptionattorneys.org

Mike Yeksavich; 4815 South Harvard, Suite 315, Tulsa, OK 74135 Tel: (918) 592-6050 ● miketheattorney.com ● m_yeksavich@yahoo.com
A graduate of University of Tulsa Law School, he has been practicing law since 1968. He has completed over 300 adoptions in his career, both independent and agency adoptions.

Phyllis L. Zimmerman; 15 W. 6th Street, Suite 1220, Tulsa, OK 74119; Tel: (918) 582-6151 ● p.zimmerman@adoptionattorneys.org
A graduate of the Washington College of Law at American University, she has been practicing law since 1963.

OREGON

State Adoption Office: Oregon Department of Human Services: Human Services Building, Adoption Unit, 2nd Floor; 500 Summer Street NE, E-71; Salem, OR 97310-1068; Phone: (503) 947-5358; http://www.dhs.state.or.us/children/adoption

State Adoption Exchange: Oregon's Waiting Children: http://www.nwae.org

State laws and procedures:

General Information. Oregon permits both independent and agency adoption. Approximately 70% of Oregon's infant adoptions are completed via independent adoption; 30% via agencies. Advertising is permitted if the adoptive parents have a completed home study, are represented by an Oregon attorney, and they have obtained a Certificate of Approval upon the home study by an Oregon agency. To file a Petition for Adoption within Oregon either the adoptive parents, the child to be adopted, or the birth parent whose consent to the adoption is required must reside there for at least six months prior to filing the Petition for Adoption (making non-resident adoption possible). Normally, adoptions are finalized approximately four to seven months after the child's placement with the adoptive parents. The adoptive parents and the child are usually not required to appear in court at the final hearing.

Independent Adoption. A pre-placement home study of the adoptive parents by a licensed adoption agency is required, as well as ten hours of adoption education. The fee for the pre and post-placement home study is approximately $1,500.

It is not required by law that the adoptive parents and birth mother meet in person and share identities, although most all do so voluntarily. The adoptive parents are permitted to assist the birth mother with pregnancy-related expenses. The child may be placed with the adoptive parents directly from the hospital, although each hospital's forms and policies vary.

The consent to adoption can be signed anytime after the birth. It must be witnessed by a notary. Most consents are signed within days of the birth, sometimes in the hospital only 12-24 hours after birth. The birth mother has the right to seek to withdraw her consent until the adoption is final. However, if the birth mother also signs a *Certificate of Irrevocability* (which is commonly done) after having been provided advice from an independent attorney, the consent is irrevocable, except upon proof of fraud or duress, provided that all the following conditions are met: the child is physically placed with the adoptive parents, the Petition for Adoption and home study have been filed with the court, the child's medical history has been obtained, and the judge signs an order naming a temporary guardian for the child.

Oregon does not have a putative birth father registry, although men who file a paternity action (called a "filiation" proceeding) must notify the state Vital Statistics office, which some people incorrectly think of as a true birth father registry. Notice must be given to putative birth fathers only when he has signed a voluntary acknowledgment of paternity with the birth mother, filed a paternity action, or the birth mother's affidavit states the birth father did one of the following: has supported or attempted to support her before and/or after the birth; lived with the child; or promised in writing to support the child. Putative fathers who did not do the above are not entitled to notice.

Agency Adoption. The information provided above regarding independent adoption is identical regarding agency adoption, except the following. The consent to adoption may be signed any time after birth. It may be witnessed by a notary or a representative of the adoption agency. Once the consent has been signed, and the child has been placed with the adoptive parents, the consent is irrevocable if the birth mother also signed a Certificate of Irrevocability, but for fraud or duress.

Some agencies in Oregon agree to do identified adoptions. Some also agree to do immediate hospital "at risk" placements, before the consents are irrevocable.

American Academy of Adoption Attorney members:

Timothy F. Brewer; 590 West 13th Avenue, Eugene, OR 97401
Tel: (541) 683-1814 ● tfbrewer.com ● tim@tfbrewer.com
A graduate of the University of Oregon School of Law, he has been practicing law since 1985.

Stefanie L. Burke; 717 Murphy Road, Medford, OR 97504
Tel: (541) 779-8900 ● roguelaw.com ●
s.burke@adoptionattorneys.org

John Chally; 2722 NE 33rd Street, Portland, OR 97212
Tel: (503) 238-9720 ● adoptionnorthwest.com ●
j.chally@adoptionattorneys.org

Catherine M. Dexter; 25260 SW Parkway Avenue, Suite C,
Wilsonville, OR 97070
Tel: (503) 582-9010 ● oregonadopt.com ● cdexter@oregonadopt.com
A graduate of the Northwestern University School of Law at Lewis
and Clark College, she has been practicing law since 1982. She
estimates she has completed more than 1,800 adoptions in her career.
Her practice is limited to adoptions (typically 80% independent; 15%
agency; 5% intercountry). She reports 60% of her clients find a birth
mother through her office; 40% find their own birth mother.

J. Eric Gustafson; 154 Treasure Cove Lane, Manzanita, OR (mailing
address, see bio in Washington); Tel: (800) 238-5437 ●
northwestadoptions.com ● egustafson@lyon-law.com
A graduate of the Northwestern School of Law of Lewis and Clark
College at Portland, he has been practicing law since 1973. He is also
licensed to practice law in Washington. He estimates he has completed
more than 800 adoptions in his career.

John R. Hassen; 717 Murphy Road, Medford, OR 97504
Tel: (541) 779-8900 ● roguelaw.com ● jrh@roguelaw.com
A graduate of the Stanford University School of Law, he has been
practicing law since 1965.

Sandra L. Hodgson; 2722 NE 33rd Street, Portland, OR 97212
Tel: (503) 238-9720 ● adoptionnorthwest.com ●
s.hodgson@adoptionattorneys.org

Susan C. Moffet; 25260 SW Parkway Avenue, Suite C, Wilsonville,
OR 97070; Tel: (503) 582-9010 ● oregonadopt.com ●
smoffett@oregonadopt.com

A graduate of the Northwestern University School of Law at Lewis and Clark College, she has been practicing law since 1987.

Robin E. Pope; 4500 SW Hall Boulevard, Beaverton, OR 97005
Tel: (503) 352-3524 ● robinpope.com ●
r.pope@adoptionattorneys.org

Laurence H. Spiegel; 4040 Douglas Way, Lake Oswego, OR 97035
Tel: (503) 635-7773 ● adoption-oregon.com ● lhspiegel@msn.com
A graduate of the Lewis and Clark School of Law, he has been practicing law since 1981. He estimates he has completed 2,000 adoptions in his career and completes 60 annually: 25% independent; 50% agency; 25% international. He does assist in creating adoptive matches. He is an adoptive parent.

PENNSYLVANIA

State Adoption Office: Pennsylvania Department of Public Welfare; Office of Children, Youth, and Families: 7th & Foster Streets, P.O. Box 2675; Harrisburg, PA 17105-2675; Phone: (717) 705-4401; http://www.dpw.state.pa.us

State Adoption Exchange: Pennsylvania Adoption Exchange (PAE): Phone: (717) 772-7011; klollo@state.pa.us; http://www.adoptpakids.org

State laws and procedures:

General Information. Pennsylvania permits both independent and agency adoption. Approximately 50% of Pennsylvania's infant adoptions are completed via independent adoption; 50% via agencies. Advertising is permitted. To file a Petition for Adoption within Pennsylvania either the adoptive parents, the birth parents, or the child must reside there (making non-resident adoption possible). If it is an agency adoption the Petition for Adoption can also be filed in Pennsylvania if the agency having custody of the child is located there. If all parties agree, enforceable post-contact agreements can exist when approved by the court. Normally, adoptions are finalized six months to one year after the child's placement with the adoptive parents. The adoptive parents and the child are required to appear in court for the final hearing.

Independent Adoption. A pre-placement home study of the adoptive parents is required before a child can be placed in their home. An interim placement can be made with court approval, if a home study is underway, and the social worker recommends the early placement occur. The home study is conducted by a licensed adoption agency or licensed social worker. The fee varies.

It is not required by law that the adoptive parents and birth mother meet in person and share identities, although some do so voluntarily. The adoptive parents are permitted to assist the birth mother with pregnancy-related medical expenses, although living expenses are not permitted. The child may be released from the hospital directly to the adoptive parents, although hospital forms and policies differ.

The consent to adoption can be signed no sooner than 72 hours after the birth. It must be witnessed by two witnesses. The birth mother has the automatic right to withdraw her consent for 30 days. On the 31st day it becomes irrevocable, except upon proof of fraud or duress. Usually about one to two months after the consent has become irrevocable, a court hearing will confirm the consent and issue an order terminating parental rights.

Pennsylvania has a putative birth father registry, but unlike most registries, it is not integral to the termination of a putative father's rights. Notice is required, unless with due diligence, he can't be found. A petition to terminate parental rights must be filed, and his rights severed if he defaults. If he elects to object, the adoptive parents must prove 4 months of abandonment if the child is a newborn, 6 months of abandonment if an older child, rape of the birth mother, or his inability to parent. A putative birth father can sign a consent to adoption before or after the birth, but may withdraw it within 30 days after the birth, or when he signed the consent, whichever is later.

Agency Adoption. There is no difference regarding the process in which a birth mother signs her consent to adoption in an independent or agency adoption. The information provided above regarding independent adoption (e.g. when the consent can be signed, before whom, legal burden to seek to withdraw a signed consent) is identical regarding agency adoption.

Many agencies in Pennsylvania agree to do identified adoptions. Immediate hospital "at risk" placements, where the child is placed with the adoptive parents before the consents to adoption are irrevocable.

American Academy of Adoption Attorney members:

Denise M. Bierly; 112 W. Foster Avenue, State College, PA 16801
Tel: (814) 237-6278 ● d.bierly@adoptionattorneys.org
A graduate of the Dickenson School of Law of the Pennsylvania State University, she has been practicing law since 1990.

Craig B. Bluestein; 28 Winding Hill Road; P.O. Box 55, Pocono Pines, PA 18350; Tel: (215) 646-5006 ● craigslegal.com ● c.bluestein@adoptionattorneys.org
A graduate of the Duquesne University School of Law, he has been practicing law since 1979.

Harry L. Bricker, Jr.; 921 Bradford Road, Harrisburg, PA 17112
Tel: (717) 233-2555 ● h.bricker@adoptionaattorneys.org
A graduate of the Dickinson School of Law, he has been practicing law since 1958.

Barbara L. Binder Casey; 527 Elm Street, Reading, PA 19601
Tel: (610) 376-9742 ● ababystepadoption.com ● bcasey@infantadoptions.com
A graduate of the University of Pennsylvania Law School, she has been practicing law since 1978. She estimates she has completed more than 500 adoptions in her career and completes 90 annually: 20% independent; 75% agency; 5% international. She does assist in creating adoptive matches.

Debra M. Fox; 355 W. Lancaster Avenue, Haverford, PA 19041
Tel: (610) 896-9972 ● transitionsadoption.com ● mail@transitionsadoption.com
A graduate of the Temple University School of Law, she has been practicing law since 1985. She estimates she has completed 1,000

adoptions in her career and completes 50 annually: 43% independent; 43% agency; 14% international. She does not assist in creating adoptive matches.

Jay H. Ginsburg; 527 Swede Street, Norristown, PA 19401
Tel: (610) 277-1999 ● adoptionadvocatesofpa.com ●
j.ginsburg@adoptionattorneys.org

Tara E. Gutterman; 2343 B Wallace Street, Philadelphia, PA 19130
Tel: (215) 748-1441 ● t.gutterman@adoptionattorneys.org
A graduate of the Temple University School of Law, she has been practicing law since 1991.

Deborah L. Lesko; 373 Vanadium Road, Pittsburgh, PA 15243
Tel: (412) 276-4200 ● leskolawandmediation.com ●
d.lesko@adoptionattorneys.org
A graduate of the University of Pittsburgh School of Law, she has been practicing law since 1983. She estimates she has completed over 3,000 adoptions in her career and completes 160 annually: 45% independent; 50% agency; 5% international.

Martin S. Leventon; 1011 Cedargrove Road, Wynnewood, PA 19096
Tel: (610) 642-7182 ● m.leventon@adoptionattorneys.org
A graduate of the Temple University School of Law, he has been practicing law since 1981.

Mary Ann Petrillo; 412 Main Street, Irwin, PA 15642
Tel: (724) 861-8333 ● maryannpetrillo.com ●
m.petrillo@adoptionattorneys.org
A graduate of the University of Pittsburgh School of Law, she has been practicing law since 1983. She estimates she has completed 1,000 adoptions in her career and completes 50 annually: 60% independent; 20% agency; 20% international. She does not assist in creating adoptive matches. She is an adoptive parent.

William Rosen; 1000 Madison Avenue, Suite 110, Audubon, PA 19403; Tel: (610) 688-8600 ● w.rosen@adoptionattorneys.org
A graduate of the Deleware-Widener University, he has been practicing law since 1988.

Stuart S. Sacks; 4431 N. Front Street, Harrisburg, PA 17110
Tel: (717) 234-2401 ● sasllp.com ● ssacks@sasllp.com
A graduate of the Washington University School of Law, he has been
practicing law since 1973. He is an adoptive parent.

Deborah E. Spivack; P.O. Box 56182, Philadelphia, PA 19130
Tel: (215) 763-5550 ● familybuildinglaw.net ●
d.spivack@adoptionattorneys.org

Samuel C. Totaro; 87 N. Broad Street, Doylestown, PA 18901
Tel: (215) 348-7700 ● mellonwebster.com ●
stotaro@mellonwebster.com
A graduate of the University of Memphis School of Law, he has been
practicing law since 1975. He estimates he has completed 3,000
adoptions in his career and competes 60 annually: 45% independent;
50% agency; 5% international. He is a past president of the American
Academy of Adoption Attorneys.

RHODE ISLAND

State Adoption Office: Rhode Island Department of Children, Youth
and Families (RIDCYF): Adoption & Foster Care Preparation &
Support; 101 Friendship Street; Providence, RI 02903; Phone: (401)
528-3799; http://www.dcyf.ri.gov/adoption.htm

State Adoption Exchange: Adoption Rhode Island: Phone: (401)
724-1910; adoptionri@ids.net; http://www.adoptionri.org

State laws and procedures:

General Information. Rhode Island permits both independent and
agency adoption. Advertising is not permitted. To file a Petition for
Adoption within Rhode Island the adoptive parents must reside there.
If it is an agency adoption the Petition for Adoption can also be filed
there if the agency having custody of the child is located there
(making non-resident adoption possible). Normally, adoptions are
finalized approximately six to eight months after the child's placement

with the adoptive parents. The adoptive parents and the child are required to appear in court for the final hearing.

Independent Adoption. A pre-placement home study of the adoptive parents is not technically required before a child is placed in their home, but virtually all Rhode Island adoptive families elect to have one as it is the norm in the state. The post-placement home study may be conducted by the state adoption office but is usually done by private agencies. The fee for both pre and post-placement home studies is about $1,200-$1,300.

It is not required by law that the adoptive parents and birth mother meet in person and share identities, although some elect to do so voluntarily. There are no specific laws governing whether the adoptive parents are permitted to assist the birth mother with pregnancy-related expenses, including living assistance, so most agencies and attorneys view it as permitted. The child may be released directly from the hospital to the adoptive parents, although this is usually done by discharging the baby to the birth mother or a relative, who in turn places the child with the adoptive parents.

The consent to adoption can be signed any time after the birth. It has no enforceability, however, until the birth mother affirms her desire to consent to the adoption before a judge in a Placement Hearing. This hearing usually occurs about three months after the child's placement with the adoptive parents but can be as late as at the final adoption hearing (when it could be done concurrently), about six months after the placement. Once the court approves the consent at this hearing, state law provides that the consent is irrevocable and can only be withdrawn upon proof of fraud or duress. Once the adoption is finalized by the court (usually six to seven months after the child's placement with the adoptive parents), however, the consent is irrevocable.

Rhode Island does not have a putative birth father registry. A putative father is entitled to notice if his whereabouts are known, and if not, notice by publication is required. Notice will be given of a termination of parental rights hearing, and if he fails to appear and object, his rigths will normally be terminated.

Agency Adoption. The information provided above regarding independent adoption is identical regarding agency adoption, except for the following. A pre-placement is always required in an agency adoption. The adoption agency can file a Petition to Terminate Parental Rights no sooner that the fifteenth day after the birth, with the birth mother's agreement that her rights be voluntarily terminated. Once the court has issued its order terminating her parental rights she has lost the automatic right to stop the adoption. There are no state laws governing a request to withdraw consent, but case law indicates it can only be done upon proof of fraud or duress.

Most agencies in Rhode Island agree to do identified adoptions. Agencies will sometimes agree to make immediate hospital "at risk" placements but many still use initial foster parent placement.

American Academy of Adoption Attorney members:

William J. Gallogly; 1220 Kingstown Road, Wakefield, RI 02879 Tel: (401) 789-8810 ● w.gallogly@adoptionattorneys.org

SOUTH CAROLINA

State Adoption Office: South Carolina Department of Social Services; Division of Human Services: PO Box 1520; Columbia, SC 29202-1520; Phone: (803) 898-7707; http://www.state.sc.us

State Adoption Exchange: South Carolina Council on Adoptable Children: Phone: (803) 256-2622; gail-coac@sc.rr.com; http://www.sc-adopt.org

State laws and procedures:

General Information. South Carolina permits both independent and agency adoption. Approximately 70% of South Carolina's infant adoptions are completed via independent adoption; 30% via agencies. Advertising is permitted only by adoption agencies and attorneys licensed in South Carolina and prospective adoptive parents with a completed home study. To file a Petition for Adoption within South Carolina either the adoptive parents must reside there, or the child be physically present there. Non-residents can file a Petition for Adoption if the child is present in state at the time of filing, but the placement of a South Carolina child placed with non-residents must be approved by court order prior to placement. (This may be done pre-birth.) If it is an agency adoption the Petition for Adoption can also be filed in South Carolina if the agency having custody of the child is located there. Normally, adoptions are finalized three to six months after the child's placement with the adoptive parents. The adoptive parents and the child are required to appear in court for the final hearing. Other than in adoptions between blood relatives, adoptions by non-residents are normally required to be finalized within South Carolina, rather than the adoptive parents' state of residence.

Independent Adoption. A pre-placement home study of the adoptive parents is required before a child can be placed in their home. The home study is conducted by a licensed adoption agency or social worker approved by the State Department of Social Services to conduct home studies. The fee is approximately $700-900.

It is not required by law that the adoptive parents and the birth mother meet in person and share identities, although a small number elect to do so voluntarily. The adoptive parents are permitted to assist the birth mother with pregnancy-related medical and living expenses. The child may be released from the hospital directly to the adoptive parents, although hospital forms and policies differ.

The consent to adoption can be signed anytime after the birth. It may be witnessed by a judge, an attorney not representing the adoptive parents, or a certified adoption worker. Consents are usually signed one to two days after the birth. Once signed, the consent is irrevocable, except upon proof of fraud or duress, and that the child's best interests would be served by being removed from the adoptive parents.

South Carolina has a putative birth father registry, applicable to birth fathers not married to the birth mother. Birth fathers who register must be given notice of the adoption or a termination of parental rights action. Once notice is given he has 30 days after the birth and the notice to object, or his rights are considered waived in most cases. However, failure to register does not terminate his rights to object in seeking to establish parental rights, however. If the birth father objects timely in court, he will have to establish that (assuming the child was placed for adoption when less than six months of age) he lived with the birth mother, or if the baby has been born, with the child, for six consecutive months prior to the child's placement, or provided reasonable financial support based upon his ability to provide. (Different standards apply if the child is placed when over six months of age.)

Agency Adoption. There is no difference regarding the process in which a birth mother signs her consent to adoption in an independent or agency adoption. The information provided above regarding independent adoption (e.g. when the consent can be signed, before whom, legal burden to seek to withdraw a signed consent) is identical regarding agency adoption.

Few agencies in South Carolina agree to do identified adoptions. Some also agree to make immediate hospital "at risk" placements, where the child is placed with the adoptive parents before the consents to adoption are irrevocable.

American Academy of Adoption Attorney members:

Frederick Corley; 1214 King St., P.O. Box 2265, Beaufort, SC 22901
Tel: (843) 524-3232 ● f.corley@adoptionattorneys.org
A graduate of the University of South Carolina School of Law, he has been practicing law since 1976. He estimates he has completed more than 400 adoptions in his career and completes 110 annually: 60% indpendent; 40% agency. He does not assist in creating adoptive matches.

L. Dale Dove; 125 Hampton Street, Suite 200, Rock Hill, SC 29730
Tel: (803) 327-1910 ● dove-barton.com ● lddove@rhtc.net
A graduate of the University of South Carolina School of Law, he has been practicing law since 1983. He is an adoptive parent.

Thomas P. Lowndes; 128 Meeting Street, Charleston, SC 29401
Tel: (843) 723-1688 ● t.lowndes@adoptionattorneys.org
A graduate of the University of South Carolina School of Law, he has been practicing law since 1966.

James Fletcher Thompson; 302 E St. John Street, P.O. Box 1853, Spartanburg, SC 29304; Tel: (864) 573-5533 ● adoptionsc.com ● jfthompson@thompsonlawfirm.net
A graduate of the University of South Carolina School of Law, he has been practicing law since 1989.

Stephen Yacobi; 408 North Church St, Suite B, Greenville, SC 29601 Tel: (864) 242-3271 ● scadoptlaw.com ● s.yacobi@adoptionattorneys.org
A graduate of the University of South Carolina, he has been practicing law since 1980.

SOUTH DAKOTA

State Adoption Office: South Dakota Department of Social Services; Department of Child Protective Services: 700 Governor's Drive; Pierre, SD 57501-2291; Phone: (605) 773-3227; http://www.state.sd.us

State Adoption Exchange: South Dakota Department of Social Services; www.dss.sd.gov/adoption/childrenwaiting/

State laws and procedures:

General Information. South Dakota permits both independent and agency adoption. Approximately 40% of South Dakota's infant adoptions are completed via independent adoption; 60% via agencies. The state statutes don't say if adoptin advertising is permitted or not, so it is generally presumed to be permitted. To file a Petition for Adoption within South Dakota the adoptive parents must reside there. Out-of-state residents can file their Petition for Adoption in South Dakota if the agency having custody of the minor is located there. This is not automatic, however, as court approval is required. Normally, adoptions are finalized approximately six months after the child's placement with the adoptive parents. The adoptive parents and the child are required to appear in court for the final hearing.

Independent Adoption. A pre-placement home study of the adoptive parents is required before a child can be placed in their home. The home study may be conducted by a licensed adoption agency or a certified social worker with a private independent practitioner certificate. The fees for pre and post-placement home study services typically varies from $800 to $1,500.

It is not required by law that the adoptive parents and birth mother meet in person and share identities, although some do so voluntarily. The adoptive parents are permitted to assist the birth mother with pregnancy-related expenses, including living expenses, but prior court approval is required. The child may be released to the adoptive parents directly from the hospital, although most hospitals will require written permission from the birth mother identifying the adoptive parents. If they wish to do an adoption without exchanging names, the baby is usually discharge to the birth mother, who then places the child with the adoptive parents outside the hospital.

The consent to adoption is made by the birth mother filing a Petition for Voluntarily Termination of Parental Rights, which cannot be filed prior to the fifth day after birth. The court's hearing on the petition can often occur immediately upon filing, or may take as long as about 25 days. The birth mother must have received counseling prior to the hearing, unless a judge waives the requirement. The birth mother must appear in court for the court to grant the order that her parental rights be voluntarily terminated. Prior to this hearing the birth mother has the right to withdraw her consent with no legal burden. Once the court has made the order, the consent is irrevocable, although the birth mother has a 30 day appeal period in which she may withdraw her consent if she can prove fraud was employed to obtain her consent.

South Dakota does not have a putative birth father registry. Notice must be given to any putative father identified by the birth mother. Usually this will be 30 days notice of an action to terminate his parental rights. If he is unknown, there is a 60 day period in which he must step forward and acknowledge paternity, or his rights will be terminated.

Agency Adoption. There is no difference regarding the process in which a birth mother signs her consent to adoption in an independent or agency adoption. The information provided above regarding

independent adoption (e.g. when the consent can be signed, before whom, legal burden to seek to withdraw a signed consent) is identical regarding agency adoption.

Some agencies in South Dakota agree to do identified adoptions. Some agencies also agree to make immediate hospital "at risk" placements, where the child is placed with the adoptive parents before the consents to adoption are irrevocable.

American Academy of Adoption Attorney members:

John R. Hughes; 224 N. Phillips Avenue, Suite 207, Sioux Falls, SD 57102; Tel: (605) 339-3939 ● adoptionhelp.net ● j.hughes@adoptionattorneys.org

TENNESSEE

State Adoption Office: Tennessee Department of Children's Services: Cordell Hull Building, 8th Floor; 436 Sixth Avenue North; Nashville, TN 37243-1290; Phone: (615) 253-6351; www.tennessee.gov/youth/

State Adoption Exchange: Tennessee Department of Children's Services: www.tn.gov/youth/adoption.htm

State laws and procedures:

General Information. Tennessee permits both independent and agency adoption. Approximately 60% of Tennessee's infant adoptions are completed via independent adoption; 40% via agencies. Advertising is permitted. To file a Petition for Adoption within Tennessee the adoptive parents must be residents for at least six months prior to filing the Petition for Adoption. Normally, adoptions are finalized six months after the child's placement with the adoptive parents. The adoptive parents are required to appear in court at the final hearing.

Independent Adoption. A pre-placement home study of the adoptive parents is required before a child is placed in their home. The post-placement home study may be conducted by a licensed adoption agency. The fee varies but usually does not exceed $1,200.

It is not required by law that the adoptive parents and the birth mother meet in person and share identities, although it is voluntarily done in most adoptions. The adoptive parents are permitted to assist the birth mother with pregnancy-related expenses, although living expenses may not be provided beyond 90 days prior to, and 45 days after, the birth. The child may be released directly from the hospital to the adoptive parents, although hospital policies differ. Some hospitals simply require a written release, while others require a copy of the birth mother's consent to the adoption.

The consent to adoption, called a *surrender*, cannot be signed before the fourth day after the birth, unless a court waives this period. It must be witnessed by a judge. Once signed, the birth mother has the right to withdraw the consent for a period of 10 business days. Once the 10 day period has elapsed the consent is irrevocable, but for fraud or duress.

Tennessee has a putative birth father registry. The registry must be checked for putative birth fathers ten days prior to filing the Petition for Adoption and the petition to terminate his parental rights. A man who has registered, as well as any man personally named by the birth mother, must be given notice. A primary ground for granting the action to terminate his parental rights is the putative birth father's failure to file a paternity action within 30 days of notice.

Agency Adoption. There is no difference regarding the process in which a birth mother signs her consent to adoption in an independent or agency adoption. The information provided above regarding independent adoption (e.g. when the consent can be signed, before whom, legal burden to seek to withdraw a signed consent) is identical regarding agency adoption.

Some agencies in Tennessee agree to do identified adoptions. Some agencies also agree to make immediate hospital "at risk" placements.

American Academy of Adoption Attorney members:

Lisa L. Collins; 3100 West End Ave. #1210, Nashville, TN 37203
Tel: (615) 269-5540 ● tnadopt.com ● l.collins@adoptionattorneys.org
A graduate of the Vanderbilt University School of Law, she has been
practicing law since 1993.

Dawn Coppock; P.O. Box 388, Strawberry Plains, TN 37871
Tel: (865) 933-8173 ● dawncoppock.com ●
d.coppock@adoptionattorneys.org
A graduate of the Wythe Scool of Law at the College of William and
Mary, she has been practicing law since 1987.

Michael S. Jennings; 130 Jordan Drive, Chattanooga, TN 37421
Tel: (423) 892-2006 ● m.jennings@adoptionattorneys.org
A graduate of the University of Georgia School of Law, he has been
practicing law since 1984.

Sharon T. Massey; 221 S. Third Street, Clarksville, TN 37040
Tel: (931) 906-0555 ● sharonmasseylaw.com ●
smassey@sharonmasseylaw.com
A graduate of Nashville School of Law, she has been practicing law
since 1998. Shes estimates she completes 150 adoptions annually:
40% independent; 40% agency; 20% international. She does not assist
in creating adoptive matches.

Robert D. Tuke; 222 4th Avenue North, Nashville, TN 37219
Tel: (615) 256-8585 ● tntlaw.net ● rtuke@tntlaw.net
A graduate of the Vanderbilt University School of Law, he has been
practicing law since 1976.

TEXAS

State Adoption Office: Texas Department of Family and Protective Services: 701 West 51st Street, MC E-558; PO Box 149030; Austin, TX 78714-9030; Phone: (512) 438-4760; http://www.tdprs.state.tx.us

State Adoption Exchange: Texas Adoption Resource Exchange (TARE): Toll-Free: (800) 233-3405; http://www.adoptchildren.org

State laws and procedures:

General Information. Texas permits both independent and agency adoption. Approximately 40% of Texas' infant adoptions are completed via independent adoption; 60% via agencies. Advertising is permitted only by licensed adoption agencies. To file a Petition for Adoption within Texas either the adoptive parents must reside there, or the child to be adopted must have been born there or reside there (making non-resident adoption possible). If it is an agency adoption the Petition for Adoption can also be filed in Texas if the adoption agency having custody of the child is located there. Normally, adoptions are finalized approximately five to six months after the birth or the placement of the child with the adoptive parents. The adoptive parents are required to appear in court for the final hearing, although the court may waive this requirement and allow only one parent to be present.

Independent Adoption. A pre-placement home study is not required before a child can be placed in their home, but a "pre-adoptive home study" is required prior to the court's order terminating parental rights. The home study may be conducted by a licensed adoption agency or licensed social worker approved by the court. The fee for pre and post-placement home studies is typically under $2,000.

It is not required by law that the adoptive parents and birth mother meet in person but it is required that they share identities. The adoptive parents are permitted to assist the birth mother with pregnancy-related medical, counseling and legal expenses. Non-medical expenses may be provided to her only through a licensed adoption agency. The child can be released directly from the hospital to the adoptive parents with the birth mother signing a release form which varies hospital to hospital.

The consent to adoption, called a *relinquishment*, can be signed no sooner than 48 hours after the birth. It must be witnessed by a notary and two witnesses. Most consents are signed within several days of the birth. There are two options in relinquishment forms. One is that it is irrevocable from signing for a period of up to 60 days. During those 60 days the adoptive parents' attorney must have a court terminate the birth mother's rights based upon her relinquishment. Failure to do so will make the consent revocable. The other option is to make the consent revocable for ten days, and any time thereafter the court order may be sought. The norm is the first method. The only grounds to set aside an irrevocable relinquishment is upon proof of fraud or duress.

Texas has a putative birth father registry. Putative birth fathers must register no later than the 31st day after the birth. Any birth father who registers must be given notice of a termination of a parental rights action. A birth father who is then served with a citation must file his response by the first Monday after the elapsing of 20 days from notice.

Agency Adoption. There is little difference regarding the process in which a birth mother signs her relinquishment in an independent or agency adoption. However, a birth mother's relinquishment in an agency adoption is irrevocable upon signing without the 60 day, period after which she has the right to seek to withdraw her relinquishment if a court order terminating her rights was not obtained.

Some agencies in Texas agree to do identified adoptions. Some agencies also agree to make immediate hospital "at risk" placements, allowing the child to be placed before the consents to adoption are final.

American Academy of Adoption Attorney members:

Vika Andrel; 1220 Deer Creek Circle, Dripping Springs, TX 78620
Tel: (512) 334-9229 ● v.andrel@adoptionattorneys.org
A graduate of the University of Texas at Austin School of Law, shehas been practicing law since 1985.

Gerald A. Bates; 3200 River Front Dr., #204, Fort Worth, TX 76107
Tel: (817) 338-2840 ● txadoptions.com

C. Harold Brown; 201 Main Street, Suite 801, Fort Worth, TX 76102
Tel: (817) 338-4888 ● brownpruittlaw.com ●
c.brown@adoptionattorneys.org
A graduate of the University of Texas School of Law, he has been
practicing law since 1960.

Lester R. Buzbee; 116 S. Avenue C, Humble, TX 77338
Tel: (281) 540-8060 ● l.buzbee@adoptionattorneys.org
A graduate of South Texas College of Law, he has been practicing
law since 1977. He estimates he completes 90 adoptions annually:
20% independent; 80% agency.

Carla M. Calabrese; 5944 Luther Lane, Suite 875, Dallas, TX 75225
Tel: (214) 939-3000 ● calabreselaw.com ● carla@calabreselaw.com
A graduate of the University of Cincinnati College of Law, she has
been practicing law since 1986.

David Charles Cole; 3631 Fairmont St., #201, Dallas, TX 75219
Tel: (214) 363-5117 ● adoptlegal.com ●
d.cole@adoptionattorneys.org
A graduate of Pepperdine University School of Law, he has been
practicing law since 1987.

Heidi Bruegel Cox; 6300 John Ryan Drive, Fort Worth, TX 76132
Tel: (817) 922-6043 ●gladney.org ● h.cox@adoptionattorneys.org
A graduate of the Texas Tech Univeristy School of Law, she has been
practicing law since 1986.

Eric C. Freeby; 201 Main Street, Suite 801, Ft. Worth, TX 76102
Tel: (817) 338-4888 ● brownpruittlaw.com ●
e.freeby@adoptionattorneys.org
A graduate of University of Arkansas, Little Rock, he has been
practicing since 2005. He estimates he completes 200 adoptions
annually: 20% independent; 50% agency; 30% international. He does
not assist in creating adoptive matches.

Dale R. Johnson; 7303 Blanco Road, San Antonio, TX 78216
Tel: (210) 349-3761 ● d.johnson@adoptionattorneys.org

Michael R. Lackmeyer; 2212 Sunny Lane, Killeen, TX 76543
Tel: (254) 690-2223 ● adopttexas.net ●
m.lackmeyer@adoptionattorneys.org
A graduate of the Baylor University School of Law, he has been
practicing law since 1970.

Melissa H. McClenahan; 7303 Blanco Rd., San Antonio, TX 78216
Tel: (210) 269-5244 ● m.mcclenahan@adoptionattorneys.org

Charles E. Myers; 5257 Wyndham Court, Abilene, TX 79606
Tel: (325) 674-1325 ● c.myers@adoptionattorneys.org

Susan I. Paquet; 201 Main Street, Suite 801, Fort Worth, TX 76102
Tel: (817) 338-4888 ● brownpruittlaw.com ●
s.paquet@adoptionattorneys.org
A graduate of the University of Arizona, she has been practicing since
1983. She estimates she completes 275 adoptions annually: 20%
independent; 50% agency; 30% international. She does not assist in
creating adoptive matches.

Irv W. Queal; 8117 Preston Road, Suite 800, Dallas, TX 75225
Tel: (214) 696-3200 ● i.queal@adoptionattorneys.org

Donald Royall; 1177 W. Loop South, Suite 650, Houston, TX 77027
Tel: (713) 462-6500 ● adoptiontexas.com

Melody Royall; 1177 W. Loop South, Suite 650, Houston, TX 77027
Tel: (713) 462-6500 ● adoptiontexas.com ●
m.royall@adoptionattorneys.org

Steve Watkins; P.O. Box 876, Greenville, TX 75403
Tel: (903) 454-6688 ● watkins-perkins.com
A graduate of the Texas Tech University School of Law, he has been
practicing law since 1980.

Jenny L. Womack; 15455 N. Dallas Pkwy., #440, Addison, TX 75001; Tel: (214) 744-4440 ● wilsonlakelaw.com ● j.womack@adoptionattorneys.org
A graduate of the University of Texas School of Law, she has been practicing law since 1998. She estimates she has completed 140 adoptions in her career and completes 30 annually: 40% independent; 20% agency; 40% international. She does not assist in creating adoptive matches. She serves as general counsel of an adoption agency.

Ellen A. Yarrell; 50 Briar Hollow Lane, #425 W, Houston, TX 77027
Tel: (713) 621-3332 ● e.yarrel@adoptionattorneys.org
A graduate of the University of Texas at Austin School of Law, she has been practicing law since 1979..

Harold Zuflacht; 12000 Huebner Road, #200, San Antonio, TX 78230
Tel: (210) 349-9933 ● h.zuflacht@adoptionattorneys.org

Linda M. Zuflacht; 5370 Prue Road, San Antonio, TX 78240
Tel: (210) 699-6088 ● adoptionservicesassociates.org ● lzuflacht@satx.rr.com
A graduate of St. Mary's School of Law, she has been practicing law since 1978. She estimates she completes 50 adoptions annually: 1% independent; 98% agency; 1% international. In 1984 she founded Adoption Services Associates, a licensed child-placing adoption agency.

UTAH

State Adoption Office: Utah Department of Human Services; Division of Child and Family Services: 195 North 1950 West; Salt Lake City, UT 84116; Phone: (801) 538-4437; http://www.hsdcfs.utah.gov

State Adoption Exchange: Utah Adoption Exchange: Phone: (801) 265-0444; ks@adoptex.org; https://www.utdcfsadopt.org

State laws and procedures:

General Information. Utah permits both independent and agency adoption. Approximately 30% of Utah's infant adoptions are completed via independent adoptions; 70% via agencies. Advertising is permitted by adoptive parents. To file a Petition for Adoption within Utah the adoptive parents must reside there, the child is born there, or the relinquishing birth parent must reside there at the time of the placement (making non-resident adoption possible). Normally, adoptions are finalized six months after the child's placement with the adoptive parents. The adoptive parents and the child are normally required to appear in court for the final hearing, but courts can waive this requirement for good cause.

Independent Adoption. A pre-placement home study of the adoptive parents is required before a child can be placed in their home, unless a court order is obtained allowing the placement in advance of a pre-placement home study. The home study is conducted by a licensed adoption agency or licensed social worker. The fee for pre and post-placement home study services is typically $1,000.

It is not required by law that the adoptive parents and birth mother meet in person and share identities, but it is usually done voluntarily. The adoptive parents are permitted to assist the birth mother with pregnancy-related medical, legal, counseling and living expenses. The child may be released directly from the hospital to the adoptive parents, usually via a release form prepared by the adoptive parents' attorney.

The birth mother's consent to adoption can be signed no sooner than 24 hours after the birth. It must be witnessed by a judge or a person appointed by the court. Most consents are signed within three days of the birth. Once signed, the consent to adoption is irrevocable, but for proof of fraud or duress. A birth father's consent may be signed before or after the birth.

Utah has a putative birth father registry. Prior to when the birth mother signs her consent to adoption, the putative birth father must file a paternity action and register notice of that action, as well show as he has paid pregnancy expenses, if the birth father lives in Utah. If he fails to do so before the birth mother's consent is signed, he loses his rights. If he lives outside of Utah, he must meet the same standard, if he knows or should have known prior to the birth mother's consent that the adoption may occur in Utah, but he is given 20 days to do so from the date of such knowledge, or before the birth mother signs her consent, whichever occurs later. If he does not know the adoption may take place in Utah, prior to the birth mother's consent he must comply with the laws of the state where conception occurred or where the birth mother last resided, to establish parental rights.

Agency Adoption. There is no difference regarding the process in which a birth mother signs her consent to adoption in an independent or agency adoption, although the consent may usually be witnessed by a notary and agency representative. The information provided above regarding independent adoption (e.g. when the consent can be signed and the legal burden to withdraw the consent) is identical regarding agency adoption.

Some agencies in Utah agree to do identified adoptions. Virtually no agencies will agree to make immediate hospital "at risk" placements, allowing the child to be placed with the adoptive parents before the consents to adoption are final.

American Academy of Adoption Attorney members:

Dale M. Dorius; 29 S. Main; P.O. Box 895, Brigham city, UT 84302 Tel: (435) 723-5219 ● d.dorius@adoptionattorneys.org

David J. Hardy; 500 Eagle Tower, 60 E. South Temple, Suite 1800, Salt Lake City, UT 84111 ● kmclaw.com ● d.hardy@adoptionattorneys.org

Larry S. Jenkins; 60 East South Temple Street, Suite 500, Salt Lake City, UT 84111; Tel: (801) 366-6060 ● woodjenkinslaw.com ● lsjenkins@woodjenkinslaw.com
A graduate of the Brigam Young University School of Law, he has been practicing law since 1986. He estimates he has completed 2,000 adoptions in his career and completes 300 annually: 25% independent; 70% agency; 5% international. He does not assist in creating adoptive matches.

Lance Rich; 500 Eagle Tower, 60 E. South Temple, Salt Lake City, UT 84111; Tel: (801) 366-6060 ● woodjenkinslaw.com ● l.rich@adoptionattorneys.org

VERMONT

State Adoption Office: Vermont Department for Child and Families; Family Services Division: 103 South Main Street, Osgood 3; Waterbury, VT 05671-2401; Phone: (802) 241-2669; http://www.projectfamilyvt.org

State Adoption Exchange: Vermont's Waiting Children: Phone: (802) 241-2122; http://www.projectfamilyvt.org

State laws and procedures:

General Information. Vermont permits both independent and agency adoption. Approximately 40% of Vermont's infant adoptions are completed via independent adoption; 60% via agencies. Advertising is permitted. To file a Petition for Adoption within Vermont the adoptive parents must be residents. If it is an agency adoption the Petition for Adoption may also be filed in Vermont if the agency having custody of the child is located there (making non-resident adoption possible). (At the time of this book's publication, legislation was pending to stop non-resident adoptions, but it is not yet known if it will become law.) Normally, adoptions are finalized approximately seven months after the child's placement. The adoptive parents are required to appear in court for the final hearing.

Independent Adoption. A pre-placement home study of the adoptive parents is required before a child is placed in their home. The post-placement home study may be conducted by a licensed adoption agency. The fee for the pre and post-placement home study varies but is usually $1,200.

It is not required that the adoptive parents and the birth mother meet in person and share identities, although it is usually done voluntarily. The adoptive parents are permitted to assist the birth mother with pregnancy-related expenses, including living costs. The child may be released directly to the adoptive parents from the hospital, although each hospital may employ a different release form.

The consent to adoption can be signed no sooner than 36 hours after the birth. It must be witnessed by a judge. Most consents are signed within days of the birth. Once signed, the birth mother has the automatic right to withdraw the consent for 21 days. After the 21-day period has expired, the consent is irrevocable except upon proof of fraud or duress.

Vermont has a putative birth father registry. Putative birth fathers file a notice of their intent to retain parental rights in the probate court. The court then notifies the state registry of the filing, which is cross-checked with a Petition for Adoption is filed.

Agency Adoption. There is no difference regarding the process in which a birth mother signs her consent to adoption in an independent or agency adoption. The information provided above regarding independent adoption (e.g. when the consent can be signed, before whom and the legal burden to withdraw the consent) is identical regarding agency adoption.

Some agencies in Vermont agree to do identified adoptions. Some agencies also agree to make immediate hospital "at risk" placements, allowing the child to be placed with the adoptive parents before the consents to adoption are final.

American Academy of Adoption Attorney members:

Kurt M. Hughes; 131 Main St., P.O. Box 363, Burlington, VT 05402
Tel: (802) 864-9811 ● adoptvt.com ● khughes@mhtpc.com
A graduate of the Vermont Law School, he has been practicing law since 1985. He estimates he has completed several hundred adoptions in his career, and last year completed approximately 50 (25 independent; 25 agency). He accepts contested adoption cases.

Linda W. McIntyre; P.O. Box 125, Barnard, VT 05031
Tel: (802) 457-4551 ● lindamcintyre.net ●
l.mcintyre@adoptionattorneys.org

VIRGINIA

State Adoption Office: Virginia Department of Social Services; Family Services, Adoption Unit: 7 North 8th Street; Richmond, VA 23219; Phone: (804) 726-7575; http://www.dss.virginia.gov

State Adoption Exchange: Adoption Resource Exchange of Virginia (AREVA): Phone: (804) 726-7524; Fax: (804) 726-7499; http://www.adoptuskids.org/states/va

State laws and procedures:

General information. Virginia allows both independent and agency adoption. Approximately 75% of Virginia's newborn adoptions are completed via independent adoption, 25% via agencies. Advertising is permitted. To file a Petition for Adoption within Virginia the adoptive parents must reside there, or if the consent to adoption is taken there (making non-resident adoption possible). The Petition for Adoption can also be filed in Virginia if the agency having custody of the child is located there. Normally, adoptions are finalized 4 to 7 months after the child's placement with the adoptive parents in independent adoption, and 9 months in agency adoptions. The adoptive parents and the child are generally not required to attend a final hearing in which the adoption is finalized, as typically the order granting the adoption is signed by the judge simply upon receipt of the social worker's report, without any hearing.

Independent Adoption. A pre-placement home study of the adoptive parents is not mandatory before a child can be placed in the adoptive parents' home, although the birth mother's consent will not be accepted by the court until a home study has been completed. The home study is usually conducted by a licensed adoption agency, but occasionally is done by a County Department of Social Services.

It is required by law that the adoptive parents and birth mother meet in person, but sharing identities can be waived. The adoptive parents are permitted to assist the birth mother with pregnancy-related medical, counseling and legal expenses. Living costs may also be provided, but requires written confirmation from her physician that she is physically unable to work. The child can be released directly from the hospital to the adoptive parents, although each hospital may employ a different release form.

The birth mother's consent to adoption may be signed no sooner than the child's third calendar of life. It must be witnessed by a judge. (The birth father's consent, married or unmarried to the birth mother, can be signed either before or after the birth, with a 7 day period from the date of signing to revoke.) The courts give preference to adoption matters and try to schedule the signing of adoption consents within ten days of the filing of the petition. Once the birth mother's consent is signed, the birth mother has the automatic right to withdraw her consent for a period of 7 days or until the child is 10 days old, whichever occurs first. After the child's tenth day of life the consent is irrevocable, except upon proof of fraud or duress. The birth mother may waive her 7 day revocation period if she is represented by legal counsel.

Virginia has a putative father registry. Notice must be given to any named putative birth father. The notice explains the existence of the registry and that he has 10 days from the birth, or the notice, whichever is later, to file. If he files with the registry he must be given notice of the adoption. The standard at the hearing is the child's best interests. Putative birth fathers wishing to agree to the adoption may sign their consent before, or after, the birth before a notary.

Agency Adoption. The information provided above regarding independent adoption is identical regarding agency adoption, except for the following. A pre-placement home study of the adoptive parents is required. The consent to adoption, called an *entrustment agreement* in an agency adoption, can be signed anytime after birth and is to be witnessed by a notary. The entrustment becomes irrevocable 7 days after execution, upon the child reaching 10 days of age, or when the child is placed with the adoptive parents, whichever is later.

Some agencies will make immediate "at risk" placements.

American Academy of Adoption Attorney members:

Gary Allison; 291 Independence Bl., #541, Virginia Beach, VA 23462
Tel: (757) 518-8000 ● pittsadopt@verizon.net
A graduate of University of Akron, hehas been practicing law since 1975. He estimates he completes 120 adoptions annually: 75%

independent; 15% agency; 10% international. He does not assist in creating adoptive matches.

Mark Eckman; 311 Maple Avenue, Suite E, Vienna, VA 22180
Tel: (703) 242-8801 ● hagarcenter.org ●
meckman@datzfoundation.org
A graduate of the Catholic University School of Law, hehas been practicing law since 1984. He estimates he has completed more than 1,000 adoptions in his career and completes 50 annually: 30% independent; 20% agency; 85% international. He does not assist in creating adoptive matches. Mr. Eckman speaks Spanish, French, German and Italian.

Sharon Fast Gustafson; 4041 N. 21st Street, Arlington, VA 22207
Tel: (703) 527-0147 ● sharonfastgustafson.com ●
s.gustafson@adoptionattorneys.org

Barbara C. Jones; 7016 Balmoral Forest Road, Clifton, VA 20124
Tel: (703) 222-1101 ● b.jones@adoptionattorneys.org
A graduate of the George Mason University School of Law, she has been practicing law since 1988.

Robert H. Klima; 9256 Mosby Street, Manassas, VA 20110
Tel: (703) 361-5051 ● r.klima@adoptionattorneys.org
A graduate of the George Mason University School of Law, he has been practicing law since 1978.

Karen S. Law; 42909 Riverstone Court, Ashburn, VA 20148
Tel: (703) 723-4385

Mark T. McDermott; 910 17th Street, N.W., Suite 800, Washington, DC 20006; Tel: (202) 331-1440 ● theadoptionadvisor.com ●
mcdermott@mtm-law.com
Mark McDermott has been practicing law since 1974. He estimates he completes 60 adoptions annually: 65% independent; 10% agency; 25% international. He does not assist in creating adoptive matches.

Thomas Nolan; 215 Wayles Lane, Suite 125, Charlottesville, VA 22911; Tel: (434) 817-4001 ● vepcharlottesville.com ● tom@vepcharlottesville.com
A graduate of the University of Virginia School of Law, he has been practicing law since 1984.

Rosemary G. O'Brien; 109 South Fairfax Street, Alexandria, VA 22314; Tel: (703) 549-5110 ● r.obrien@adoptionattorneys.org

Janet Ours; 9306 Grand Avenue, Manassas, VA 20110
Tel: (703) 361-9700 ● oaslaw.com ● jours@oaslaw.com
A graduate of George Mason University School of Law, she has been practicing since 1999. She estimates she completes 25 adoptions annually: 50% independent; 50% agency. She does assist in creating adoptive matches.

Betsy H. Phillips; 12576 Wards Road, Rustburg, VA 24588
Tel: (434) 821-5100 ● b.phillips@adoptionattorneys.org
A graduate of the University of Richmond School of Law, she has been practicing law since 1983.

Stanton Phillips; 1921 Gallows Rd. #110, Tysons Corner, VA 22182
Tel: (703) 891-2400 ● stantonphillips.com ● s.phillips@adoptionattorneys.org
A graduate of the George Mason School of Law, he has been practicing law since 1980. He estimates he has completed 2,500 adoptions in his career and completes 150 adoptions annually: 50% independent; 25% agency; 25% international. He does assist in creating adoptive matches.

Rodney M. Poole; 4901 Dickens Rd., #108, Richmond, VA 23230
Tel: (804) 358-6669 ● pooleandpoole.com ● r.poole@adoptionattorneys.org
A graduate of the University of Virginia, he has been practicing law since 1973. He estimates he has completed 2,500 adoptions in his career and completes 75 annually: 44% independent; 28% agency; 28% international. He does not assist in creating adoptive matches. He is an adoptive parent and a past-president of the American Academy of Adoption Attorneys.

Colleen M. Quinn; 4928 W. Broad Street, Richmond, VA 23230
Tel: (804) 545-9406 ● virginia-adoption-attorney.com ●
c.quinn@adoptionattorneys.org
A graduate of the University of Virginia, she has been practicing law
since 1988. She estimates she has completed 2,500 adoptions in her
career and presently completes 100 annually: 65% independent; 20%
agency, 15% international. She assists in creating adoptive matches.

Ellen S. Weinman; 111 East Main Street, Salem, VA 24153
Tel: (540) 389-3825 ● e.weinman@adoptionattorneys.org

Please be aware than several AAAA members in neighboring states,
particularly Maryland and the District of Columbia, practice in
Virginia, including Mark McDermott (DC) and Peter Wiernicki (MD).

WASHINGTON

State Adoption Office: Washington Department of Social and Health
Services (DSHS); Division of Children and Family Services: 1115
Washington Street, SE -- PO Box 45713; Olympia, WA 98504; Phone:
(360) 902-7968; http://www1.dshs.wa.gov

State Adoption Exchange: Washington Adoption Resource
Exchange (WARE): Phone: (206) 441-7242; Fax: (206) 441-7281;
http://www.warekids.org

State laws and procedures:

General Information. Washington permits both independent and
agency adoption. Approximately 70% of Washington's infant
adoptions are completed via independent adoption; 30% via agencies.
Advertising is permitted, but only when placed by adoption agencies,
attorneys licensed by the State of Washington, or adoptive parents
with an approved Washington home study. To file a Petition for
Adoption in Washington either the adoptive parents, the child, or the
birth mother must reside there (making non-resident adoption
possible). Normally, adoptions are finalized two to three months after

the placement of the child with the adoptive parents. The adoptive parents are usually required to appear in court for the final hearing, although the court may waive this requirement.

Independent Adoption. A pre-placement home study of the adoptive parents is required before a child may be placed in their home. The home study may be conducted by the state adoption office, a licensed adoption agency, or licensed social worker or other person approved by the court. The fee varies but is usually $500 to $2,000.

It is not required by law that the adoptive parents and the birth mother meet in person and share identities, although most do so voluntarily. The adoptive parents are permitted to assist the birth mother with pregnancy-related expenses with court approval. The child can be released directly from the hospital to the adoptive parents. Some hospitals only require a hospital release form but most others require a court order.

The consent to adoption may be signed before or after the birth. It must be witnessed by a witness selected by the birth parent. Birth parents under the age of 18 must have a guardian ad litem appointed to make sure they understand the proceedings. The consent to adoption becomes effective only after it has been filed and approved by the court, at which point the court terminates the parental rights of the parent. This can occur no sooner than 48 hours after birth, or the signing of the consent, whichever occurs later. Before the court has approved the consent, the birth mother has the automatic right to withdraw her consent without any legal burden. After the court has approved the consent, the consent is irrevocable, except upon proof of fraud, duress or mental incompetency.

Washington does not have a putative birth father registry. Putative birth fathers must be given notice (usually 20 days if by personal service and 30 days if by publication) of a hearing to terminate their parental rights. If they do not object, their rights can be terminated by default. If they do object the court will examine the best interests of the child and whether the putative father failed to perform parental dueies showing a substantial lack of regard for his obligations.

Agency Adoption. There is no difference regarding the process in which a birth mother signs her consent to adoption in an independent or agency adoption. The information provided above regarding

independent adoption (e.g. when the consent can be signed, before whom and the legal burden to withdraw the consent) is identical regarding agency adoption.

Some agencies in Washington agree to do identified adoptions. Some agencies also agree to make immediate hospital "at risk" placements, allowing the child to be placed with the adoptive parents before the consents to adoption are final.

American Academy of Adoption Attorney members:

David V. Andersen; 5507 35th Avenue NE, Seattle, WA 98115
Tel: (206) 267-7200 ● holmancahill.com

Rita L. Bender; 1301 Fifth Avenue, Sutie 3401, Seattle, WA 98101
Tel: (206) 623-6501 ● skellengerbender.com ●
rbender@skellengerbendercom
A graduate of the Rutgers University School of Law, she has been practicing law since 1968.

Mark M. Demaray; 145 3rd Avenue South, #201, Edmonds, WA 98020; Tel: (425) 771-6453 ● washingtonadoptionattorney.com
● m.demaray@adoptionattorneys.org
A graduate of the Lewis and Clark Law School of Portland, he has been practicing law since 1981. He estimates he has completed more than 3,000 adoptions in his career. He is an adoptive parent.

J. Eric Gustafson; P.O. Box 1689, Yakima, WA 98901
Tel: (509) 248-7220 ● northwestadoptions.com ● egustafson@lyon-law.com
A graduate of the Northwestern School of Law of Lewis and Clark College at Portland, he has been practicing law since 1973. He estimates he has completed more than 1,000 adoptions in his career, and last year completed approximately 50 (36 independent; 6 agency; 2 intercountry). He is an adoptive parent.

Michele Gentry Hinz; 33035 52nd Avenue South, Auburn, WA 98001
Tel: (253) 740-0667 ● michelehinz.com ● michelehinz@hotmail.com
A graduate of the University of Washington School of Law, she has been practicing law since 1978. Approximately of her 75% of her

practice consists of adoptions (typically 90% independent; 5% agency; 5% intercountry).

Margaret Holm; P.O. Box 13350, Olympia, WA 98508
Tel: (360) 943-6933 ● m.holm@adoptionattorneys.org
A graduate of the Seattle University School of Law, she has been practicing law since 1983.

Mark R. Iverson; 921 W. Broadway, Suite 301, Spokane, WA 99201
Tel: (509) 462-3678 ● adoptionwa.com ●
m.iverson@adoptionattorneys.org
A graduate of Gonzaga University School of Law, he has been practicing since 1988. He estimates he completes 300 adoptions annually: 60% independent; 30% agency; 10% international. He does assist in creating adoptive matches.

Albert G. Lirhus; 1200 5th Ave, Suite 1550, Seattle, WA 98101
Tel: (206) 728-5858 ● lk-legal.com ● a.lirhus@adoptionattorneys.org
 A graduate of the University of Washington School of Law, he has been practicing law since 1973. He estimates he has completed more than 3,000 adoptions in his career and completes 250 annually: 205 independent; 60% agency; 20% international. He does assist in creating adoptive matches.

Raegen N. Rasnic; 1301 Fifth Avenue, Suite 3401, Seattle, WA 98101
Tel: (206) 623-6501 ● skellengerbender.com
A graduate of the University of California, The Hastings College of Law, she has been practicing since 1995.

Joyce E. Robson; 201 St. Helens Avenue, Tacoma, WA 98402
Tel: (253) 572-5104 ● j.robson@adoptionattorneys.org
A graduate of the University of Puget Sound School of Law, she has been practicing law since 1988.

Marie N. Tilden;1014 Franklin Street, Vancouver, WA 98660
Tel: (360) 695-0290 ● marietilden.com ● marie@marietilden.com
A graduate of the University of Texas School of Law, she has been practicing law since 1985.

WEST VIRGINIA

State Adoption Office: West Virginia Department of Health and Human Resources; Office of Social Services: 350 Capitol Street, Room 691; Charleston, WV 25301; Phone: (304) 558-3431; bobbyjmiller@wvdhhr.org

State Adoption Exchange: West Virginia Adoption Resource Network; Bureau for Children and Families: (same as above); Phone: (304) 558-2891; cstalnaker@wvdhhr.org; http://www.adoptawvchild.org

State laws and procedures:

General Information. West Virginia allows both independent and agency adoption. Approximately 50% of West Virginia's infant adoptions are completed via independent adoption; 50% via agencies. Advertising is permitted. To file a Petition for Adoption within West Virginia the adoptive parents must reside there. Normally, adoptions are finalized six to nine months after the child's placement with the adoptive parents. The adoptive parents and the child are usually required to attend the court hearing in which the adoption is finalized.

Independent Adoption. A pre-placement home study of the adoptive parents is not required. The post-placement home study may be conducted by a licensed adoption agency or a person approved by the court. The fee varies but is typically $1,400.

It is not required by law that the adoptive parents and the birth mother meet in person and share identities, although this is sometimes done voluntarily. The adoptive parents are only permitted to assist the birth mother with medical, counseling and legal expenses. Anything outside those categories requires court approval, which is rarely given. The child can be released directly from the hospital to the adoptive parents, although hospital forms and policies vary.

The consent to adoption may be signed no sooner than 72 hours after the birth. It must be witnessed by a notary. If the birth mother is under the age of 18, the consent must be witnessed by a judge. Two consent options can be used. If the consent is an *Irrevocable Consent,* the consent is irrevocable effective immediately. It can only be withdrawn upon proof of fraud or duress. Birth mothers are alternatively permitted to sign a *Conditional Consent*, however, in which they may give themselves the right to stop the adoption within the conditions set forth in the consent (such as a number of days to reconsider, or if the birth father were to object).

West Virginia does not have a putative birth father registry. Notice must be given to any putative father at his last known address or by publication if unfindable. The notice is of the final adoption hearing. Birth fathers wishing to consent must wait 72 hours, like birth mothers, to sign a consent.

Agency Adoption. There is no difference regarding the process in which a birth mother signs her consent to adoption, called a relinquishment, in an independent or agency adoption. The information provided above regarding independent adoption (e.g. when the consent can be signed, before whom and the legal burden to withdraw the consent) is identical regarding agency adoption. However, a pre-placement home study is required.

Some agencies in West Virginia agree to do identified adoptions. Some agencies also agree to make immediate hospital "at risk" placements, allowing the child to be placed with the adoptive parents before the consents to adoption are final.

American Academy of Adoption Attorney members:

David Allen Barnette; P.O. Box 553, Charleston, WV 25322
Tel: (304) 340-1327 ● dbarnette@jacksonkelly.com
A graduate of the University of Dayton School of Law of Lewis, he has been practicing law since 1979. He estimates he has completed 1,850 adoptions in his career, and last year completed approximately 45 (10 independent; 15 agency; 20 intercountry). Approximately 10% of his practice consists of adoptions (typically 25% independent; 25% agency; 50% intercountry), and of these 30% are newborn placements, 70% are toddlers or above. He accepts contested adoption cases.

WISCONSIN

State Adoption Office: Wisconsin Department of Health and Family Services: 1 West Wilson Street; PO Box 8916; Madison, WI 53703; Phone: (608) 266-3595; http://www.dhfs.state.wi.us

State Adoption Exchange: Adoption Resources of Wisconsin: Phone: (414) 475-1246; info@wiadopt.org; http://www.wiadopt.org

State laws and procedures:

General Information. Wisconsin permits both independent and agency adoption. Approximately 60% of Wisconsin's infant adoptions are completed via independent adoption; 40% via agencies. Advertising is permitted if the adoptive parents have a favorable home study. To file a Petition for Adoption within Wisconsin the adoptive parents must be residents. Normally, adoptions are finalized approximately six months after the child's placement with the adoptive parents. The adoptive parents are required to appear in court for the final hearing.

Independent Adoption. A pre-placement home study of the adoptive parents is required before a child is placed in their home. The home study may be conducted by a licensed adoption agency. The fee varies.

It is not required by law that the adoptive parents and the birth mother meet in person and share identities, although it is often done voluntarily. The adoptive parents are permitted to assist the birth mother with necessary pregnancy-related medical, living and legal expenses. However, assistance with living expenses cannot exceed $5,000. The child may be released directly from the hospital only into a licensed foster home. This can be the home of the adoptive parents, if they have a foster home license, which is traditionally part of their pre-placement home study. If so, the child is placed with them in a "legal risk placement." If his is not possible, the child can be placed with them by court order of temporary guardianship.

The consent to adoption is made by means of a *Petition for Voluntary Termination of Parental Rights*, which is filed with the court anytime after the birth. The birth mother then appears in court to consent to the termination of her parental rights, which usually occurs two to four weeks after the birth or placement with the adoptive parents. The adoptive parents normally attend this hearing as well, and should have had their initial home study previously filed with the court. The court then signs a *Termination of Parental Rights Order*. Before the court's order terminating parental rights, the birth mother has the automatic right to withdraw her consent. After the court's order, the consent is irrevocable, although there is a 30-day period in which an appeal can be filed to withdraw the consent based upon fraud, duress or court error.

Wisconsin has a putative birth father registry, of sorts. Two methods are available to adoptive parents to notify birth fathers. The traditional method is to give notice of a termination of parental rights hearing to any putative birth father named by the birth mother. This can be done regardless of the child's age. The newer method requires notice to all birth fathers of their right to file with the putative birth father registry. If the birth father registers within 14 days of the birth, or 21 days from when notice was received, whichever is longer, he must be given notice of an action to terminate his parental rights. This method is only available when the child is one year of age or less.

Agency Adoption. There is no difference regarding the process in which a birth mother signs her consent to adoption in an independent or agency adoption. The information provided above regarding independent adoption (e.g. when the consent can be signed, before whom and the legal burden to withdraw the consent) is identical regarding agency adoption.

Some agencies in Wisconsin agree to do identified adoptions. Many agencies will agree to make immediate hospital "at risk" placements.

American Academy of Adoption Attorney members:

Lynn J. Bodi; 450 S. Yellowstone Drive, Madison, WI 53719
Tel: (608) 821-8212 ● law4kids.com ● lbodi@law4kids.com
A graduate of the University of Wisconsin Law School, she has been practicing law since 1987. She estimates she has completed 200 adoptions in her career and completes 10 annually; 20% independent; 80% agency. She does not assist in creating adoptive matches.

Carol M. Gapen,; 434 S. Yellowstone Drive, Madison, WI 53719
Tel: (608) 821-8211 ● law4kids.com ● egapen@law4kids.com
A graduate of the University of Wisconsin Law School, she has been
practicing law since 1988.

Stephen W. Hayes; N14 W23777 Stone Ridge Drive, Suite 200,
Waukesha, WI 53186; Tel: (262) 798-8220 ● ghnlawyers.com
A graduate of the University of Illinois College of Law, he has been
practicing law since 1969.

Elizabeth A. Neary; N14 W23777 Stone Ridge Drive, Suite 200,
Waukesha, WI 53188; Tel: (262) 374-2001 ● ghnlawyers.com

Judith Sperling-Newton; 450 S. Yellowstone Dr., Madison, WI
53719; Tel: (608) 821-8210 ● law4kids.com ● j.sperling-
newton@adoptionattorneys.org

Theresa L. Roetter; 211 S. Paterson St., #340, Madison, WI 53703
Tel: (608) 251-6700 ● annenroetter.com ● troetter@annenroetter.com
A graduate of the Marquette University School of Law, she has been
practicing law since 1993. She estimates she has completed 350
adoptions in her career and completes 50 adoptions annually: 55%
independent; 40% agency; 5% international. She does not assist in
creating adoptive matches.

Richard B. Schoenbohm; 600 E. Northland Ave., Appleton, WI
54911
Tel: (920) 735-5858 ● schoenbohmlaw.com
A graduate of the Indiana University at Bloomington School of Law,
he has been practicing law since 1980.

Victoria J. Schroeder; 2574 Sun Valley Dr. #200, Delafield, WI
53018
Tel: (262) 646-2054 ● v.schroeder@adoptionattorneys.org
A graduate of the University of Wisconsin Law School, she has been
practicing law since 1980. She estimates she has completed 1,000
adoptions in her career and completes 75 annually: 14% independent;
85% agency; 1% international. She does not assist in creating
adoptive matches.

Emily Dudak Taylor; 450 S. Yellowstone Drive, Madison, WI 53719
Tel: (608) 821-8214 ● law4kids.com ●
e.taylor@adoptionattorneys.org
A graduate of Tulane University School of Law, she has been
practicing law for six years. She has completed 150 adoptions in her
career. She does not assist in creating adoptive matches.

WYOMING

State Adoption Office: Wyoming Department of Family Services;
130 Hobbs Avenue; Cheyenne, WY 82009; Phone: (307) 777-3570;
http://dfsweb.state.wy.us

State Adoption Exchange: Wyoming Department of Family
Services: Phone: (307) 473-3924; Rfry@state.wy.us; http://
dfsweb.state.wy.us

State laws and procedures:

General Information. Wyoming permits both independent and agency
adoption. Advertising is permitted. To file a Petition for Adoption
within Wyoming the adoptive parents must be residents. Normally,
adoptions are finalized approximately six months after the child's
placement. The adoptive parents are required to appear in court for at
least one court hearing, either the initial court appearance for an
interlocutory decree, or the final hearing to grant the adoption.

Independent Adoption. A pre-placement home study of the adoptive
parents is not required before a child is placed in their home. In fact,
Wyoming law does not even require a post-placement evaluation,
unless ordered by the court. The home study may be conducted by a
licensed adoption agency or licensed social worker. The fee for the
post-placement home study is typically $350-$550.
   It is not required that the adoptive parents and the birth mother
meet in person and share identities, although it is often done
voluntarily. Wyoming law has no provisions for or against the
adoptive parents being permitted to assist the birth mother with
pregnancy-related expenses. Typically, adoptive parents obtain court

approval and can provide pregnancy-related medical, living and legal assistance if needed. Normally, the child may be released directly to the adoptive parents from the hospital, although some adoptive parents prefer that the child be released to an intermediary, often an attorney, to maintain confidentiality.

The consent to adoption may be signed anytime after the birth. It must be witnessed by a notary, representative of a licensed adoption agency or a judge. Once signed, the consent is irrevocable except upon proof of fraud or duress.

Wyoming has a putative birth father registry. Notice must be given to any putative birth father identified by the birth mother, as well as any man listed in the registry. The putative birth father has 30 days in which to file a paternity action. He must also be given notice of the action to terminate his parental rights.

Agency Adoption. There is no difference regarding the process in which a birth mother signs her consent to adoption in an independent or agency adoption. The information provided above regarding independent adoption (e.g. when the consent can be signed, before whom and the legal burden to withdraw the consent) is identical regarding agency adoption. However, a home study will be required.

Some agencies in Wyoming agree to do identified adoptions. Some agencies also agree to make immediate hospital "at risk" placements, allowing the child to be placed with the adoptive parents before the consents to adoption are final.

American Academy of Adoption Attorney members:

Peter J. Feeney; 104 S. Wolcott, Suite 800, P.O. Box 436, Casper, WY 82602; Tel: (307) 266-4422 ● p.feeney@adoptionattorneys.org A graduate of the University of Wyoming School of Law, he has been practicing law since 1974.

Douglas H. Reiniger; 320 E. Broadway, Suite 2A, P.O. Box 1215, Jackson, WY 83001; Tel: (307) 690-6625 ● reinigerlaw@wyoming.com

Appendix A

NATIONAL AND REGIONAL ADOPTION EXCHANGES

National exchange:

Children's Bureau, Department of Health and Human Services
(AdoptUSkids)
8015 Corporate Drive, Suite C
Baltimore, MD 21236
(888) 200-4005
Website: www.adoptUSkids.org
Email: info@adoptuskids.org

Regional exchanges:

National Adoption Center
1500 Walnut Street, #701
Philadelphia, PA 19102
(800) TO-ADOPT
Website: www.adopt.org

Children Awaiting Parents, Inc. (The CAP Book)
595 Blossom Road, #306
Rochester, NY 14610
(888) 835) 8802
Website: www.capbook.org
Email: info@capbook.org

The Adoption Exchange
14232 E. Evans Avenue
Aurora, CO 80014

(303) 755-4756
Website: www.adoptex.org
Email: kids@adoptex.org

Northwest Adoption Exchange
600 Stewart Street, Suite 313
Seattle, WA 98101
(800) 927-9411
Website: www.nwae.org
Email: nwaesource.org

Adopt America Network
(800) 246-1731
Website: adoptamericanetwork.org
Email: mking@adoptamericanetwork.org

State exchanges:

Chapter 15 (state-by-state review) lists each state's individual
adoption exchange.

For general assistance:

The North American Council for Adoptable Children (NACAC) and
the Child Welfare League of America (CWLA). Information is
provided in Appendix C.

Appendix B

HELPFUL ORGANIZATIONS, PUBLICATIONS AND WEBSITES

Helpful Organizations:

North American Council for Adoptable Children (NACAC)
Website: www.nacac.org • Email: info@nacac.org
   NACAC is committed to the needs of waiting children and the families who adopt them.

National Council for Adoption
Website: www.adoptioncouncil.org • ndfa@adoptioncouncil.org
   An advocate for state laws that promote sound adoption policy and is a resource for state and federal lawmakers.. It was responsible for the nation's first photolisting of waiting children, now done by www.adoptuskids.org.

The Child Welfare League of America (CWLA)
Website: www.cwla.org
   An association of more than 900 public and private non-profit agencies that assist more than 2.5 million abused and neglected children and their families each year.

Resolve
Website: www.resolve.org • Email: info@resolve.org
   A highly respected, non-profit national infertility organization.
The Child Welfare Information Gateway
Website: www.childwelfare.gov • Email: info@childwelfare.gov
   A service of the U.S. Department of Health and Human Services. It offers a tremendous database of adoption information.

American Academy of Adoption Attorneys
Website: www.adoptionattorneys.org
A not-for-profit fellowship of adoption attorneys and judges who have distinguished themselves in the field of adoption.

The Evan B. Donaldson Adoption Institute
Website: www.adoptioninstitute.org ● info@adoptioninstitute.org
An internationally recognized organization, its goal is to translate policy into action, achieving ethical and legal reforms.

The American Adoption Congress
Website: www.americanadoptioncongress.org
Dedicated to promoting legislation and public awareness regarding adoptee and birth parent access to identifying information.

Concerned United Birthparents, Inc. (CUB)
Website: www.cubirthparents.org
A national organization focusing on the needs and concerns of birthparents.

Publications:

Adoptive Families Magazine
Website: www.adoptivefamilies.com
Offering articles of tremendous assistance to both new adoptive parents, as well as those whose adopted children are now adults.

Websites:

Adoption101.com (Free online articles on adoption in an advertising-free setting and a huge online adoption bookstore.)

Adoption.com (A highly commercial site with dozens of URLs leading to it. Despite the many advertisements it carries, there are many excellent articles, and other helpful information provided, making it a helpful resource.)

Appendix C

SAMPLE PHOTO-RESUME LETTER

Hi,

We're Brian and Shelly and we are hoping with all our hearts to adopt. We live in a wonderful suburban community in southern California. Our neighbors are some of our best friends and many of them have young children, or are just starting their families. We are about five minutes to the ocean and we love to spend weekends at the beach. Brian likes to bodysurf while I prefer to sit under an umbrella and read a good book. What we'd really love to be doing is building sandcastles with our child, but we know that day will come. Besides the beach, Brian likes to barbeque and also enjoys playing softball and doing home projects. I like sports like jogging and tennis, but I also like being a homebody and just relaxing at home. Sunday mornings we do the crossword puzzle together and see who can get the most answers – winner gets a massage. (Sometimes I even let him win!)

Brian is a fireman and loves his job. He also feels good about having a job where he can help people and make a difference in our town. My job is not so exciting. I'm the assistant manager of a clothing boutique, but I have fun helping people choose clothes that make them feel good about themselves. I plan to be a stay-at-home mom.

We are working with an adoption attorney/agency, _____, to make sure we do everything correctly. To learn more about us, you can call him/her/them toll free at _____. Many adoptions nowadays are open, allowing us to meet, share identities and get to know each other, so you can be sure you are picking the right parents for your baby. We can't wait to meet you!

Brian and Shelly

Appendix D

SAMPLE "TRADITIONAL" NETWORKING COVER LETTER

Hi!

We are hoping to adopt a baby. We are sending you our photo-resume letter with the hope you will keep it on hand, and when the time comes, that you will pass it along to a woman who is facing an unplanned pregnancy and might be considering adoption as a loving option for her child. We are able to help with pregnancy-related expenses.

We have selected "open" adoption because it allows adoptive and birth parents to get to know each other before the birth, with no hidden identities.

Thank you!

Hi!

We are hoping to adopt a baby. We are sending you our photo-resume letter with the hope you will keep it on hand, and when the time comes, that you will pass it along to a woman who is facing an unplanned pregnancy and might be considering adoption as a loving option for her child. We are able to help with pregnancy-related expenses.

We have selected "open" adoption because it allows adoptive and birth parents to get to know each other before the birth, with no hidden identities.

Thank you!

Note: printing two cover letters per page will allow you to cut it in half, giving you two copies. Then affix one to each photo-resume letter, allowing half the cover letter to show from behind it.

Appendix E

SAMPLE "PERSONAL" NETWORKING COVER LETTER

Dear Friends:

We are hoping to adopt a baby and we hope that you can help us. As you may know, there are many couples like us unable to conceive a child who turn their hopes to adoption. Unfortunately, there are more couples waiting to adopt than there are babies. Nowadays, most adoptions are started by the baby's biological mother, learning of a couple who is hoping to adopt, usually from one of her healthcare providers, or a friend.

e process is very open and women considering adoption can meet us in person to decide if they would like to select us as the adoptive parents. That's where you come in! We hope you will help us by *personally* giving a copy of our resume letter (we've enclosed five) to people you know who will keep it on hand for when they may come into contact with a woman with an unplanned pregnancy. Specifically, please give one directly to your family doctor the next time you have an appointment, as well as your OB/GYN. Not their receptionist, but directly to the doctor. Other people you could give it to could be your minister, and any friends you have who work in medical clinics, as counselors, etc. Even where you get your hair and nails done can be great places to get the word out. If you have any questions, please call us. We have an adoption attorney/agency helping us to be sure we do everything correctly.

There is nothing more important to us than having a family, and we thank you for helping us create ours.

Ryan and Robin

Index